LENIN AND
WORLD REVOLUTION

Lenin and
World Revolution

STANLEY W. PAGE

McGraw-Hill Book Company

New York • St. Louis • San Francisco • London • Düsseldorf
Kuala Lumpur • Mexico • Montreal • Panama • Rio de Janeiro
Sydney • Toronto • Johannesburg • New Delhi • Singapore

Library of Congress Catalog Card Number: 59-6250

First McGraw-Hill Paperback Edition, 1972

07-048082-6

1 2 3 4 5 6 7 8 9   MU   MU   7 9 8 7 6 5 4 3 2

To   Joyce and Nicole

PREFACE

Most of my research was done at the excellently equipped Slavonic Room of the New York Public Library, the staff of which could always be counted upon for speedy and courteous service. Similar co-operation was also received from the Butler Library at Columbia and from the Widener Library at Harvard.

For permission to draw upon my previously published articles I am indebted to *The American Slavic and East European Review, The Journal of Modern History,* and to Harvard University Press and Mouton & Company (The Hague, Holland), publishers conjointly of *Russian Thought and Politics.*

All dates are given in accordance with the Western calendar.

Material in brackets within quotations usually comprises a simplified or abbreviated version of what was actually stated. At times, however, I have used this device to make a comment of my own without interrupting the quotation as a whole.

Four abbreviated designations are used frequently: USPD stands for the Independent Socialist party of Germany; KPD for the Communist party of Germany; KAPD for the Communist Workers' party of Germany; and VKPD for the United Communist party of Germany.

STANLEY W. PAGE

CONTENTS

Introduction   xi

Chapter 1   The Russian Proletariat and World Revolution: Lenin's Views to 1914   1

Chapter 2   Lenin's Assumption of International Proletarian Leadership   12

Chapter 3   The April Theses and the Three Crises   27

Chapter 4   The Seizure of Power   55

Chapter 5   Trotsky and Lenin   74

Chapter 6   Brest-Litovsk: The Opening Moves   81

Chapter 7   Brest-Litovsk: The End Game   91

Chapter 8   After Germany—the World!   111

Chapter 9   The Third International   119

Chapter 10   Violence When Necessary   134

Chapter 11   Lenin and the East   141

Chapter 12   The Second Congress of the Comintern   154

Chapter 13   The Course Is Set   185

Notes   201

Bibliography   245

Index   249

INTRODUCTION TO THE
PAPERBACK EDITION

As ONE AFTER ANOTHER of the great industrial nations of Western Europe failed to fulfill the phophecy of proletarian upheaval, Marx, Engels and their spiritual successors allowed their thoughts to drift steadily eastward as they sought to locate the elusive center of insurrectionary ferment. In 1845 Engels wrote of a possible bloodletting in England which would make the French revolution seem like child's play. In 1848, *The Communist Manifesto* saluted Germany as the workingmen's inspiration "because that country [was] on the eve of a bourgeois revolution that [was] bound to be carried out under more advanced conditions of European civilization, and with a much more developed proletariat, than that of England was in the seventeenth, and of France in the eighteenth century, and because the bourgeois revolution in Germany [would] be but the prelude to an immediately following proletarian revolution."

In 1849, writing in *Die Neue Rheinische Zeitung*, Marx and Engels, by that time disappointed in Germany, defined partitioned Poland as "the revolutionary section of Russia, Austria and Prussia," and "the hearth of European democracy," since even the Polish nobility "adhered to the democratic agrarian revolution with unprecendented devotion. . . . As long as [we Germans] help to oppress Poland, [by keeping] part of Poland riveted to Germany, we ourselves will remain riveted to Russia and to Russian policy. . . . The creation of a democratic Poland is the first condition for a democratic Germany."

The savage outburst of class war in Paris of 1871, coming after two "dry" decades, momentarily rekindled the Marx-Engels hopes for something of the same for the West in general. But the glorious "storming of the heavens" by the Communards was crushed within two months, and, except for an echo in Algeria, this first "proletarian dictatorship" disappeared without a ripple. In 1877 Marx predicted the start of a revolution in Russia. "The revolution this time will begin in the East, formerly the impregnable citadel and reserve army of counter-revolution." That statement was in line with a tradition, the origins of which are explained in the first chapter of this book, wherein Marxism had made tsarism the major reason for the failure of revolutionary action in the West. In the same vein, Engels, in 1890, charged Russian diplomacy with "constituting some new form of Jesuit order," a gang, which "shirking neither treachery . . . nor murder from ambush" had "made Russia the most powerful inspirer of fear and had opened the path for her domination of the world." Similarly, in 1896, Karl Kautsky declared that St. Petersburg had become "a much more important revolutionary centre than Warsaw," because the Russian revolutionary movement had a greater international significance than did that of Poland. (After World War I, it might be added, Kautsky in part justified his party's voting for war credits on the basis of German Marxism's "old belief that the war against Russia was the 'holy war' of German Social Democracy.")

It is readily understandable why these German prophets, dourly observing the rapidly improving living standards of proletarians in the booming centers of nineteenth-century capitalism, should have turned their eyes toward the impoverished East in searching for the star on whose coming they had, so to speak, staked their lives. It is equally understandable why the Russian Marxists, around 1900, paid virtually no attention to the flattering attention their country had been receiving. For as Marxists they could not take seriously the idea that Russia (made up so largely of vodka-swilling peasants, driving ox-drawn carts along quagmire roads into villages of thatched-roofed huts) stood ready to initiate a European proletarian revolution. But a single Russian Marxist, Lenin, eagerly took this notion to his bosom, and, as the first chapter of this book explains, made it into a central motif of his interpretation of the Marx-Engels teaching.

What could possibly have prompted Lenin to react in this way? Was it his simple conviction that the prophets spoke the truth and that it was his duty to obey their commands? Was it a sense of internationalism, so solidly founded that allowed him to feel no embarrassment at the thought of asserting (not as a German, but as a Russian) what might so easily have been deemed to be an expression of national pride? Was it an awareness on Lenin's part that only in Russia, home of anarchist, nihilist and narodnik martyrs, was there a revolutionary vanguard of the kind needed to provide the impetus for social overturn? Such thinking may well have stirred Lenin and hundreds of other radicals of his day. But Lenin alone, among all the Russian Marxists, found a special importance in the marginal (one might call it a last resort) Marxian postulation that a European revolution might be sparked by one in Russia. This makes it simple to deduce that Lenin expected one Russian at least to steer his native land onto its world-historic course.

And who was a more likely candidate for this task than he who wanted it done, which means that, consciously or not, Lenin was prepared to assume a role of some importance in leading the way to the world revolution. The chain of thinking that may be implied further reveals not only Lenin's self-confidence, but, more than that, his belief in the power of an individual to affect the course of history. Such a belief, since it contradicted the deterministic essence of Marxism, should have logically compelled Lenin to reject either Marxism or the notion, which, of course, may not have been conscious, of his personal importance to the end result. Since he did neither, it means that he was tailoring the theory; that is, was consciously or unconsciously reshaping Marxism to fit his emotional structure, and that, therefore, he would be compelled to reject all interpretations but his own as incorrect. This would account for his lifelong war against liberal intellectuals (who try to see all aspects of a problem) since they would, by definition, feel a need to challenge his personal and personality-oriented arbitrariness on the subject of Marxism. Lenin never tired of excoriating the talkers, rather than doers, for bemuddling the class struggle's basic issue, *Kto Kovo?* ("Who Will Conquer?"), thereby delaying the final conflict.

The adolescent trauma commonly said to have shaped Lenin's impatience with cowardly vacillators was the shunning of his family in Simbirsk by "liberal" friends and neighbors, when they learned of the arrest of his elder brother, the student Alexander Ulyanov, for an attempt upon the life of tsar Alexander III in March, 1887. Long afterward Lenin recalled their behavior with utter contempt. Not a single person could be found who would accompany his mother on the long wintry ride by horse-drawn vehicle to catch the train to St. Petersburg so that she could visit her son in prison. "He learned the true worth of all liberal rant at an early age," writes his wife and biographer, Nadezhda Krupskaya.

In the years following his brother's execution, Lenin, part of the time under police surveillance, avidly studied and devoured the writings of Chernyshevsky and Marx, both calling for uncompromising hatred of the ruling classes. During the catastrophic famine of 1891, Lenin scorned the attempts of liberals to ameliorate the peasant sufferings by philanthropic measures, which might draw the attention of the vanguardist youth from their primary purpose, revolutionary struggle with the autocratic order. Late in 1893, Lenin, a twenty-three-year-old lawyer, made his initial appearance among St. Petersburg Marxists. His powerful presence was soon felt in a pamphlet which directed a broadside against the narodnik champions of the peasant commune and advocates of "small deeds," i.e., progress through legal means. Lenin charged them with thwarting the progress of capitalism and hence of socialism in Russia and with obstructing the Marxists, who were the wave of the future. Among the Marxists too, Lenin found compromisers, and in another tract he assailed the hypocrisy in the bourgeois tendencies of Peter Struve, a leading Russian Marxist. Sounding the trumpet for a revival of the Marx and Engels spirit of 1848, young Lenin fiercely opposed the comfortable assumption of "liberals" that an invisible economic hand was ineluctably leading to socialism. Instead he called for a Marxism armed with a hatred not alone of the tsar and the rich, but of those as well, who calling themselves socialists, were not ready to bloody their hands.

Making a "pilgrimage" to the West in 1895, to meet Plekhanov and Axelrod, the legendary founders of Russian Marxism, Lenin startled them by his assertion that there was no place for liberals in Russian Social Democracy. Although upset by his intolerance, both men recognized his capacity for leadership, a trait which came strongly to the fore upon his return to St. Petersburg and his arrest in December of 1895 for agitation, along with others of his Marxist circle, among striking factory workers. In a Petersburg prison until February, 1897, he continued to exert important influence on Russian Marxism and began at the same time to write *The Development Of Capitalism In Russia*. The book, completed in Siberian exile, demonstrated through statistics that Russia, though a land of villages, had, since the emancipation of 1861 displayed a typically capitalist development, slower than the West, only because of the survival in Russia of many "ancient institutions." In the supposedly harmonious village commune, the handicrafts industry had pitted exploiters against exploited. In addition to the wage laborers in the villages, the increasing use of machinery in agriculture was promoting the proletarization of the peasantry. Lenin also demonstrated that the number of workers in large capitalist enterprises had more than doubled from 1865 to 1890, proving "that commodity circulation and, hence, commodity production were firmly implanted in Russia. Russia," Lenin asserted, "is a capitalist country." In his preface to the second (1907) edition of the book, Lenin further stressed the growing formation among the peasantry of bourgeois and proletarian classes.

"With this economic basis," he wrote, "the revolution in Russia is, of course, inevitably a bourgeois revolution. This Marxist proposition is absolutely irrefutable. It must never be forgotten. It must always be applied to all the economic and political problems of the Russian Revolution."

A more dogmatic declaration can scarcely be imagined, but Lenin was trying to hammer home the point, by no means obvious, that a revolutionary Marxist mentality was already practical, even though Russia had not yet caught up with the West industrially. The thrust of Lenin's book had been to shove Russia onto the Marxist map of Europe, to the satisfaction of many of Lenin's revolution-minded countrymen, who saw in Lenin Marx's apostle to backward but progressive Russia.

News from Europe and even from European Russia came but scantily into the Minussinsk region of Lenin's exile (1897-1900). But Lenin was deeply perturbed to learn of Russian Marxist attempts to convert Marxism into a legal movement and the "Economist" activities to direct the workers into trade unionist compromises. He was especially outraged by Bernstein's book, foretelling the peaceable evolution to socialism, that became the bible of Marxian revisionism. Beneath the lip service paid to the cause of social revolution, Bernstein had correctly gauged the temper of West Europe's leftists, which, indeed, many Russian Marxists too were ready to share. The open renunciation of the Marxist spirit by the moderates was to come in 1914 when the war shattered the last pretense that the Social Democratic parties were indomitably internationalistic. But in 1899, and even until the events of August, 1914 disenchanted him, Lenin refused to accept the ideas expressed by Bernstein as a true reflection of Western socialist sentiment. He was delighted soon thereafter to obtain Kautsky's indignant rejection of Bernstein's point of view.

Toward the end of his term of exile Lenin conceived the idea of organizing a centrally directed Marxist movement in Russia. As the first step to this end he hoped to set up a newspaper outside Russia, copies to be smuggled into the country and placed at the disposal of the working class. At the same time he began to make plans for the establishment of a revolutionary party whose members, under rigid discipline, would be carefully trained in the methods of illegal revolutionary work. During Lenin's years in Siberia, Social Democratic groups had formed in different parts of the Russian Empire. In 1898 nine delegates of such Social Democratic units met at Minsk and drew up a manifesto proclaiming the existence of the Russian Social Democratic Workers' party. This was about all they were able to achieve, for they were immediately seized by the police and banished. When Lenin returned to Russia, therefore, the growing Marxist movement still lacked a co-ordinating center.

In 1900 Lenin and various other Marxists, among them Martov and Potressov, with both of whom Lenin had previously corresponded about his plans, met secretly to discuss the founding of the guiding Marxist organ to be published abroad. With the aid of Klara Zetkin and other German Social Democrats, the paper came to life in Leipzig on December 21, 1900. *Iskra*, the "Spark," as Lenin named it, was soon flowing into Russia through innumerable illegal pipelines, and so the directional center and basis for a single party was established.

The editorial board of *Iskra* was originally composed of the revolutionary veterans Plekhanov, Axelrod, and Zasulich, who had long been living in exile, and the much younger triumvirate of Lenin, Martov, and Potressov. Friction developed from the very outset. Plekhanov, who had expected to direct the paper's policies, strongly resented Lenin's early assertion of superiority. On another level the three senior members feared that the vigorous juniors, fresh from contact with the Russian movement, would edge them out of their rightful primacy. Therefore on one issue of policy after another, the editorial board found itself deadlocked by a vote of three against three. To break the tie in his own favor Lenin, early in 1903, proposed that Trotsky, then a pink-cheeked emigré from Russia, be added to the board. Plekhanov, easily reading Lenin's intent, opposed the move.

The conflict of generations also revealed itself on the question of the sort of party that ought to be formed. The elders favored a moderate line with respect to Russian revolutionary practice and agreed that the lower middle class should play a conspicuous part in its development. Lenin, with the reluctant support of Martov and Potressov, fought this "soft" attitude. His pamphlet *What Is To Be Done*, published in 1902, called for a revolutionary party made up of a secretly organized and centrally directed band of professional revolutionaries. In such a party there could be no place for quibbling intellectuals. The opposing conceptions within the *Iskra* group—in time it would be Lenin alone against the other five—foreshadowed the famous Menshevik-Bolshevik split that first manifested itself at the Second Congress of the Russian Social Democratic party, in actuality the founding congress.

Before the convocation of the congress Lenin made all manner of arrangements designed to ensure for him and for his view of party organization the support of delegates who would come from Russia. By July 30, 1903, when the congress opened its sessions in Brussels, Martov and Potressov had abandoned Lenin's "hard" position and gone over to the "softs." Martov, addressing the congress, expressed his opposition to the idea of a party whose members had "abdicated their right to think." He advocated a broad party, open to all who agreed to work under its direction; one in which each member would have the right to influence the party's decisions. The congress balloting on the issue of party organization showed Martov's side victorious by a vote of 28 to 22.

Lenin was never one to accept a majority decision when it went against his fundamental convictions about what ought to be done. Using the arts of persuasion as well as the bludgeon, he moved delegates to change their positions. Aided by the sudden departure from the congress of two factions whose seven votes had earlier supported Martov, Lenin succeeded in overturning the original decision. His majority gained—"Bolshevik" means "member of the majority"—Lenin was able to dictate the party's constitution. *Iskra*, he insisted, should control the Central Committee. To make sure that he would control *Iskra*, he proposed a new editorial board of only three members. Besides himself they were to be Plekhanov, who had sided with Lenin at the congress, and Martov, leader of the Menshevik, or minority, faction. Martov indignantly declined the honor, but the new editorial board was nevertheless elected. In the newly formed Central Committee all three members were staunch followers of Lenin.

Lenin's victory split the Russian Marxist movement. The Mensheviks simply ignored the Bolshevik Central Committee and even many of those who had voted with Lenin at the Second Congress tried to bridge the gap which their leader had created. Lenin, becoming increasingly isolated, found it necessary to resign from the editorial board of *Iskra*, turning that organ over to the Mensheviks. He started *Vpered*, a new periodical, in Geneva, and his faction scheduled a new party congress for 1905, which the Mensheviks agreed to boycott. The debate over the structure of the party continued vigorously in the course of 1904, and Lenin's *One Step Forward, Two Steps Back*, explained that the issue was reduced to the alternative: "consistent application of the principle of organization [i.e., centralized control], or the sanctification of disunity and anarchy?" Lenin asked, "By what logic does the fact that we are the party of a class warrant the conclusion that it is unnecessary to make a distinction between those who *belong* to the party [those who would take orders] and those who *associate* themselves with it [those who would refuse to take orders]?"

In Geneva, Lenin told Valentinov, a Bolshevik colleague, that at one of the Menshevik meetings "some orator or other had tried to show that Lenin needed 'a conductor's baton' in order to introduce [military] discipline in the party." After Lenin had amplified his comments, Valentinov concluded that Lenin fully believed that he had a right to the conductor's baton. "I was at first shocked by his unshakeable faith in himself," writes Valentinov, ". . . in his conviction that he was preordained to carry out some great historical mission." Valentinov's initial feeling of shock soon wore off because he discovered that in Lenin's entourage in Geneva, "no one for a moment doubted his right to hold the conductor's baton and to issue orders. Adherence to Bolshevism seemed somehow to imply a kind of oath of loyalty to Lenin, a vow to follow his lead unquestioningly. Since at that time there were no programmatic or tactical disagreements [between Bolsheviks and Mensheviks], conflict was reduced to differences in ideas on the structure of the party and the way it should be led, and this in the end always necessarily and inevitably came down to the role which Lenin wanted to play in the party and which his opponents refused to let him play."

The revolutionary year of 1905 momentarily overshadowed the bitterness within Russian Social Democracy over Lenin's intransigence. All Marxists joined forces in the hope of overthrowing autocracy and out of this tactical collaboration grew a vain attempt to mend the rupture, the so-called Unification Congress (Fourth Party Congress) of 1906. In the parliament, which grew out of the revolution, Mensheviks and Bolsheviks sat as separate delegations and acrimony continued, particularly over Lenin's refusal to halt the practice of robberies (expropriations) to supply funds for the party treasury. By 1912, the Mensheviks had renounced the need for an illegal Marxist or conspiratorial party center because of the improved conditions in Russia for political freedom. Lenin then proclaimed that the Mensheviks had, in effect, "liquidated" the party, and secretly convoking a conference of Bolsheviks, which met January, 1912 in Prague, he designated this assemblage the Sixth Congress of the Russian Social Democratic Party.

But even among the Bolsheviks, in the period 1907-1912, serious friction had arisen, as so-called leftists had opposed Lenin's "unprincipled" willingess to have Bolsheviks participate in the parliament, the trade unions and other legal channels of political activity. Lenin also found it necessary, like some high priest of a religious body, to label as sceptics and heretics, among them Maxim Gorky, those who challenged the materialist bedrock of Marxism. "In a fashion which was to become characteristic," writes R. V. Daniels, "Lenin's left wing critics were lumped together and identified as enemies of Bolshevism.... The threat to unity was ended as Lenin himself put an end to unity and expelled the opposition. The intolerant expulsion of the Leftists produced an indignant [right wing] Bolshevik trend for conciliation with the Mensheviks, and this in turn required Lenin to anathemize all in the Russian Social Democratic Workers' Party who were not in complete agreement with him on all possible interpretations of Marxism in Russia."

Lenin's career to 1912 clearly reveals the ever recurrent pattern of his lifelong political behavior. He always needed to be in sole command and free to act as he thought best. Hence, while demanding an ortho-

---

*N. Valentinov, *Encounters with Lenin,* London, Oxford University Press, 1968, pp. 113-114 (translators from Russian, Paul Rosta and Brian Pearce).

doxy among party members in terms of fealty, he was constantly introducing abrupt changes in ideological interpretation along with concomitant tactical alterations. Such sudden shifts in party line would usually outrage those who had convictions of their own and who, therefore, had no choice but to become Lenin's outright antagonists. Those who held no strong principles were able to follow Lenin unquestioningly through the years, however bizarre the pattern of his politics, thus giving rise to a party, like cement in unity, but like jelly in its principles. To account for Lenin's leitmotiv there are two possible explanations.

It might on the one hand be said that only Lenin possessed the necessary devotion and intellect to lead to victory the revolution in Russia. Since the Cause came before all else, it was Lenin's duty to assert without modesty his rightful claim to leadership in the Russian Marxist movement. Therefore he also had the right to manipulate as he saw fit all others in the movement.

Or, did Lenin have a compulsive need to dominate, out of which grew his justifications for seizing the controls and the expedient and pharisaical ways in which he did it?

Few psychologists would have difficulty in deciding which explanation was basic. Motivations do not float through the ether in rigid patterns to light fully formed upon an unwary ego. It is the ego, formed and made sensitive in special ways through early impressions, that selects from an indifferent and chaotic environment such challenges and stimuli as give it a crystalline structure of conscious and unconscious action. It would be putting the cart before the horse to assume that an inbred revolutionary fanaticism led Lenin to become the spearhead of what was first the most revolutionary party of Russia and then of the entire world. Lenin was indeed a revolutionary fanatic out to destroy the existing social order and build anew upon its ruins. But his fanaticism was only the outward form of a demon-driven ego intent upon dominating the processes of destruction and of rebuilding. That, at any rate, is what this book intends to establish. Lenin, of course, never openly admitted—he was probably not even conscious of the fact—that he had a compulsive need to dominate and that all else was subordinated to that personal end. It is then only through an analysis of Lenin's behavior in continuous historical situations that the proof of this fact finally becomes overwhelmingly clear.

What, it might be asked, is the purpose of such a study? Does it matter in the final analysis whether Lenin acted out of one or another basic motivation?

It is of the greatest importance because Lenin's conviction that he was personally indispensable to the success of the world revolution colored his ideas. By dissecting the words and deeds of Lenin and deducing the great leader's underlying motives, it becomes evident that his famous political canons, which are taught to hundreds of millions the world over as the disembodied voice of history and the objective truth, are a series of rationalizations designed to mask his personal strivings. This investigation, moreover, helps to explain how Marxism has grown into something quite different from what its founding fathers thought it to be. The present condition of Communism could not possibly have been foreseen from a reading of Marxist scripture as it had accumulated to about the year 1900, when Lenin began contributing to it. However, a reading of Lenin's *Collected Works* will present the scholar with all the theoretical foundations for present-day Russia and China and the other national monarchies that characterize the Communist parts of the world.

1

THE RUSSIAN PROLETARIAT AND WORLD

REVOLUTION: LENIN'S VIEWS TO 1914

IN HIS PAMPHLET *What Is To Be Done,* written in the period 1901–1902 and dealing with the "crucial questions" of the formative Russian Social Democratic movement, Lenin declared:

> History has now placed us before an immediate task which is far more revolutionary than the immediate tasks of the proletariat of any other country. The completion of this task, the destruction of the strongest bulwark of European, and we may even say Asiatic, reaction would make of the Russian proletariat the vanguard of the international proletarian revolution.[1]

Lenin's challenging statement meant that the Russian proletariat, by overthrowing tsarism, would open the path to proletarian revolution in the West. The idea that Russian autocracy was the great obstacle to European revolt dates from the time of Nicholas I (1825–1855), whom every liberal knew as the "Gendarme of Europe." Marx harbored a particular animus toward Nicholas, whose intervention in German affairs in 1849 he blamed for the failure of the "bourgeois" unification movement. In Russia's constant readiness to render military support to the Prussian monarch, Marx saw a major deterrent to the "natural" flow of revolutionary events in Germany, the country which in 1849 Marx still thought of as the eventual center of Europe's proletarian rising.

In later years Marx became almost paranoiac on the subject of Russian intrigue, which to his mind supported the entire system of European reaction. Actually Marx gave the Russian government too much credit. After the Crimean War and the death of Nicholas I, Russian autocracy became far too preoccupied with its own problems to concern itself much with those of other governments. By

July, 1866, after Prussia's startling blitzkrieg victory over Austria, even Marx could grudgingly admit that Prussia, rather than Russia, was the greatest military force in Europe, that Russia was "less to be feared than ever before." [2] This admission implied that the Prussian government would not need Russian help to suppress a revolutionary uprising in Germany.

Eleven years later, even as he predicted the overthrow of the tottering Russian monarchy, he still spoke of it as the "last prop" of the Hohenzollerns and suggested that the fall of autocracy in Germany would follow upon the collapse of tsarism in Russia.[3] The conception of a monarchy too weak to sustain itself but strong enough to support its neighbor exhibits Marx's tendency to find convenient, if undernourished, dialectical scapegoats to explain why revolutionary events anticipated by him had not occurred.

The English working class, which Marx had ample opportunity to observe at firsthand, time and again disappointed his hopes for revolt. In 1868, when the English city workers got their first chance to vote, Marx confidently expected them to cast a significantly radical ballot. Instead they elected Tory candidates. It was then that Marx discovered "enslaved Ireland" as the cause of English proletarian conservatism, and postulated the theory that a nation (the proletariat of a nation) could not be free while it held another nation in bondage. Before 1868 Marx had scarcely considered the Irish worth mentioning. In like fashion the old bugaboo of tsarism was brought out to account for the strength of the (modern) House of Hohenzollern, which Bismarck had built, and for the failure of antimonarchical action in Germany.

In any case the Gendarme of Europe by 1877 no longer frightened anybody, least of all Marx. Yet in 1902 Lenin revived the Russian menace and proceeded to use it as an argument for the immense significance of the Russian proletariat to the European, possibly Asiatic, and hence world revolution. How could Lenin have formed an opinion so untenable in the light of the contemporary historical situation? This opinion was actually the culmination of a devious route of political rationalization. The starting point was Lenin's need, as the would-be leader of the Marxist party in Russia, to explain why, in a backward agrarian country, the industrial proletariat should assume the leadership role in the revolutionary movement.

In Russia the bourgeoisie was still weakly developed, capitalism and industry both being in their infancies, and the proletariat was very small in number. Nonetheless, as Lenin saw it, the Russian proletariat, having last arrived upon the European scene, was precisely therefore, and despite its smallness, eminently qualified to lead the revolution. Had it not before it the revolutionary experiences of Western proletariats? Was it not, then, the proletariat in Europe most advanced in theory and thereby able to apply the most effective revolutionary technique? [4] Certainly the weak and backward capitalist class could not be expected to lead an antitsarist revolution. The bourgeoisie still needed the protection of the monarch against the masses. They feared what a fully successful revolution might do to their status as owners of property and hence could not be expected to support any revolution more than halfway.[5] But, since a revolution of some kind was imminent, should the proletariat meekly follow the halfway middle-class effort, which he feared would leave tsarism in existence, strengthen the bourgeoisie, but be of no benefit to the lower classes? Lenin was much too aware of the tremendous revolutionary potential in Russia to be satisfied with such an outcome. He could see great things in store for the revolution if the workers could ally themselves temporarily to the seething peasantry. Together, with the proletariat leading, they might not only overthrow the autocracy but might even, by quickly establishing a revolutionary republic (a dictatorship of the proletariat and the peasantry), prevent a bourgeois government from taking power.

All this, while presenting reasons why the proletariat must take the lead and showing the manner by which it could win the revolution, made no promise of socialism. Even a victory of the proletarian-led revolution in Russia could not promise that, since Russia was industrially not yet ready for socialism. Also, there was no guarantee that the preponderant peasant element in the proletarian-peasant alliance would not soon come to dominate the scene of victory and turn the revolution into bourgeois channels. In addition, there could be every expectation of antirevolutionary intervention by the reactionary governments of Europe. If, then, the Russian proletariat, even by victory, could guarantee neither socialism nor even the end of bourgeois domination, wherein was it traveling the Marxian road?

The answer to this problem had to be found in the envisioned effect of the Russian revolution upon Western Europe. If the Russian revolution could stir up a successful Europe-wide proletarian revolt, then and only then could (1) the revolutionary government of Russia survive and remain proletarian in its direction, and (2) the industrial advances of the West be imported into Russia in the quantity necessary to make it possible for the revolutionary government to think in terms of a planned economy in anything like an immediate future. Lenin then found it necessary to restore the outdated Marxian concept of tsarism as the bastion of European reaction. This bastion overthrown by the Russian proletariat meant European revolution, which in turn would lead to socialism in Russia. Thus did Lenin discover the hitherto missing link between the Russian proletariat and its Marxian reason for striving to lead the Russian revolution.

Not only was the role of the proletarian party thus justified within Russia, but even better, the Russian working class at the same time might claim international significance and hence recognition from Marxists of countries far ahead of Russia in industrial development. Nor were Lenin's personal ambitions hurt by his formulation of this shaky thesis. For naturally this self-appointed leader of Russian Marxism would rise with the position of the party he led—and Lenin, instead of remaining an obscure politician on the fringe of the movement, might become a central figure in the world socialist crusade. Whatever the thought process by which Lenin constructed this article of faith, this concept of the Russian proletariat as a trigger to world revolution quickly became an established part of the Bolshevik doctrine.

The revolution of 1905, as Lenin saw it, was to have a twofold purpose: (1) The overthrow of the tsarist government and the establishment of a democratic republic, based on an alliance of proletariat and peasantry, would make the greatest strides toward social democracy possible to Russia at that time, in view of her historical and economic development. (2) It would set the European revolution in motion. In Lenin's words, it would "light the lamp of revolution before the dark and beaten mass [of Europe]." The accomplishment "with yet unheard of completeness [of] all the democratic reforms, our entire minimum program," [6] the "building of a Russian revolutionary movement, not of several months but a movement of many years, [would] lead not only to small concessions on the part of the existing authorities but to a complete destruction of these authorities. And, if this succeeds, then—then the revolutionary fire will strike Europe; the European worker, exhausted [in the struggle with] bourgeois reaction will rise in his turn and show us 'how it is to be done'; then the revolutionary upheaval of Europe will turn upon Russia and out of the epoch of several revolutionary years [in Russia] comes the epoch of several revolutionary generations." [7]

The Russian proletariat, though not successful in overthrowing the tsar in 1905, had nevertheless exhibited a strength out of all proportion to its numbers. If Lenin was disappointed in the outcome, which, among other things, resulted in the immediate suppression of all revolutionary organizations and the execution or exile of thousands of workers, his writings hardly show it. Most of all, Lenin seems to have been proud of the performance of the Russian proletariat, of the general strike in October, which had forced the tsar to proclaim the Constitutional Manifesto, and particularly of the December uprising in Moscow, Bolshevik-led, which cost the tsarist soldiery considerable effort to put down. Lenin, fully realizing that this uprising would be futile and bloody for the workers involved, nevertheless, seemingly for its subsequent value as propaganda, ordered the one-sided battle to take place.

In a speech delivered on the twelfth anniversary of January 22, 1905 ("Bloody Sunday"), Lenin, addressing a group of young workers in Zurich, declared that the revolution of 1905 had "not only wakened . . . the largest and most backward country of Europe and created the revolutionary populace led by the revolutionary proletariat—it had also brought all of Asia into the movement." As evidence of the "deep traces" of "the mighty upheaval of 1905" in Asia, Lenin mentioned the revolutions of 1908–1911 in Turkey, Persia, and China.[8] Lenin was even more concerned with demonstrating that the revolution of 1905 had affected Western Europe, as evidenced by the victory of the universal suffrage movement in Austria and street demonstrations in Vienna and Prague about November 1, 1905.[9] Lenin went on to attack the opinion, common in Western Europe, that a revolution in backward Russia had no relationship to conditions in the West and hence no practical significance there. Admitting that the "forms and the causes for the coming struggles in the immediate European revolution" would "differ greatly in many particulars from the form of the [impending] Russian revolution," Lenin declared that the Russian revolution

would nonetheless, and "precisely because of its proletarian character, in the special sense of the word which I stressed before," [10] be
a prelude to the coming European revolution.

The revolution of 1905, then, had awakened Russia and Asia,
had stirred the West, and had above all shown the proletariat of
the West the methods of successful proletarian revolt—the general
strike and street fighting; this despite the fact that the Russian revolution had been proletarian in form only, not yet socialist in content.[11] Europe, however advanced, would have to take its pattern of
revolution from Russia.

Lenin was to stress this last point on various occasions during the
years following 1905. As though to underline the fact that his conclusions as to the importance of the revolution of 1905 in producing
the correct pattern of revolt were shared also by Western Marxists,
he cited Kautsky, the later "renegade" who, in the period 1905–
1914, agreed with most of Lenin's ideas regarding revolution within
Russia. On the specific subject of street fighting Kautsky had
termed the Moscow uprising of December, 1905, a success, if only
because even at that late date, and against a modern-equipped
army, the Russian workers had held out for a full week, supported
as they were "of course" by the people of Moscow.[12] "But who could
say with certainty," Lenin quotes Kautsky, "that some similar [suc-
cess] could not be possible in Western Europe?" [13] From this
guarded question of Kautsky's, Lenin feels safe to declare

> that the workers' party sees in the direct revolutionary fight of the
> masses, in the October and December struggles of the year 1905, the
> greatest movement of the proletariat since the [Paris] Commune, that
> only in the development of such forms of struggle rests the pledge of
> future successes of revolutions, that these forms of battle must serve
> us as guide lights in the business of educating new generations of
> fighters.[14]

The implication is clear. The comparison between Moscow in
1905 and the Commune of 1871 meant nothing less than that the
modern (1908) center of proletarian martyrdom and guide to
action was Russia rather than France or any other part of Western
Europe.

In many ways Lenin's exulting over the importance of the
Russian proletariat in the period 1906–1908 was a kind of whistling
in the dark. Actually the Russian revolutionary movement was in

terrible straits, with vengeful reaction rampant in Russia, the Social Democratic chieftains in lonely exile, and the party as a whole disrupted by numerous schisms. Lenin was no doubt striving to keep up morale within the weakened party and also, perhaps, trying to defend his policies of 1905, which had demanded the futile armed uprising. At the same time he was attempting to keep alive among Russian revolutionaries the feeling that within Russia itself, even in this darkest hour, militant revolutionary action was still possible and necessary. The grim experiences following 1905 had soured many on the idea and led them to believe that such activity, in the immediate postrevolution period, "was out of the question."[15]

Not long after this the political climate of Europe became highly charged with threats of intracontinental war. Lenin well recalled the effect of the Russo-Japanese War on Russia in 1905. If a war, which scarcely disturbed the daily routine of Russian existence, could produce revolution, what impact must a major European war have upon the Russian masses? And when by 1912 the Russian proletariat began anew to stir in the direction of strikes and other gestures of opposition to the government, and, shadows of 1905, there were revolutionary disturbances in the navy, Bolshevik hopes again rose to fever pitch. And if war could produce revolution in Russia, why not in the West, where the proletariat, forced to bear the brunt of bloodshed and suffering, would be more than ever ready to follow the Russian example?

During the period 1906–1912 Lenin or his delegates faithfully attended the conferences of the Second International. There they struggled against the growingly moderate tendencies of Western Social Democratic leaders and tried to commit them to internationalist revolutionary action if war should break out. In 1912 the Socialist Congress met at Basel shortly after the first Balkan Wars had started, when European war seemed closer at hand than ever. Despite the evasive statements of various delegates concerning revolutionary action, Lenin considered the general tone of the meeting satisfactory. For the first time the Socialists universally characterized the coming war as imperialist, the era of national wars having come to an end. The manifesto of this congress declared, among other things, that

proletarians consider it a crime to fire at each other for the benefit of capitalist profits, the ambitions of dynasties, or for the greater glory

of secret diplomatic treaties. . . . The proletariat will make use of all
its forces to prevent the destruction of the flower of all peoples, threatened with all the horrors of mass murder, starvation and pestilence.[16]

Lenin took this to mean that the Socialist parties of the West might
very likely act in the spirit of their words. As he said to Zinoviev,
on reading the manifesto of the Basel Congress, "They [the Western
Social Democrats] have given us a large promissory note; let us see
how they will meet it." [17]

The Bolsheviks were particularly pleased by the statement in the
manifesto on the subject of Russia:

> It is with great joy that the Congress [of Basel] greets the Russian
> workers' strikes of protest as a guaranty that the proletariat of Russia
> and Poland is beginning to recover from the blows dealt it by the
> Tsarist reaction. The Congress sees in this the strongest guaranty
> against the criminal intrigues of Tsarism. . . . For Tsarism is the hope
> of all the reactionary powers of Europe and the bitterest foe of the
> democracy of the peoples whom it dominates; to bring about the de-
> struction of Tsarism must, therefore, be viewed by the entire Inter-
> national as one of its foremost tasks.[18]

Having thus delivered this tribute to the Russian proletariat, the
manifesto went on to say: "But the most important task in the
International's activities devolves upon the working class of Germany, France and England." [19] As the main source of danger the
Second International saw the antagonism between Germany and
England; this the Socialists of both countries must strive to put an
end to.

It is interesting to note how the Bolsheviks magnified the statement on Russia in the manifesto to cast upon the Russian proletariat
a light far brighter than that in which the West viewed it. On January 25, 1913, in the Bolshevik organ *Sotsial-Demokrat*, Kamenev reported as follows on the Russian aspects of the Basel Manifesto:

> Comrades will find above in full the passage which the Basel
> Congress devoted in its manifesto to Russian Tsarism and the tasks of
> the Russian workers. The existence of the Romanov monarchy is one
> of the chief obstacles in the solution of the problem which confronts
> the socialist proletariat of Europe. The overthrow of the monarchy,
> which is pressing equally upon the free development of both Europe
> and Asia, is a vital [literally "blood"] task not merely of the Russian

Social Democracy and the Russian proletariat but also of the proletariat of the entire civilized world. Seven years after the great [1905] Russian revolution, the Basel Congress recalled that the overthrow of the regime of "renovated Russia," the regime of June 16 [the date of the dispersal of the second Duma by Stolypin, June 16, 1907] is essentially an *international* task. Not "improvement" of the regime of June 16, not "expansion" of the June 16 Constitution, but the overthrow of the monarchy—this is how the question has been posed not merely by conditions within Russia but by the entire international situation. First of all this stone must be removed from the path in order that the European proletariat can assure itself free development toward socialism. In greeting the new tide of the Russian proletarian movement, the Socialist International at the same time declares that the task which falls to the share of the Russian proletariat is one of the most responsible tasks at this moment. The conditions which have developed in Europe and Asia by the second decade of the twentieth century are such that the Russian proletariat happens to be in the center of international events. Much depends on the voice of the Russian proletariat. Proletarian Europe, and Asia which is becoming revolutionary, listen attentively to its voice and its voice must resound ever louder in the struggle against the Romanov monarchy. Only people who do not see the forest for the trees can fail to notice that the revolution and republican preaching are the most urgent, the most vital demands of the moment, demands which have been evoked by all the circumstances under which the new revival of the Russian laboring class is proceeding. Only under this slogan can the socialist proletariat of Russia fulfill the tasks with which it has been brought face to face by history and which were emphasized by the Basel Congress. *Revolution in Russia*—this is the Achilles' heel of the entire system of relations in Europe and Asia. Only a new revolution in Russia can open a new period of successes of the proletarian cause in Asia. Without this revolution the solution of all questions will be postponed for a long time; among these questions, there will also be the one which has caused the representatives of the proletariat of all countries to assemble at Basel. The Basel Congress could not conceal from itself the fact that the matter of assuring the peace of Europe demands at least one *war:* a victorious war of all the peoples of Russia against the Romanov monarchy.[20]

From the foregoing it seems clear that just before World War I, the Bolshevik party had convinced itself of the axiomatic quality of the following ideas: (1) The world revolution was impossible unless it started with revolution in Russia and overthrow of the tsar. (2) It was therefore the duty of the international proletariat (spe-

cifically that of Western Europe) to do all in its power to help that
revolution take place. The Bolsheviks were further convinced
that the Western Socialists shared their views with regard to the
importance of the Russian revolution.

In view of this belief, it is more than ever understandable how
stunning a shock it was to the Bolsheviks when they learned of the
war-induced abandonment of internationalism by the Social Democratic parties of the West. For not only had Western Marxists betrayed the international proletariat: they had even more directly
sold out the Russian working class, which ever since 1905 had been
making the utmost sacrifices for the sake of Western and world
revolution.

Among Socialists of the West, the standard justification of their
opportunist position was that their countries were defending themselves against governments more reactionary than their own. The
Socialists of republican France claimed to be fighting imperial
Germany, a greater evil. The Socialists of Germany and Austria, in
turn, declared that they must defend their governments in view of
the even worse reaction represented in their Russian tsarist opponent. To this last view a Bolshevik manifesto of November, 1914,
replied:

> The German and Austrian Social Democrats attempt to justify their
> support of the war by saying that thereby they struggle against
> Russian Tsarism. We, Russian Social Democrats, declare that such a
> justification is simple sophism.[21]

On the eve of the war, the manifesto pointed out, the Russian
revolutionary movement, having "once again grown to great dimen-
sions," had been all but ready to proceed to the overthrow of the
tsar. But nothing could have done more to assist the tsar in the fight
against "the whole Russian democracy" than the war, "which placed
at the disposal of [his] reactionary aims the purse of the English,
French and Russian bourgeoisie." As a primary obstruction to the
revolutionary struggle the manifesto cited "the conduct of the
leaders of German and Austrian Social Democracy, a conduct con-
tinually held up as an example for us by the Russian chauvinist
press." The Bolsheviks had nevertheless continued to "fulfill their
duty before democracy and the International." Despite the annihila-
tion of the party press, the outlawing of the majority of trade unions,
and the persecution of numerous party workers, the Bolshevik group

in the Duma had courageously voted against war credits and had demonstratively left the Duma chambers. At the same time "the Russian worker-comrades [were] already publishing their first illegal proclamations against the war." [22]

The same note was sounded again by the Bolshevik Shlyapnikov at the Congress of Swedish Social Democrats on November 24, 1914. He described the rising tide of revolutionary activity that started in 1912 and reached its peak in the days of mobilization in the form of antiwar demonstrations by the workers.

> We class conscious workers did not believe in the possibility of a world war. We turned our eyes full of hope toward the West, toward our organized brothers, Germans, French, Austrians. There we expected to find support and to hear a powerful appeal for struggle against the devilish plot of the bourgeoisie. But bitter reality brought us something else. The governmental press and the bourgeois newspapers, as well as our countrymen who fled abroad, informed us of the treason of the leaders of the powerful German Social Democracy and, thereafter, of many others who considered the situation from the "point of view of national self-defense. [23]

Thus in 1914, according to the Bolsheviks, just when the rising revolutionary tide plus the war should have proved the end of tsarism, the Second International undermined Bolshevik defeatist efforts and compelled the Russian workers to join the tsarist war. And by frustrating the Russian revolution, the Western Socialists had delayed the starting point of world revolution.

2

LENIN'S ASSUMPTION OF INTERNATIONAL

PROLETARIAN LEADERSHIP

EARLY IN SEPTEMBER, 1914, Lenin, who had just arrived in Switzerland, wrote his famous "Theses on the War." [1] These described the war as bourgeois-imperialist and flayed the Socialist betrayers of the proletariat. All the warring governments, Lenin wrote, had equally plunderous intentions. From the workers' point of view, therefore, the defeat of the enemy was not, as the Socialist leaders of France and Germany maintained, a lesser evil than the defeat of the fatherland. To the toiling masses of the Russian Empire, Lenin boasted, the lesser evil was precisely the downfall of the tsarist monarchy and the destruction of its army. [2]

The theses proposed three slogans for European social democracy. They were: (1) Propaganda to convert the imperialist war into civil war in each country, coupled with a merciless struggle against the chauvinism and "patriotism" of the bourgeoisie and particularly "against the leaders of the contemporary Second International." (2) Agitation in favor of German, Polish, Russian, and other republics, along with the transformation of all the separate states of Europe into a republican United States. (3) "Thirdly and particularly, a struggle against the tsarist monarchy and the Great Russian, pan-Slavist chauvinism, and the preaching of a revolution in Russia." [3]

The third slogan, requiring that European social democracy "particularly" seek a revolution in Russia, stamps Lenin as a Russian immersed in the problems of his own country. It also reveals his need to place the Russian proletarian revolution in the forefront of world attention. Utterly impractical as a rallying cry in Europe, slogan 3 was essentially a directive to the Bolsheviks still in Russia. The war theses as a whole, for that matter, were composed for ap-

Notes begin on page 203.

plication in Russia rather than in Western Europe. They were soon adopted by the Bolshevik party and used as a guide to action inside Russia throughout the war.[4]

The aim of slogan 2 of the theses stands in direct contradiction to that of slogan 1, which calls for proletarian revolutions in every warring country; but slogan 2 speaks of a republican United States of Europe. This suggests merely bourgeois-type revolutions in Russia, Germany, and Austria and the leaving of these and the other states of Europe within the national or bourgeois-capitalist framework. The only explanation for this cross-purpose of aims within the same text is that Lenin, being both Marxist and Russian, found himself in a dilemma. As a Marxist he might well call for universal proletarian revolution, but he knew that his own country was not yet ready for such a move. Thus while advocating proletarian revolution he also proposed republicanism, the only kind of revolution that made sense in Russia. At the same time, though far from modest regarding his own potentialities for leadership, Lenin could not but have felt embarrassed by the fact that his was the sole important Socialist voice calling for proletarian revolution—this, by default, making him the inheritor of the prophet's mantle. But could the Russian feel secure in a spot that, by all the tenets of the creed he preached, should have been occupied by some Western Marxist? If not, then perhaps it was still best to remain the Russian leader and keep one's feet on firm ground.

The web of Lenin's theorizing, more often than not, was spun around very specific political or personal contingencies. But practical considerations are not the best guides to pure theory. Lenin's reasoning sometimes became so fuzzy that fellow Bolsheviks found it necessary to confront him with hardheaded dialectical criticism. To solve a number of problems regarding organization and theoretical orientation, the Bolsheviks in exile held a conference in Bern from February 27 to March 4, 1915. At this time, as G. Shklovsky, chairman of the conference relates, Lenin clearly revealed his confusion regarding the slogan on the republican United States of Europe. Shklovsky writes: [5]

What concerns the course of the conference, only the question of the United States of Europe stirred up any great amount of controversy. . . . Our objections to the slogan [Shklovsky and one other participant at the conference voted against it] consisted of the following: (1) Under imperialism true democracy is impossible . . . therefore so is a United States of Europe. (2) It is further impossible because of the conflicts of interests among the European capitalist countries. (3) If it were to be formed, it would only be for the purpose of an onslaught upon the more advanced United States of America.

In the discussion Ilyich argued that to proceed from our line of reasoning would mean giving up a whole series of points of our minimum program as impossible under imperialism; that we, nonetheless, do not discard them, although true democracy can be achieved only under socialism. He further reproached us with having missed completely the economic side of the question. This we disputed on the grounds that the formation of a U.S. of Eur[ope] under imperialism would not constitute the highest form of democracy but a reactionary league of warring states, which, unable to defeat each other, should have banded together for war against America. . . .

Although Vlad[imir] Ilyich fully convinced the conference, which voted unanimously for his theses, he was not able to convince himself. That evening he met with comrade Radek . . . and questioned him in detail as to the opinion of various European comrades on this point.

The following morning, Vlad[imir] Ilyich took the floor. "Although," he said, "we yesterday decided on the question of the Unit[ed] St[ates] of Europe, in view of the fact that the question has aroused disagreement in our ranks, and because the discussion was one-sided and did not concern itself with the economic side of the question, the latter remaining quite unclear, this question must not be considered as definitively decided." He mentioned also his meeting with Radek, who had told him that Rosa Luxemburg, too, was opposed to the Unit[ed] St[ates] of Europe. He proposed, therefore, that the point on the Unit[ed] St[ates] of Europe be removed from the theses for the time being, suggesting that a discussion on this matter be opened in the C.[entral] O.[rgan] which should focus principal attention on the economic side of the matter.

The conference agreed with the opinion of Vlad[imir] Ilyich. However, no discussion of any sort has taken place, and the sole article in the C.[entral] O.[rgan] devoted to this theme was the article by Vlad[imir] Ilyich . . . and this was directed against the slogan and for reasons not purely economic.

It is clear that Shklovsky was annoyed with Lenin for having brushed aside his objections to the slogan by accusing him, among other things, of not having touched the economic side of the question; for bulldozing the conference to vote in favor of the slogan, despite the fact that he himself was not convinced of its dialectical soundness; for twisting the conference around, the following morning, and persuading it to cross the slogan out of the theses temporarily because the economic side of the question was unclear—the point Lenin had in effect charged Shklovsky with not properly comprehending; and because Lenin's change of heart or mind came only after he had learned of Luxemburg's objections, proving that Lenin had not considered Shklovsky important enough to give his arguments the attention they deserved.

As an added bit of wry comment, Shklovsky points out that no discussion of the question was ever raised in the central organ and that the sole article Lenin did write on the subject was opposed to the slogan for reasons not purely economic and not essentially on the grounds with which he had countered Shklovsky's objections. Shklovsky could not have understood the emotional conflict of the Russian leader, who desired to assume the crown of international proletarian chieftain but feared as yet to grasp the scepter. Of this inner conflict Lenin's confusion at the Bern Conference was merely the outward symptom. However, by August 23, 1915, Lenin was much more certain about his future course of action. It was then that the above-mentioned article appeared in *Sotsial-Demokrat*. Entitled "On the United States of Europe Slogan," [6] it vividly indicates the direction of Lenin's thinking.

The first portion of the article deals with the political implications of the United States of Europe idea. In this respect Lenin considered it progressive, since "[democratically oriented] political revolutions [could] . . . under no circumstances either obstruct or weaken the slogan of a socialist revolution." [7] Nonetheless, as he wrote in the second part of the article, the slogan was wrong from the economic side. Lenin then proceeded to give a number of arguments against the slogan, among which were the very ones advanced by Shklovsky at Bern. Small wonder that Shklovsky's memoirs evince annoyance.

The United States of Europe, Lenin explained, was impossible under capitalism, since such a unity presupposed some equitable redivision of colonial possessions among the powers of Europe. This the nature of imperialism made impossible, among other reasons because imperialism rises out of states in which the pace of capitalist development is unequal, so that each capitalist country has varying expansionist needs. Even if the European powers reached a temporary agreement, it would be nothing more than a defensive maneuver against European socialism or against the rival imperialism of the United States or Japan. In either case the reactionary governments entering into such an alliance were not fit to be supported by Bolsheviks.

Only socialism, Lenin declared, can give rise to a union of free nations,[8] and then it would be a United States of the World not merely of Europe. That would come about "only when the full victory of communism [had] brought about the final disappearance of every government, including the democratic ones." [9] As a separate slogan, then, even that of United States of the World was incorrect, since that presupposed communism. Thus the slogan was superfluous and meaningless.

With these arguments Lenin adequately demolished the United States of Europe slogan. His discussion could have ended right there, but he saw fit to raise additional points against the slogan or rather against its extension, the United States of the World. Why? At first glance the final paragraphs of his article appear as mere afterthoughts to an already completed thesis. Seen closer, they loom as reflections of important new ideas then rumbling about in Lenin's mind, in the process of formulation, perhaps, and not yet ready for full-scale exposition in some separate article. Lenin concluded his article [10] by pointing out that the slogan "United States of the World" was further incorrect

> because it could be erroneously interpreted to mean that the victory of socialism in one country is impossible; it would also create misconceptions as to the relations of such a country to others.
>
> Unequal economic and political development is an indispensable law of capitalism. It follows that the victory of socialism is, at the beginning, possible in a few capitalist countries, even in one, taken separately. The victorious proletariat of that country, having expropriated the capitalists and organized socialist production, would stand up against the capitalist rest of the world, attracting to its cause the oppressed classes of other countries. It would stir up among them revolt against their capitalists, and if necessary, even advance with military might against the exploiting classes and their states.

This last portion of Lenin's article is of course far more than merely an attack upon the United States of Europe idea. It is essentially a conception, entirely new to Marxism, of the manner in which the world revolution would originate and spread. Marxism had hitherto accepted without much question world revolution as an inevitable final achievement; but no Marxist had ever before attempted to blueprint in any detail the initial stages. At the same time the article as a whole must be viewed as the first expression of Lenin's decision to assume the role of leader in the cause of proletarian internationalism and hence to sidetrack his lesser function as leader of the Russian proletarian party.

That this is so can be concluded, first, from the fact that Lenin allowed himself to be talked out of his Russian-oriented plan for a United States of Europe, which contradicted the slogan of proletarian revolt in all countries. Those who study Lenin are aware that simple logic could never sway him from a theoretical position, however irrational, as long as he had politically practical motives for holding to it. The mere surrender of his opportunistically contrived slogan is testimony that Lenin no longer considered it basic to his plans.

Much clearer evidence, however, of Lenin's swinging away from a Russian-based position is the suggestion that socialism in one country was a possibility as a starting point for world revolution. In Lenin's formerly expressed ideas on this subject it was necessarily the spark from a Russian revolution that would set off proletarian revolution in Western Europe—all countries therein being conceived of as about equally ready to join in the movement. However, the ideas of "unequal development of capitalism" and "socialism in one country" suggest that the countries of Western Europe were not all equally ready, that one might spontaneously arrive at the bursting point of revolution. The implication is that such revolution could take place without the stimulus of a successful proletarian-led revolution in Russia and could "at the beginning" establish socialism in a single country.

This implication is contained in the fact that Lenin, up to and certainly well beyond this period, did not consider Russia capable of attaining socialism by herself. Therefore Russia could not possibly have been a country under consideration for this achievement. If Russia herself did not come into consideration and if a single country might alone achieve socialism, then of course it might do so without any assistance whatever from Russia. If, by Lenin's indirect admission, the overthrow of the Russian monarchy by the Russian proletariat was not crucial to the beginning of world revolution, then the conclusion is reached that the Russian proletariat is of no great

Marxian importance, nor is the party of the Russian proletariat, nor is its leader. By his own statement on the possibility of socialism in one country, the entire delicate and irrational structure that Lenin had so painstakingly developed and cherished since 1902 in order to justify his party's and his own Marxian importance was destroyed.

This is not to say that at the time anyone besides Lenin himself penetrated deeply enough into the meaning of his seemingly casual statement regarding socialism in one country to realize that he had thereby cut from under his feet the dialectical ground supporting his claim to international importance as leader of the Russian Bolshevik party. That Lenin, even with only his own conscience as witness, was willing to tamper with his home-grown and hitherto axiomatic doctrine concerning the missionary role of the Russian proletariat is a sure sign that he already foresaw the likelihood of abandoning that article of faith. In its stead he would attach himself to the star of a European revolution without Russian impetus, which would rise out of the war and in the destiny of which he hoped to play a decisive part.

There were by mid-1915 two conditions making it feasible, if not necessary, for Lenin to take so drastic a step. Isolated almost completely from contact with the Russian revolutionary movement, he found himself, where Russia was concerned, consigned to a secondary role. This was hard for him to stomach.[11] At the same time all the big-name Socialists of Western Europe had turned against internationalism. In this shift Lenin saw a unique chance to plunge himself into renewed leadership activity simply by constituting himself leader of the entire European proletariat, whose revolt he considered imminent.

In the period 1902–1905, Lenin, in preparing himself for his role in Russia's proletarian-led revolution, had prophesied that revolution and had described in meticulous detail the Marxian manner in which it would occur.[12] He had also envisioned the form of the revolutionary government—a republic whose parliament would represent only proletarians and peasants. At the Russian Social Democratic Congress of 1903, he proposed that the party of the proletariat be made up of a small and secretly organized band of professional revolutionaries. For this his opponents at the congress denounced him as an autocrat, a centralist, a Robespierre, and a would-be dictator over the proletariat. During 1914–1917 Lenin adopted a similar pattern in preparing himself to lead the European proletariat.

His prophecy of the coming European revolution Lenin substantiated in his *Imperialism: The Highest Stage of Capitalism*,[13] and also in other wartime tracts. As to his lighting upon "socialism in one country" as the predictable origin of Europe's revolution, it was the only possibility that made sense in 1915. In that year Europe was divided by the war, and the normally easy flow of ideas, principal weapon of any social revolution, was checked by walls of bayonets and censorship around the warring nations. Lenin further suggested that this single country, having achieved socialism, would advance against the exploiting classes and their states, using military force if necessary. Was this a mad dream? Not when viewed against the backdrop of Europe in 1915. Unquestionably it was Germany that Lenin had in mind at the time. Germany, home of Europe's most numerous industrial proletariat and the most courageous proletarian leader, Karl Liebknecht,[14] held out the best prospects for initiating socialist revolution.[15] That Germany was militarily powerful enough to challenge the rest of Europe, the war, by mid-1915, had amply proved.[16]

Late in 1916, when he thought revolution was closer than ever,[17] Lenin began to ponder the step beyond. Every Marxist knew about something called "dictatorship of the proletariat." But so sketchily had Marx drawn his outline of the future that few would have ventured to explain just what he had meant by it. Also, like most of Marx's revolutionary maxims, this one, or whatever there was of it, had undergone considerable revisionist dilution. Lenin decided to undertake a completely fresh study of this Marxian notion.[18] The random comments of Marx and Engels on the state, which Lenin, during January and February, 1917, assembled in a notebook [19] replete with marginalia, provided the materials later to be drawn together and published as *State and Revolution*,[20] the first intelligible elucidation of the proletarian dictatorship concept. By "dictatorship of the proletariat," Lenin explained that Marx, contrary to revisionist opinion, had meant nothing less than an actual dictatorship.[21] This dictatorship, established upon the revolution-made ruins of the bourgeois state organization, would endure until communism (perfect democracy) had been achieved and the state, dictatorship of the proletariat, could wither away.

Out of a handful of hints by Marx and Engels, Lenin had creatively synthesized a completely fashioned theory of government, one that he hoped would soon thereafter be molding the destinies of the people of Europe. At the same time, it is clear, Lenin had provided the dialectical thesis justifying the position of a future dictator over the revolutionary proletariat of Europe.

A further parallel to Lenin's ideas of 1903 is observable in 1916 in his arguments on the right of nations to self-determination. In 1903, along with his proposals on party organization, he had insisted on self-determination for the peoples of the Russian Empire as an essential point in the program of the Social Democratic party. Paradoxical as it may seem, this slogan was designed not to break up the unity of the Russian Empire but to prevent Polish and Jewish Social Democrats from maintaining autonomous sections within the All-Russian party. The purpose was to help centralize the multinational Socialist movement of the empire around a hard-core leadership—Lenin.[22] In 1916 nationalism was the most formidable obstacle to any prospective dictatorship over the masses of Europe. Having earlier faced the same problem with respect to the Russian Empire, Lenin thought he had the answer. And so at the very time that he was busily doing research on *State and Revolution,* Lenin found time to write lengthy pamphlets wherein he argued heatedly for the unconditional right of all nations to self-determination—the right of all annexed territories, come the revolution, to break away from their oppressor states.[23] But as in Russia of 1903, Lenin believed, or wanted to believe, that the complete assurance of that right to the peoples concerned would lead precisely to their rejection of the opportunities it offered. An illustration of his thinking in this matter is found in his speech on the national question given May 12, 1917, at the All-Russian Conference of Bolsheviks. By this time of course he was again for the moment relating the question of self-determination to the Russian Empire rather than to Europe. "The Finns now wish only for autonomy. We [the Bolsheviks] desire that Finland be given full freedom. When this aim of ours is brought to life, faith of the Finns in Russian democracy will be strengthened and precisely for this reason will they not separate themselves [from Russia]."[24] Instead of a revolutionary Europe broken up into proletarian-dominated states headed by separate national leaders, Lenin preferred to foresee a confluence of the European proletariat into an international society headed by a single centralized governing body.

None of the foregoing discussion is meant to suggest that Lenin ever ceased to think of himself as leader of the Russian Bolsheviks, the party of the (Russian) proletariat. What he did essentially was to extend his field of operations while quietly and inconspicuously divesting himself of the once-focal doctrine of his party—that world revolution must begin in Russia. He thus liberated himself to seize at whatever leadership opportunities arose, whether in Russia or in the international arena.

Having by mid-1915 decided that he was eligible to act as European leader, Lenin still needed a platform from which to broadcast his views. Within Russia he had created a party that for its size was most effective. Outside Russia his party amounted to a handful of exiles who had no contact whatever with the European masses. He himself was virtually unknown, and the central organ of the Bolsheviks was hardly the instrument for spreading his ideas. But unexpectedly Lenin obtained the opportunity to make himself and his program known.

The Bolsheviks were not the only ones in Europe who knew that something ailed the spirit of internationalism. To remedy the situation the Italian Socialist party, about the time of Italy's entrance into the war, conceived of convoking a full conference of the parties of the Second International. A delegate of the Italian party, sent to England and France in April, 1915, received enough encouragement if only from the minority factions of the English and French parties. At a meeting held May 15–16 the Italians called for a conference of all parties and workers' organizations "ready to come out against civil peace, to stand for united and simultaneous action of Socialists in various countries against war on the basis of the proletarian class struggle." [25] The Zimmerwald Conference, which met September 5–8, grew out of this decision, specific arrangements for it having been made at a preliminary conference at Bern on July 11. At the July conference the Italian proposal was toned down, and it was decided to invite to Zimmerwald both moderate and leftist Socialists. [26]

This scheme, however moderated, well suited Lenin's newly found leadership aspirations, and during July and August, 1915, he grew "very excited and busily wrote letters in every direction—to Zinoviev, Radek, Berzin, Kollontai, the comrades at Lausanne—anxious that at the forthcoming conference places should be secured for real left-wingers and that there should be as much solid unity among the

lefts as possible." [27] Lenin also wanted the Lefts to be provided with
documents giving the Bolshevik position,[28] and he desired, in case
they were themselves unable to attend, that they "assign their
proxies to Lenin." [29]

It is clear from these facts alone how vastly Lenin's attitude had
changed. In the prewar conferences of the Second International the
Bolsheviks had been a mere fringe group, content to remain on
the side lines, sometimes giving voice to a resolution and grateful
for occasional crumbs of acknowledgment that fell to the Russian
revolution of 1905. Not so this time. Lenin was preparing to take
the lead, or close to it, in what he conceived of as the beginnings
of an entirely new international organization. In the best politician's
tradition, Lenin, two days before the conference opened, went to
Bern and conducted a special meeting for all those whom he knew
he could count upon and "delivered a report concerning the nature
of the war and the tactics to be adopted by the international conference." [30] Those attending this special meeting later became the
Zimmerwald Left.

Lenin's following constituted an articulate minority at Zimmerwald and an even more forceful voice at the "second" Zimmerwald
conference, held at Kienthal, April 24–30, 1916. In the intervening
seven months elements in the German Socialist party had moved
decisively leftward, presaging the party's subsequent split. Within
the left wing a newly formed Spartacus League, headed by Luxemburg and Liebknecht, had taken a position similar to that of
Lenin. The Zimmerwald Left called for civil war in each country
and the formation of a Third International to replace the traitorous
leadership of the Second International. However, the majority of
the delegates, many of whom were patriotically inclined, were not
ready to go so far. Instead of civil war led by a Third International,
they called for peace on democratic principles. This pious hope
Lenin damned as deceitful to the proletariat. In March, 1916, he
wrote:

> The "peace program" of social democracy should consist finally in
> explaining that neither the imperialist powers nor the imperialist bour-
> geoisie is capable of bringing about a democratic peace. This must be
> sought and striven for—not *behind us,* in the reactionary utopia of
> *non*imperialist capitalism . . . —but in *the future* and the socialist
> revolution of the proletariat. Not a single vital democratic demand can

be achieved in any of the advanced imperialist states in any way except *through* revolutionary struggles under the banner of socialism.

And whoever promises the people a "democratic" peace and does not at the same time preach a socialist revolution and denies the struggle for it, the struggle now while the war is in progress, he deceives the proletariat.[31]

Lenin, as is clear, wanted no peace short of revolution. Whatever his dialectical justification of this position, a psychoanalyst might here accuse Lenin of wishing to prolong the massacre, if only that all his striving toward European leadership should not have been in vain. Despite basic disagreements with the majorities at Zimmerwald and Kienthal, Lenin's Left supported the manifestoes issued by the two conferences. They did include, and thus helped popularize, numerous Bolshevik ideas, among these the concept of the war as universally inimical to the interests of the working classes. Also, to Lenin & Co. the very proclamation of such ideas outside the framework of the old International Socialist Bureau represented a first step, however uncertain, in the direction of a new Socialist international.[32]

The Russian revolution of March, 1917, may have surprised Lenin, but it did not embarrass him. Whatever transitions or waverings had occurred in him, he had never openly renounced his faith in either the revolutionary potential of the Russian proletariat or its importance to world revolution. Not having done this, he was in a position to accept the Russian revolution as the beginning of the fulfillment of his prophecy of 1902. The Russian revolution had indeed come first in Europe, and Lenin unhesitatingly declared it proletarian-led. This statement, though quite beyond proof,[33] was useful in that it further bore out the prophecy. Thus Lenin easily slid back into the groove he had so amply prepared himself to occupy, leader of the Russian "proletarian" revolution.

A casual reading of Lenin's writings of March, 1917, might lead a reader to assume that except for the differences in historical moment between 1905 and 1917, and especially the impact of the war upon Lenin's reasoning, the twelve years had brought about no important changes in Lenin's fundamental attitude toward the relation between Russian "proletarian" revolution and European proletarian revolution. In his "Farewell letter to the Swiss workers" Lenin wrote:

To the Russian proletariat has fallen the great honor to *begin* the process of revolutions which the imperialist war has inevitably called forth.

However, the thought that the Russian proletariat might be the chosen revolutionary proletariat among the workers of other lands is absolutely foreign to us. We know very well that the proletariat of Russia is *less* organized, prepared, and class conscious than the workers of other countries. Not peculiar characteristics but special historical conditions have made the proletariat of Russia—*for a certain, probably very brief, period*—the spearhead of the revolutionary proletariat of the world.

Russia is a peasant land, one of the most backward of European countries. Socialism cannot win in Russia *immediately* and *directly*. But the agrarian character of the land, *can*, in view of the still tremendous landholdings of the aristocratic large estate owner . . . on the basis of experiences of 1905, give the bourgeois-democratic revolution in Russia a tremendous momentum and convert our revolution into the *prologue* to the socialist world revolution—to make it a *steppingstone* for this revolution. . . .

In Russia, socialism cannot win out directly and without delay. But the peasant masses *can* bring the inevitable agrarian revolution, conditions being ripe, to the point of *taking away* from the nobility their entire vast possessions. . . .

For *this* slogan [nationalization of the land] the proletariat will struggle, fully aware that [rural class differences will continue to exist in the form of rich peasants versus landless and poor peasants]. . . .

Such [agrarian] revolution would in itself in no way constitute socialism. But it would give the international working-class movement a tremendous incentive. It would strengthen the attitudes toward socialist revolution in Russia and increase its influence upon the landless proletariat and poor peasants. This [agrarian] revolution would give the proletariat of the city the opportunity—on the basis of this influence—to erect . . . Soviets of Workers' Deputies which would replace the old organs of the bourgeois governmental suppression—army, police, bureaucracy—and, under pressure of the unbearably heavy imperialist war and its consequences, to put through a series of revolutionary measures regarding control and distribution of production.

The Russian proletariat cannot alone *bring* the socialist revolution to a victorious conclusion. However, it can give the Russian revolution such momentum that through its action the best preconditions for this revolution are created and that it is, in a certain sense, begun. It can make it easier for its most important, truest, and most faithful comrades, the European and American socialist proletariat, to enter into the decisive struggle.

Only those of little faith despair because of the temporary victory

in European socialism of such lackeys of the imperialist bourgeoisie as
Scheidemann, . . . Renaudel, . . . and the English Fabians. We are
strongly convinced that the waves of world revolution will soon wash
away this filthy scum from the international workers' movement.

In Germany there *seethes* already the mood of the proletarian
masses. These have already done so much for mankind and socialism by
their stubborn, persistent, steadfast organization of labor in the course
of long decades of European "calm" [revolutionary calm] 1871–1914.
The future of German socialism will not represent the traitors Scheidemann, . . . David & Co., and such characterless adherents to the
"peaceable" period of politics as Kautsky, Haase, and the like.

This future will belong to that spirit which gave us Karl Liebknecht,
which created the Spartacus group, which conducted propaganda in
the Bremen *Arbeiterpolitik.*

The objective conditions of the imperialist war are vouchers for the
fact that the revolution will not stop on the *first level*—the Russian
revolution—that it will not confine itself to Russia. *The German proletariat is the most faithful and most reliable cohort of the Russian and
international proletarian revolution.*[34]

This single article is the best summary of Lenin's 1917 views on
the relation of Russian to world revolution. The ideas it contains are
basically those expressed by Lenin between 1902 and 1914, when,
still entirely in his Russian framework of activity, he was trying to
convince himself, the Bolshevik party, and the important Marxists
of Western Europe that the Russian proletariat held a vital place
in the world revolutionary scheme. Then, as on this occasion, he indicated that the Russian proletarian revolution, by overthrowing the
tsar, would act as inciting agent to the proletariat of Western
Europe, that Russia could not achieve socialism alone but must
wait for the industrial proletariat of the West to win out and carry
the basis for socialism into Russia. Though the article contains exactly Lenin's earlier ideas, the stresses placed upon them differ
considerably.

In earlier days, no doubt because of the need to make something
out of little, Lenin, while admitting that Russia was not yet ready
for socialism, was by no means reticent regarding the quality of its
proletariat. This proletariat, he implied, though small in numbers,
was in revolutionary education the most advanced in Europe.[35]
Subsequently, in 1908, he declared that the Russian proletariat, by
its street fighting and other activities in 1905, had become the model
for world proletarian action.[36]

In his "Farewell letter," however, he is at great pains to minimize the importance of Russia's proletariat, despite the fact that it had proved itself by the act of revolution. Note his emphasis upon the following ideas:

1. The Russian proletariat is not a chosen proletariat. It is less organized and less class-conscious than the proletariat of other countries. (Coupled with this statement is his affectionate mention of other proletarian movements of the world, the European, the American, and especially his extravagant praise of the German proletariat; all this as though to say that there, outside Russia, is the real Socialist movement.)

2. Only for a very brief period has the Russian working class become the spearhead of the revolutionary proletariat of the world; it is merely the steppingstone, the prologue, to greater revolutions.

3. Russia alone cannot achieve socialism. (This declaration he made four times.)

Lenin was speaking here as a scientific internationalist who could see his own backward country in its true Marxian light, as though attempting to atone for his earlier exaggerations, no longer necessary now that he was a man of world repute. In addition he momentarily expected the European revolution, which was sure to overshadow that in Russia. Wishing to play a key role in the greater revolution, he probably did not want to go on record as having made too much of the Russian one.

3

THE APRIL THESES AND THE THREE CRISES

THE TSARIST GOVERNMENT having fallen in March, 1917, Lenin burned with impatience to return to his native land and resume political activity. His repatriation, however, along with that of numerous other Russian revolutionaries, faced the deliberate obstruction of the British and French governments, which feared that such potent antiwar propagandists would further undermine the wavering Russian martial spirit. What was poison to the Allies was meat to the Germans, and Lenin was eventually able to negotiate an agreement with the German government permitting him to reach Russia through Germany. About four weeks passed before he was able to leave Switzerland, and during this hectic interim he wrote numerous letters in which he expressed his fears and hopes about events in Russia. In the famous five "Letters from Afar," written to instruct the Bolshevik party, he particularly stressed the following points:

1. Russia was a part of Europe. The March, 1917, revolution had progressed in typically European fashion: the workers had shed their blood, the bourgeoisie had reaped the fruits of victory.[1]

2. The Russian bourgeoisie was tied to its European counterpart. Therefore the war, conducted by the provisional government, was an imperialist, not a defensive war.[2]

3. The Russian proletariat was bound to that of Europe by its Marxist heritage; its revolutions of 1905 and 1917 had continued the traditions of the Paris Commune.[3] The revolution in Russia was only part of the greater process of European revolution, the March revolution having been merely "the first stage of the first revolution."[4]

Lenin, hoping at some later date to emerge as leader of Europe's revolution, had to convince the European proletariat that Russia was a part of Europe and that therefore the Russian leader was suitable as Europe's leader. But it was not enough to "prove" in words

Notes begin on page 206.

that Russia was European. Russia must act like a part of Europe. Moreover, if Lenin's aims were to be properly promoted, Russia would have to be more progressive than Europe, in the sense that under his guidance the Russian revolution would carry out the Zimmerwald Left program of breaking cleanly with any bourgeois government and its imperialist war as well as with the social traitors of the Second International.

"*Never again* along the lines of a Second International," he wrote to A. M. Kollontai on March 16. "*Never again* with Kautsky! By all means *a more revolutionary* program and more revolutionary tactics . . . war against imperialism; revolutionary propaganda . . . agitation and struggle for an *international* proletarian revolution and for the conquest of power by the 'Soviets of Workers' Deputies' (but not by the fakers of the Constitutional Democratic [i.e., bourgeois-liberal] Party)." [5]

The Petrograd Soviet of Workers' and Soldiers' Deputies, modeled upon the Soviet of 1905, came into existence on March 12. Similar councils appeared all over Russia in the days following the collapse of tsarist authority. Although the Soviet of the capital immediately assumed the role of a shadow government—permitting the provisional government to form, and generally acting as the unofficial guardian of the new democracy—few if any Russians envisaged the Soviets as permanent.[6] It was generally believed that they would vanish from the scene once the provisional government had given way to the Constituent Assembly. This body would then set up a parliament to which representatives of the people would be chosen in the traditional manner.

Taking a completely different tack, Lenin decided that the Soviets must remain in existence and give shape to the new state. Unlike the bourgeois parliament, the government based on Soviets would establish a militia, police force, and bureaucracy interested in working for and with, rather than against, the masses. Wrote Lenin in the third of his "Letters from Afar":

> We need the state but *not* of the kind needed by the bourgeoisie, with organs of power (police, army, bureaucracy) separated from and opposed to the people. All bourgeois revolutions have only improved upon *this* state machinery, only transferring *this* from the hands of one party into the hands of another.
>
> But the proletariat, to last out the battles of the present revolution and go on to win peace, bread and freedom, must "destroy," to use

Marx's expression, this "existing" machine and replace it with a new one, which *unites* police, army and bureaucracy with the *universally armed people*. Moving along the path beaten by the Paris Commune of 1871 and the Russian revolution of 1905, the proletariat must organize and arm *all* the poorest and most exploited sections of our people so that they *themselves* should take directly into their hands the organs of state power, *themselves comprising these organs.*

And the workers of Russia, already in the first stage of the first revolution, in March, 1917, have *entered* upon this course.[7]

Lenin thought the Soviets could serve a twofold purpose: (1) that of a device through which he could advertise himself and Russia as having made a revolutionary break with the old governmental form, through participation in which, incidentally, the European Socialists had betrayed the revolution; and (2) that of a specific form of organization for the European dictatorship, a form not envisioned by Lenin when, just before the outbreak of the March revolution, he had compiled his notebook of Marxian materials for *State and Revolution*. The link in Lenin's mind between Russian Soviets and Europe is clearly if unintentionally revealed in the memoirs of his wife. "Those," she writes, "who want thoroughly to understand Lenin's book, *State and Revolution*, must read [the third of the "Letters from Afar"] in [which] . . . Ilyich presents his ideas on the proletarian state." [8]

In the Paris Commune, or better in Marx's account of it, Lenin had a Marxian precedent excellent for his purposes. Marx, thoroughly frustrated after twenty-odd years of waiting for the English proletariat to rise, compensated himself by viewing the abortive Commune as a giant step toward the fulfillment of his prophecies. Marx made much of this "communistic" society, so frightening to the upper classes, whose "true secret" lay in the fact that it was "essentially a *regime of the working class,* the result of the struggle of the producing versus the taking [capitalist] class." [9] At the same time he conceded, though in less prominent terms, that the Commune regime depended for support on the petty bourgeois shopowners, craftsmen, and merchants, that is, the Parisian debtor class in general as against the creditor class.[10]

"Paris, the center and seat of the old governmental authority, and at the same time the center of gravity of the French working class," Marx crowed, "Paris had staged an armed uprising." [11] But, as Marx had to admit, Paris was also the capital of an agrarian country, and the proletarian Commune was forced to try to make common cause with the peasantry, using the slogan "Our victory is your hope!" This tactic, Marx defensively insisted, was "absolutely justified" on the ground that the peasantry, being heavily in debt (Marx at one point used the phrase "rural proletariat"), was therefore more or less proletarian in its orientation.[12]

The Soviets at the start were dominated by Mensheviks and Socialist Revolutionaries, or SRs (whom Lenin classed as petty bourgeois parties), and Russia was an agrarian country. But because Marx had so glorified and hence sanctioned the Paris Commune, Lenin had grounds for arguing that the Soviet was a Marxist rather than a merely Russian development, and he made the most of it.

In the third of his "Letters from Afar" Lenin wrote: "The whole task now consists of clearly understanding the nature of this new path and how boldly, firmly and steadfastly to advance further along it."[13]

Lenin hoped to convince both Western Marxists and his own Bolsheviks too, as will be shown, that the workers of Russia, having so brilliantly taken the first step in the trail blazed by Marx, were therefore ready, like proletarians in more advanced countries, to move toward taking control of state power. What if such a government could not introduce socialism? Marx had not expected an immediate introduction of socialism in France either. A people's government in Russia could still distribute what goods there were (bread, milk, homes, and so forth) among the poor.[14]

"Such measures," as Lenin was frank to admit, "are *not yet* socialism. They concern a distribution of commodities but not a reorganization of production. They would not yet constitute a 'dictatorship of the proletariat' but only a 'revolutionary democratic dictatorship of the proletariat and the poorest peasants.'" Then, as though fearing that this statement had deprived his argument of its Marxian base, he brushed it aside, as it were, by explaining that "the manner of classification does not matter here. It would be the greatest error if we should try to fit the complex, vital and rapidly developing practical tasks of the revolution into the procrustean bed of a narrowly conceived 'theory' instead of seeing in the theory . . . above all *a guide to action*."[15]

Lenin could not afford to be too exact about Marxian classification. Marx, it is true, had compromised with his tenets in singing such unrestrained hosannas to the "proletarian" Commune. But to depict the Russia of 1917 as a parallel to what Marx had wished to see in the Commune was to distort the dialectic quite beyond recognition. Lenin was probably aware of what he was doing. However, it must be kept in mind that he was much more concerned with form than with content. When seen from the distance of Western Europe,[16] a Soviet state, having established a universal militia, etc., might (despite Russia's predominantly peasant composition) pass for something like the Paris Commune. Lenin at this time did not expect to erect a permanent structure in Russia on such wobbly theoretical foundations. It was revolution in the West, beginning in Germany, that would, he believed, provide Russia with the real basis for proletarianism. "If in . . . Germany and in Russia," Lenin wrote late in April, "state power were to pass wholly and exclusively into the hands of the Soviets of Workers' and Soldiers' Deputies, then the passing of all countries into socialism would actually be assured." [17]

Lenin's immediate goal was a Russia camouflaged by a hastily assembled façade of the proletarian state. Then, when revolution occurred in the West, he could take charge of it as though simply making a transfer from one proletarian society (Russia) to another (the West). He would be additionally fortified in this move by being able to bring with him a form of proletarian organization, the Soviet, which would already have passed through a stage of practical experimentation. If, as Lenin probably expected, revolt in the West was to precede the establishment of Soviet power in Russia, Lenin, having proceeded in the true and undiluted Marxist tradition, would still be able to claim the distinction of having headed the first attempt since the Commune to fashion a workers' society.

To succeed in his purpose, Lenin of course needed the unconditional support of the Bolshevik party. However much he may have regarded his leadership as essential to the proper progress of the European proletarian revolution, Lenin could not possibly have presented a plan of action to the party stated in terms of his personal mission. He therefore saw it as his problem to induce the Bolsheviks to adopt a program which, while seeming to make sense as applied to Russia, was aimed primarily at catching the eye of the West, thereby serving Lenin's aspirations in that major arena of the world revolutionary conflict.

Before Lenin's return, Kamenev, Stalin, and other old-timers had maneuvered the Bolshevik party into a position that deprived it of all mobility. The party declared itself opposed to both the government and the war. Beyond this it refused to venture, considering the Russian proletariat too weak to institute a rising, especially since the government enjoyed the confidence of the Soviet of Workers' and Soldiers' Deputies. Disabled by this stand from either fighting or supporting the bourgeois authority, the Bolsheviks officially declared themselves as the party in the Soviet most sincerely devoted to keeping a sharp eye on the suspect government. *Pravda* of March 27, 1917, demanded that "the revolutionary democracy headed by the proletariat [exercise] the most unremitting control over all acting authorities, whether in the center or in the local areas."

However stern the tone of this message, in practice the Bolshevik party had placed itself alongside the Mensheviks and SRs in the Soviet, who also denounced the government and the imperialist war, yet allowed both to continue. As a natural outgrowth of this position, in fact, the Bolshevik leaders had begun to think of forming a bloc in the Soviet with at least the Internationalist wing of the Menshevik party. Lenin's return on April 16 was to dash ice water on this quasi-Menshevik accommodation of the Bolshevik leadership. To a caucus of Bolshevik members of the All-Russian Congress of Soviets, Lenin the next day read his so-called April Theses,[18] which might be described as the Zimmerwald Left program as adjusted to Russia and Russian conditions.

Of the Bolsheviks, the model party for Europe's proletarians, Lenin demanded a complete break with the bourgeois government and its moderate Socialist supporters who, like their colleagues in the West, had termed the imperialist war a "defensist" war and had made a *Burgfrieden* with the bourgeoisie. A democratic peace, the Theses said, was *"impossible"* without the overthrow of capital. This truth the Bolsheviks must explain to the masses and propagate "among the army units in the field" who were also to be instructed to fraternize with the enemy.

Instead of a parliamentary republic, the Bolsheviks must seek a republic of Soviets. This state, with the old organs of power (police, army, and bureaucracy) replaced by a universally armed people, would constitute a state modeled after the Paris Commune.

As the international parallels to the above conditions, the Theses demanded that the Bolsheviks break all ties with the Second International and the "Center"—this meant breaking with the Zimmerwald bloc—and proceed to the formation of a new International.

Other portions of the Theses called for "nationalization of *all* the land," preceded by "confiscation of all landed estates," the "immediate merger of all banks in the country into one national bank" subject to Soviet control, and the changing of the party's name from Social Democratic to Communist.

As to tactics, the Theses cautioned the Bolsheviks specifically against risking civil war. The *"immediate* task" was not the "introduction" of socialism, but "only the transfer of social production and distribution of goods to *the control* of the Soviets of Workers' Deputies." In most of the Soviets, Lenin pointed out, the Bolsheviks constituted but a tiny minority "as compared to the *bloc of all* the petty bourgeois opportunist elements [SRs, Mensheviks, etc.] who have surrendered to the influence of the bourgeoisie and have been extending this influence to the proletariat." Lenin's instructions to the party included the following:

> It must be made clear to the masses that the Soviet of Workers' Deputies is the *only possible form of revolutionary government*. And therefore, while *this* government submits to the influence of the bourgeoisie, *our task can only be* the patient, systematic, and persistent explanation of its errors and tactics in a manner adapted particularly to the needs of the masses.
>
> While we are in the minority, we conduct ourselves as critics, pointing out errors, teaching, at the same time, the necessity of transferring the entire power of the state to the Soviets of Workers' Deputies, so that the masses, from experience, may learn to overcome their errors.

Opposing Lenin's Theses, the old guard Bolsheviks recalled that Lenin himself in 1905 had held the view that the completed bourgeois revolution would be followed by a proletarian-peasant republic. But by April, 1917, the peasants had not yet made their revolution so that the bourgeois revolution could not be considered as completed. Though the time for even the proletarian-peasant republic had not yet arrived, Lenin was placing something like a Paris Commune on the order of the day. This the "old Bolsheviks" likened to the Narodnik notion of skipping the capitalist period on the road to socialism—a non-Marxian scheme implying minority seizure of power, a Blanquist program of adventurism.

Lenin promptly counterattacked. The bourgeoisie, he maintained, did hold state power, and to "that extent the bourgeois-democratic revolution [had been] *completed*." [19] A skipping of the bourgeois revolution was therefore no longer possible. In Petrograd, at the same time, real power was "actually in the hands of the workers and soldiers." [20] Thus the proletarian-peasant dictatorship was already achieved. Those who constituted it, however, believed as yet that the overthrow of the tsar had changed the nature of the war. Therefore they supported the government and its imperialist war, thinking it was being waged in defense of their revolution.

As for Russia at large, the peasants had not yet seized the land and were for the moment part of the unconscious proletarian-peasant alliance as represented by the Petrograd Soviet,[21] "and just as freely [did] they *give away* their power to the bourgeoisie." [22] But allowing for the inevitable peasant revolution, Lenin denied that this would signify the outright triumph of bourgeois power. For there was a "very deep gulf between the agricultural laborers and poorest peasants on the one hand and the peasant landowners on the other." [23] Even after the seizures of land, Lenin pointed out, 90 per cent of the peasants would side with the workers in a Soviet government.[24]

By a flexible use of the concept of power and an ingenious if artificial division of the peasant question into present and future stages, Lenin was able to present an oversimplified picture of the situation in Russia. In this view a tiny bourgeois oligarchy was holding out against an overwhelmingly multitudinous revolutionary demos. The latter, given the necessary enlightenment, would easily assume its Soviet power. The use of forceful or adventurist methods, Lenin scorned as alien to his program. He wrote, mocking Trotsky:

This danger might threaten me were I to say: "No tsar, but a workers' state." But I have not said this. . . . I said that power in Russia can at present go from [the provisional government] *only* to the Soviets and these are dominated by the peasants, by soldiers, by the petty bourgeoisie. . . . In my Theses I absolutely secured myself against any leaping over of a not yet fulfilled peasant or other petty bourgeois movement, against any *playing* with "seizure of power" by a workers' government, against any type whatever of Blanquist adventure, for I alluded directly to the experience of the Paris Commune. This, . . . as Marx . . . and Engels . . . carefully pointed out, completely excluded Blanquism, guaranteed direct, immediate, unconditional *majority* rule and mass activity only to the extent of the *conscious* action of the majority.[25]

But until the majority became "conscious," Lenin asked in effect, was it not the duty of bolshevism to guide the masses toward their best interests—to help them in the pre-Socialist interim to improve their economic lot? Was it the function of Bolsheviks to allow the masses to be deceived into supporting a government that carried on an imperialist war? Was there any way of attaining peace except through a government whose interests were not bound to those of world imperialism, i.e., a government of Soviets? [26]

But the "old Bolsheviks," Lenin charged, were out of line with the realities of 1917, and hence with Marxism. They continued to cling dogmatically to the old formulas and had failed to note the achievement of power by the masses, the actuality of revolutionary power existing in the Soviets.

"Who *now*," Lenin wrote, "speaks only of 'revolutionary-democratic dictatorship of proletariat and peasantry' remains behind life, has in effect gone over to the petty bourgeoisie and opposes the proletarian class struggle. Such a one should enter the archive of 'Bolshevik' prerevolutionary antiques (one might call it archive of 'old Bolsheviks')." [27]

The "old Bolsheviks" were not only hurt by Lenin's attack but also more than a little baffled. Said Kalinin at the April 27 conference of the Petrograd Bolsheviks:

I belong to the old Bolshevik Leninists, . . . and see no essential disagreement between ourselves and Comrade Lenin. The only thing new in the Theses . . . is the proposition that the Soviet of Workers' Deputies is the sole form of government. This is not true—but it is true that the Soviet at the present time appears to be the only possible authority. . . .

What is different in the point about the agrarian program compared to what Bolsheviks said in the past? Nothing. . . . The point about the banks has no practical propagandistic significance. About the name of the party, we could just as easily show the [Mensheviks] that despite the name, the masses come to us. But for practical considerations, I propose that we first advertise the name Socialist-Communists and then take on the new party name—in the interim retaining the bolshevik title. I understand the feelings of comrades coming from abroad where the word social democrat has become so dirtied. But that is not so [in Russia].[28]

Kalinin justly viewed as unreasonable Lenin's proposition that Soviet power was the only possible alternative to the existing situation. At the April 21 session of the party's Petrograd Committee, Sergei Bogdat'ev had earlier attacked this and other points of Lenin's Theses. Bogdat'ev declared it absurd, in one and the same program, to demand a bourgeois-free government of Soviet power, whose first task, according to Lenin, would be the convocation of a constituent assembly which by democratic necessity would include bourgeois representatives. "Why not call the Soviet the parliament of a republic?" [29] Bogdat'ev wanted to know, wondering wherein a Soviet government would differ from an old-fashioned republican legislative assembly.

The method to Lenin's madness eluded both Kalinin and Bogdat'ev. Nor was Lenin in a position to explain that he was trying to get them to accept a program whose main purpose was to disguise peasant Russia as a more advanced country by garbing her in something that might appear to the West as a resurrected Paris Commune. In essence, Kalinin and Bogdat'ev accused Lenin of quibbling over terminology. But it was largely terminology that Lenin was concerned with, for it would be the idea, not the actual shape of the thing, that would be carried abroad. If, as Kalinin said, seizing the banks had no propaganda value in Russia, it did, as Lenin saw it, have the function of telling the West that his program ran parallel to that of Marx. The latter's polemics on the Paris Commune make much of the fact that the Communards failed to seize the banks of Paris. The change of party name to Communist, to Kalinin [30] another trifling matter, had to Lenin the importance of a headline to the West—dramatizing his break with the betrayers of Marx in the Social-Democratic parties of Europe, and was furthermore directly connected with Lenin's demand that the Bolsheviks undertake to found a new International. An analysis of Lenin's detailed explanation of this demand, as given in the pamphlet *Tasks of the Proletariat in Our Revolution*,[31] reveals the extent to which Lenin was ready to distort the natural course of the Russian revolution for the sake of his European ends and further explains why the "old Bolsheviks," not suspecting the crass opportunism that underlay his thoughts, were unable to make much sense out of Lenin's line of reasoning.

Outlining the existing trends in European socialism,[32] Lenin characterized the majority (or right-wing) Socialists in the various countries as "Socialists in words and chauvinists in fact," the "Center" (the rightist majority of Zimmerwald), of which Kautsky was "the main leader," as "a domain of gentle petty bourgeois phrases, of internationalism in words, cowardly opportunism and fawning before the social chauvinists in deeds." The third trend, that of "internationalists in deeds," he wrote, "is most nearly expressed by the 'Zimmerwald Left.'"

Lest the Bolsheviks think it presumptuous if not fantastic to be themselves proclaiming the birth of a European international, Lenin explained to them that they did not yet realize that the Zimmerwald majority was of Kautskyan disposition, "a basic fact . . . of which Western Europe [was already] fully aware." [33] Since Western Europe's workers had recognized Kautsky's "Center" for what Lenin said it was (certainly a stupendous exaggeration), and since they were therefore ready for the formation of a new international, the Bolsheviks would be blazing no new trail but would merely be following an established European trend.

Only in Russia, Lenin declared, had a working class generated such great revolutionary energy. "But to whom much is given, much is also asked." Consequently, it was the international duty of the Bolsheviks to "break at once with this [chauvinist] International . . . . It is precisely we, who must now, without delay, found the *new* proletarian international, or rather [lest he be contradicting his argument that Europe already stood on new internationalist ground] not be afraid to admit for all to hear, that it is already *founded* and functioning."

"This is the international of those 'internationalists in deeds' [such as Liebknecht of Germany, MacLean of Scotland, Pannekoek of Holland, among those that Lenin named]. These alone are the representatives and not the corrupters of the revolutionary internationalist masses."

Lenin anticipated the question of whether a handful of individuals could be said to represent a universal desire of Western Europe for the new international.

"If there are few of *such* Socialists," he said, "let each Russian worker ask himself how many conscious revolutionaries there were in Russia *on the eve* of the [March] revolution. The matter is not one of numbers, but of a correct expression of the ideas and politics of a truly revolutionary proletariat."

But if there was in the West so potent if small a revolutionary force, why could it not take the initiative in forming the new international? To this question too, which his faulty argumentation had raised, Lenin had a ready answer.

" 'To wait' for international congresses and conferences [to take the decisive step]," Lenin warned, "means to be *traitors* to internationalism." This was so, Lenin pointed out, because "even from Stockholm true international Socialists are not allowed to come to us, nor even to write to us, despite the full opportunity for [applying to their letters] the severest type of military censorship." There being no hope then of Western Socialists taking the necessary action, Lenin urged his party not to "wait" but "to found the Third International—and hundreds of Socialists in German and English prisons would sigh with relief." That the "best" Socialists of the West were in prison constituted another of Lenin's reasons why the Russians had to take the first step.

"In no other land on earth is there *now* the freedom that exists in Russia. Let us use this freedom," Lenin exhorted, ". . . to found the type of third international Liebknecht would want, one that will be daring, honest and proletarian and equally hostile to traitors—whether they are social chauvinists or waverers of the 'Center.' " [34]

As to tactics, Lenin's Theses agreed with the previously determined Bolshevik line in so far as Lenin disavowed direct revolutionary action. But the slogan "All Power to the Soviets," which demanded an open antigovernment stand and a definite break with revolutionary defensism, constituted a clear departure from the party's pre-April 17 position. Lenin's stand precluded any sort of bloc with the Mensheviks, even with their so-called Internationalist wing.[35] Initially, almost the entire Bolshevik leadership reacted negatively to Lenin's proposals.[36] Soon, however, particularly within the Petrograd section of the party, the tide began to flow Leninward. Within two weeks the "old Bolsheviks" were left high and dry, clinging to the bare crags of their moderate program.

This development is explainable by the fact that the senior Bolsheviks, being largely theoreticians, had no direct contact with the masses. The lesser leaders, on the other hand, were in touch with the rank and file of the party and therefore responsive to the mass mood. In the pre-Lenin days this mood had not yet crystallized into an index of political direction, and so the lesser Bolsheviks were content to take their bearings from the prestige-laden elders. But Lenin's Theses, rejected by the latter on the first reading, had also been severely attacked, and hence publicized, by the bourgeois and socialist press. *Yedinstvo,* a Menshevik paper, charged Lenin with having issued a call to civil war. The second and subsequent readings of the Theses came to the Bolshevik leadership from the factory workers and most emphatically from the Petrograd garrisons. To the soldier-peasants particularly the combined themes of peace and land had brought a thrilling message. Had Lenin called for civil war? He denied it, but the Mensheviks and others said he had. In any event, there was confusion as to what he meant. One thing though seemed clear enough: he had spoken against the government and had called for arming the people. To the excitable and impatient masses the Theses came as a jumble of notions, but the general impression was that of a call to direct action and this was what they wanted to hear. It was inevitable that the second-line Bolsheviks would follow the mass mood and place their weight behind the Theses, or at least that part of the Theses which concerned Russia. Of the Theses' international aims, the masses, of course, had no understanding whatsoever, and hence exerted no pressure toward their fulfillment.

Whether out of feelings of conviction or from a need to save face, the "old Bolsheviks" continued to oppose the Theses.[37] But once Lenin's message, however misunderstood, had been seized upon by the masses,[38] it would no longer have made sense to fight it on the theoretical level. Kamenev, chief spokesman for the opposition, concentrated his oratory upon a single theme—adventurism.

The second session of the Petrograd Party Conference met April 28 to discuss a resolution, based on the Theses, dealing with the party's attitude toward the provisional government. After listing seven major crimes of the government in a tone bound to stir up the masses, the resolution concluded mildly enough: "For the transfer of all governmental power into the hands of the Soviets . . . there must be prolonged work toward clarifying the proletarian class consciousness." [39]

Kamenev protested on the ground that lively agitation without specific direction by the party would result in spontaneous mass action. Troubling him also was the obvious fact that the party had gone beyond hinting. Among the members there had risen an increasing preference for the slogan "Down with the Provisional Government," a slogan with unquestionably explosive possibilities. Kamenev declared:

At the moment [we cannot adopt] the slogan of overthrowing the . . . government. Between the government and the Soviet there exists an agreement. . . . If you propose that this agreement be destroyed tomorrow, it is necessary to say so today. Shall we not tell the soldiers what they must do today? In the motivational part of the resolution there are no directives for a transfer of power to the proletariat; it lacks that which would make it possible for our agitators to bring it to life. As long as you do not call for the overthrow of the . . . government, call now, as our [erstwhile] resolution has it, for control over it.

Just before the session came to a vote, Kamenev, aware of his impending defeat, attempted to add two corrections to the resolution. The second of these called for large-scale propaganda explaining the true class character of the provisional government, but asked that the conference for the present express its opposition to the slogan of "overthrowing the government," as a disorganizing idea. Lenin, who only days earlier had angrily denied that his Theses had issued a "call to civil war," sat quietly, refusing to back up Kamenev's proposal. It was defeated by a vote of 20 against, 6 for, and 9 abstaining. The resolution as a whole was adopted, 24 votes being cast in its favor.[40]

On May 3, just two days after the excitement generated by the revolution's first May Day,[41] the Soviet learned that Miliukov, Foreign Minister in the provisional government, had sent the Allies a note informing them that Russia was in the war to the end and would live up to the "imperialist" agreements previously made. This led to protest demonstrations of soldiers and workers who clashed with progovernment elements on the night of May 3 and particularly on May 4.[42] The Bolshevik party had had no part in initiating the riotings,[43] but the tone of the inscriptions borne by the demonstrators was clearly a sign of the party's influence.[44] A direct Bolshevik contribution, once the demonstration was in motion, was the slogan "Down with the Provisional Government," which had been introduced by extremist elements of the Petrograd Bolshevik Committee. These, stampeded by the roar of the mob, had deliberately disregarded their committee's decision, made on the night of May 3, not to employ the slogan for the occasion but to organize a peaceable demonstration.[45]

While the Mensheviks scoffed at the disorder in the Bolshevik ranks, Lenin, in a May 6 article, sharply expressed his displeasure at the use of the slogan.[46] "I fully agree with Comrade Lenin," commented a caustic Kamenev next day at the first session of the All-Russian Bolshevik Conference, "but I think that the warning should have been given somewhat sooner." Kamenev then restated his plea that the party agree to control the government through the Soviet, but refrain from offering nondirective explanations.[47] Lenin, somewhat flustered by what he considered a dangerously premature act by party members,[48] proceeded in demagogic fashion to absolve himself of all blame. He began by deriding Kamenev for harping on the theme of Bolshevik adventurism, whereupon he himself declared "Down with the Provisional Government" to be an "adventurer's slogan." The "deviation to the left" of the undisciplined men of the Petrograd Committee, Lenin described as "a most serious crime," the "greatest crime . . . disorganization." [49] He failed to mention his own silent approval of the slogan, which had of course encouraged the "deviation."

Though retreating from the more exposed position of tacitly approving the provocative slogan, Lenin refused to budge from his basic program. Kamenev cautioned anew that the Theses as a whole, not the single slogan, had caused the trouble. He predicted that the Theses, lacking specific directives, would again arouse the masses to take spontaneous revolutionary action and force the party, whose slogans they would follow, into undesired adventurism.[50] Lenin argued that the fault lay not in the program, but in the inadequacy of the party's organization. Given the necessary organization, the party membership and hence the masses, he thought, could be held under perfect control.[51] Lenin also stressed and restressed the point that Soviet power was identical with majority rule. To advocate it therefore was the very antithesis to adventurism.[52]

However pious Lenin's words, his deeds previous to the May outbursts show that he was not averse to reinforcing the "patient explanations" called for in the Theses by certain less patient methods of inciting the masses. This proves that the Theses in their entirety, however camouflaged by Lenin's argumentation, were in fact designed to prod the masses leftward, and did therefore contain at least some of the adventuristic quality referred to by Kamenev. On the other hand, as his attitude toward the May crisis reveals, Lenin did not intend that his Theses should stir up armed revolt; indeed, he was definitely opposed to allowing this tendency to gain the upper hand. Further evidence to this effect can be derived from

Lenin's resolution offered to the All-Russian Party Conference on May 10, which dealt with the way in which a Soviet government would proceed in attempting to end the war.

To answer the "slander" which reported that the Bolsheviks favored a separate peace with Germany, Lenin declared that "the German capitalists [were] bandits equally with the capitalists of Russia, England, France, etc.," and that Wilhelm was "a crowned bandit on the same order as Nicholas II or the monarchs of England, Italy, Rumania, etc." But

> the revolutionary class, upon having seized the state power, would inaugurate a series of measures to undermine the economic rule of the capitalists [and] render them completely harmless politically, and would immediately and frankly offer to all peoples a democratic peace on the basis of complete relinquishment of every possible form of annexation or indemnity. Such measures and such an open offer of peace would bring about an attitude of complete confidence of the workers of the belligerent countries toward each other . . . and would inevitably lead to uprisings of the proletariat against such imperialist governments as might resist the offered peace.[53]

The above view was largely the same as that which Lenin had expressed in an article in *Sotsial Demokrat*, October 13, 1915. There he had stated that if the Bolsheviks came to power during the war (there were, of course, no Soviets in 1915), they would offer a democratic peace "to all belligerents on the conditions that they liberate their colonies and *all* dependent, oppressed and underprivileged peoples." His conclusion was that none of the great powers could accept these conditions. Then the Bolsheviks would prepare for and carry on revolutionary war by putting into effect their entire minimum program. This would rouse to action the suppressed peoples of Russia, the colonial and dependent nations of Asia, and the socialist proletariat of Europe.[54]

Despite the fact that Russia, as he did not really expect in 1915, had actually produced the first revolution, Lenin, in May, 1917, still thought in terms of a "minimum" program. This is indicated by the moderate language he used with reference to removing the capitalists from power and even more so by a further comment contained in his May 10 report:

> If the revolutionary class assumes power in Russia, and there are no risings in the other countries, what will the revolutionary party do? This question is answered in the last paragraph of our resolution:

"Until the revolutionary class in Russia shall have taken over the entire state power, our party will with all means support those proletarian parties and groups in foreign countries as are already, during the continuance of the war, conducting a revolutionary struggle against their own imperialist governments and their bourgeoisie." [55]

The minimal aspects of Lenin's May aims are seen in the distinction he made between the "revolutionary class" and the "revolutionary party" and in the remark "until the revolutionary class . . . shall have taken over the entire state power." The time when the "revolutionary class" would have attained Soviet power, Lenin conceived of as the first stage of the revolution's development. Only later, when the "revolutionary [Bolshevik] party" would have gained control over the Soviets, would, in Lenin's view, the "revolutionary class" have taken over the "entire" state power. Only this would have made it possible for the Bolsheviks to replace their minimum program with their maximum program of proletarian dictatorship.

In the period from 1904 to 1906 both Lenin and Trotsky had agreed that the Russian revolution, led by the proletariat, should with one blow eliminate the power of the tsar and the bourgeoisie. Seeing no hope for an immediate introduction of socialism in Russia, even after this should have happened, Lenin had expressed the belief that the next move should be the establishment of a proletarian-peasant republic. This republic would endure, under proletarian guidance, until the European revolution had taken place and the West would initiate Russia into socialism. Trotsky had gone further. According to him, the Russian proletariat should set up a dictatorship and proceed toward socialism. However, since the proletarian government would eventually face a peasant counterrevolution and intervention from foreign capitalist nations, it would have to adopt a policy of "permanent revolution," that is, move at once into the European arena where the workers, ripe for revolution, would join the Russian forces in the world revolutionary crusade. Lenin's more cautious program for the Russian revolution was seemingly derived from his inability to share with Trotsky and other prominent Marxists of the day the belief that Europe's proletariat was prepared to rise. For had he believed this, he should logically have arrived at conclusions similar to those of Trotsky. However, Lenin's behavior in 1917 sheds a revealing light upon what he had done in 1905 and the reverse is equally true. For in May, 1917, though Lenin himself, like Trotsky in 1905, believed in the imminence of Europe's revolution, he still refused to accept the idea of the "workers' state" for Russia.[56] Times had changed, but Lenin apparently had not. In 1905, it would appear, Lenin, unknown in Europe, had preferred the role of a leader in Russia's revolution to that of a nonentity ready to give his all in the name of world revolution. But if in 1905 he was reluctant to sacrifice his status as Russian leader, not to mention his life, in 1917 he was playing for even higher stakes—leadership of the world revolution. This would explain why, whatever incentive to European revolution the establishment of a proletarian regime in Russia might produce, Lenin had no interest in becoming the legendary hero of a Petrograd commune. This was even more the case because of the assumed imminence of European revolution. In view of what that event could be expected to achieve for Russia and for Lenin, who was by this time a European "figure," any thought of martyrdom must have appeared to him to be quite superfluous.

As previously mentioned, the early achievement of Bolshevik power was not essential to Lenin's scheme. If it were preceded by Europe's revolution, he might still point with parental pride to a Russia pregnant with unrevised Marxism and power rapidly accruing to or held by the Soviets. Without risking his prestige or neck, Lenin would have garnered the reputation, so different from that of Europe's foremost Socialists, of having preached and practiced true internationalism in the face of a bourgeois imperialist government. In the absence of stronger candidates he had reason to hope that such a record would go far toward providing him with the seat of power in a Europe aflame with revolution.

What the April Theses boil down to is Lenin's attempt, with unwitting Bolshevik support, to move the masses of Russia steadily toward the establishment of the Soviets as their organs of government. Such a development, in addition to encouraging the Western proletariat to break with its traditional governmental form, would also incline it to accept the guidance of the man most experienced in both the theory and the practice of revolutionary dictatorship. At the same time Lenin wished to avoid stirring up an explosion, which, if it ended in failure, might easily frustrate his European ambitions.

The May riots forced Miliukov and Guchkov, the two ministers most closely associated with imperialism, to resign from the government. On May 18 the second provisional government, a coalition of bourgeois and Socialist ministers, came into existence. Among the titans of the Soviet who moved "upstairs" were Chernov and Tseretelli, leaders respectively of the SR and Menshevik parties. To dispel the bad impression left upon Russian public opinion by the May 1 dispatch, Tereshchenko, the new Foreign Minister, issued a statement to the press in which he emphasized the "profoundly idealistic," hence nonimperialistic, war aims of the new government.[57] At the same time he gave the Allies firm assurances of Russia's intention to fight to the end against the Central Powers.[58] Lest there be any Allied doubts on this score, the government made plans for an early offensive.[59] This meant reactivating the army, and orders went out which were calculated to restore discipline and prevent fraternization. Kerensky, then Minister of War, sent morale-building messages to the troops. He himself toured the front to make fiery speeches calling for patriotism and sacrifice in the name of the democratic revolution.

However sincere the professed anti-imperialism of the new government, by planning an offensive it aroused the fury and suspicion of the Petrograd soldiery. By the end of May it was evident to the Military Committee of the Bolshevik party that tension in the garrisons was mounting to a point at which a repetition of the May 4 crisis was clearly at hand. The Bolsheviks had been caught unprepared the first time. Now, alert to the incalculable dangers of a spontaneous explosion of soldier sentiment, a caucus of Central Committee members, meeting June 18, decided in principle to organize this sentiment and provide it with political leadership. The committee at the same time expressed the desire that the situation be exploited for its propaganda value among those proletarians who still followed the guidance of Mensheviks or SRs. A final decision as to what action to take was therefore left to a more broadly representative Central Committee meeting, scheduled for June 21.[60] In the meantime the mood of the factory proletariat was to undergo further study.

Lenin and Zinoviev attended the Central Committee meeting of June 19, when the Bolshevik Nevsky, of the Narva Rayon, described the intense excitement among the soldiers. Nevsky suggested that the Military Committee take the initiative in organizing a demonstration, otherwise it "would occur spontaneously. . . . That very day the Pavlovsky Regiment . . . [had] designated representatives of the Petrograd garrison for the purpose of discussing the question of a demonstration." [61] The committee then accepted a motion for taking the initiative,[62] and, though informed of the fact that most soldiers desired an armed demonstration, expressed itself preponderantly in favor of a peaceable demonstration.[63] A minority faction took the position that the Bolsheviks, without advocating a seizure of power, should prepare for the event that the demonstration would take a violent turn. In that case, Smilga and others of the Petrograd Committee proposed, the Bolsheviks should not refrain from seizing such key positions as postal and telegraph offices, railroad stations, banks and arsenals.[64] There was difference of opinion also as to whether the demonstration should be purely military or whether it should include workers too. Most of the speakers agreed that a demonstration without workers would be quite lacking in political value—that only the workers could bring into the demonstration "the maximum of organization and political awareness and provide the proper slogans." [65]

The deciding vote of the June 21 meeting was a mere formality. The time and order for a peaceable demonstration were set and the Bolsheviks went about preparing the task. Party workers aided by several hundred Kronstadt sailors spread the word through the ranks of the military. On June 22, bills were posted throughout the workers' quarters announcing a worker-soldier demonstration for the following day.[66] To provide the workers with a direct interest in the demonstration the posters stressed two points: first, that the starvation level of Russian workers was due to the imperialist war and capitalist profits, and second, that a redisciplined army would become the government's weapon for counterrevolutionary purposes.[67]

Meanwhile the first All-Russian Congress of Soviets had convened. At its second session, June 17, Tseretelli, Minister of Post and Telegraph, declared in his address that there was no party in Russia willing to take power. "At any minute," said Lenin, who took the floor after Tseretelli, "[the Bolsheviks] are ready to take power." Lenin went on to explain that the war was being fought for 500–800 per cent profits for Russian capitalists, and that only by eliminating the profit motive from the war could it become a war in defense of the revolution. But to achieve this meant publishing information on war profits, arresting "fifty or a hundred of the biggest millionaires," in short, the downing of the provisional government, which, though camouflaged by socialist ministers, still carried on its business at the same old imperialist stand.[68] On June 22, the day before the demonstration was to take place, Lenin made another antiwar, antigovernment speech before the congress.

On June 22 the Executive Committee of the Petrograd Soviet, fearing the announced demonstration as a possible Bolshevik stroke for power, announced that it would not permit the demonstration. A Bolshevik conference at nine o'clock that night decided to ignore this on the ground that any party had the right to call for a peaceable demonstration.[69] Later that night the All-Russian Congress added its authority to that of the Petrograd Soviet. A resolution was passed condemning the demonstration as a Bolshevik attempt to overthrow the provisional government and forbidding any demonstration for three days. Any person disregarding this decision was to be labeled "an enemy of the revolution." Among the stated reasons for banning the demonstration, the resolution gave one wherein the congress professed to "know that the hidden counterrevolutionaries [were] preparing to take advantage of the [Bolshevik-called] demonstration." [70] Late that night the Bolshevik Central Committee met again. At two in the morning, the last possible moment, Lenin reluctantly gave the word to call off the demonstration. It was obviously impossible for the Bolshevik party to defy the All-Russian Congress of Soviets, the very organization which it claimed should hold all power.[71] But Lenin was furious. In *Pravda*, June 24, he railed at the "perplexed and frightened [Mensheviks and SRs of the Congress of Soviets] who made a fantastic 'plot' out of [the contemplated] demonstration," passing "a thunderous resolution, full of desperate and sharp words against our party." The charge that the Bolsheviks wanted to overthrow the government, Lenin termed "stupid to extremes." "A *coup d'état*," he went on, "by means of a peaceful demonstration, decided upon on Thursday, planned for Saturday and announced on Saturday morning. Well, gentlemen, whom do you really want to astound with your nonsensical insinuations?" [72] Lenin emphatically stated and restated the right of his or any other party "in a free country" to call demonstrations, adding that "even if the Soviets should become the supreme revolutionary parliament we would *not* submit [to restraint of] our freedom of agitation . . . by forbidding of peaceful demonstrations, etc. In that event we would prefer to become an illegal, officially persecuted party, rather than give up our Marxist . . . principles." [73] Tseretelli, whose speech on June 24 before the Congress of Soviets had demanded that the "Bolshevik conspiracy" be placed "outside the pale of revolutionary democracy," Lenin labeled an "out and out counterrevolutionist." [74]

While it is perfectly true that Lenin did not plan to turn the June demonstration into a seizure of power, his indignation toward the leaders of the Soviet rings a very false note. Menshevik and SR ideology clearly envisaged a legally constituted Russian government in which the bourgeoisie would play a prominent if not dominant part.[75] But the slogan "All Power to the Soviets," if not a call to violence, could mean only collaboration of all Socialists to the end of easing the weak bourgeoisie from power. Since it opposed one of their basic doctrines, Lenin's slogan, especially as it acquired armed mass support, was bound to rouse the moderate Socialists against Lenin and drive them into closer adherence to the bourgeoisie. Then instead of a struggle against a tiny and isolated bourgeoisie, which truly would have been no war at all, Lenin's campaign for Soviet power would also have to be waged against the more solidly founded SRs and Mensheviks, a matter of serious conflict, conceivably leading to armed clashes.

That the Menshevik and SR leaders in the Soviet reacted as they did in June is by no means surprising. But it is surprising at first glance that Lenin, who had never minced words about their petty bourgeois nature, should not have foreseen the direction in which he had compelled them to move. The explanation is that Lenin was suffering from self-delusion. He required the slogan of "Soviet Power" to intensify the leftward pace of the Russian revolution. But he dreaded the thought that armed action might develop prematurely and ruin his plans. Hence he blinded himself to the most reasonably expectable, almost inevitable, result of his slogan.

The June events, so clear in their import, failed to shake Lenin out of his fool's paradise. This is best indicated by the inertia that possessed him during the crisis of July 16–17. On this occasion the seeds planted by his Theses came fully to blossom as the Petrograd masses took to the streets without awaiting Bolshevik sanction, and the SRs and Mensheviks of the government adopted forceful and even fraudulent measures in their attempts to destroy Lenin. Before going on to this there rises yet one other interesting question regarding Lenin's behavior in June.

For one who had not intended to provoke the outbreak of civil war, Lenin had certainly allowed the situation to drift dangerously far in that direction. Lenin made much of the right to peaceable demonstrations and mocked the Soviet's fears of violent antigovernmental action and Bolshevik conspiracy. But the fact remains that the tone of Lenin's speeches in the days before the demonstration, his mention notably of Bolshevik readiness to take power, matched very closely in quality the extremist sentiments expressed at the Bolshevik committee meeting of June 19, when Smilga and others spoke of seizing arsenals and railroad stations. Nor was Lenin ignorant of how thin a line separated a "peaceable" demonstration of armed soldiers from action of a violent nature. Why then, if Lenin really wished the masses to control their passions, did he deliver such rabble-rousing talks?

The answer to this question appears to lie in the fact that Lenin's speeches were not essentially intended for a Petrograd audience. The Petrograd masses had suspected the provisional government from the very outset, and thanks to Bolshevik influence, had remained, or grown increasingly, suspicious of it even after it had been joined by the Socialists. But how could Lenin be certain that the country at large, perceiving the entry of Socialists into the government, had not been lulled anew into supporting the war effort? This might have destroyed the effect of Bolshevik propaganda hitherto and throughout Russia slowed the pace of revolutionary fermentation. One can scarcely doubt but that Lenin painfully recalled how the same "ministerialism" on the part of the "socialist lackeys" of the West had induced the proletariat to support the Fatherland's War and had wrecked the Second International. It is understandable then that Lenin saw in the first All-Russian Congress of Soviets a handy device through which to expose the alliance of capitalists and "almost socialists" and thus to reinvigorate the Bolshevik spirit throughout the entire country.

The bourgeois-socialist coalition must further have worried Lenin in that it blurred the picture he had been trying to throw upon the screen of Western consciousness—of a Russian proletariat following Lenin along the true path of international socialism. Whatever the risk with respect to the critical situation in Petrograd, it seems that Lenin was not averse to raising a minor proletarian storm to add thunder to his words; Lenin apparently wanted it known abroad that unlike the Haases, the Scheidemanns, and the Guesdes, he, the true Marxist leader, would keep the faith. And so, using the congress as a twofold tribunal, he unequivocally proclaimed his un-

compromising anti-imperialism, his confidence in the international
proletariat. As the following portions of his speeches reveal, Lenin
addressed himself at least as much to the workers of Europe as he
did to the masses of Russia. On June 17 he said:

> We can never make a peace without annexations and indemnities
> as long as we do not deny our own annexationism. But this is laughable,
> this is a game! In Europe every worker laughs at us, he says: They
> use splendid words, they call upon peoples to overthrow their bank-
> ers, but their own bankers they send into the government." Arrest
> them, show up their tricks; . . . this you do not do, though you have
> organs of power which nothing can oppose. . . . MacLean and Lieb-
> knecht—these are the names of Socialists who bring to life the idea of
> the revolutionary struggle against imperialism. What they said is what
> must be said to all governments if one fights for peace. One must indict
> them before the peoples. That way you place all imperialist govern-
> ments in a confusing position. But now you confuse yourselves. You
> turn to the people with the call for peace of March 14, saying, "Over-
> throw your tsars, your kings and your bankers." At the same time, you,
> having a powerful organization like the Soviet of Workers' and Soldiers'
> Deputies, enter into a bloc with the bankers, establish a coalition, an
> almost socialist government, and write projects for reforms of the kind
> which Europe has been writing for many decades. There in Europe,
> they laugh at such a battle for peace. There they will understand only
> then, when the Soviet takes power and directs the revolution.[76]

On June 22 Lenin declared:

> To nourish the illusion that you can unite with the workers of all
> countries by appeals directed toward them is possible only because of
> your Russian-bound perspective. You do not know how the press of
> Western Europe, where the workers and peasants are accustomed to
> political overturns, have seen them by the dozens, you do not know
> how this press laughs at such phrases and appeals. In Europe they do
> not know that in Russia there has actively risen a mass of workers
> who are fully aware of the predatory schemes of the capitalists
> of all lands and desire freedom of peoples from bankers. They,
> the Europeans, do not understand why you, having organizations
> like the Soviets of Workers' and Soldiers' Deputies, as no other peoples
> in the world, why you, having the weapons, send your Socialists into
> the ministries and give power back to the bankers. Abroad they not
> only accuse you of naïveté, that would be nothing, but also of hypo-
> crisy. The Europeans have forgotten how to understand naïveté in

politics, forgotten how to understand that in Russia there are tens of millions of people who have for the first time awakened to life, that in Russia one does not know the connection between class and government, between government and war.[77]

In both of Lenin's speeches the tone is clearly that of a Western Marxist showing his awareness of Russia's revolutionary backwardness as compared with the progressiveness of the West. As the speeches nonetheless suggest, the Russian proletariat had the power to take very creditable Marxian action. Such action would be admired by the Western proletarians who had their eyes on Russia and, as Lenin hoped, on Lenin as well.

On July 1, the day Kerensky's offensive began, the Soviet itself called for a demonstration in Petrograd. The demonstration was intended to serve as evidence of popular support for the Soviet, but the pro-Bolshevik orientation of the marchers was unmistakable. In many instances the banners carried were those prepared for June 23 but never used. Lenin, whose prestige soared that day, must have been pleased to note the steady advance of the revolution according to the timetable he had drawn up in April, the ever-growing mass trend in his favor and unmarred by any hitherto unmanageable situation. At this point Lenin, quite exhausted, left Petrograd to take a vacation at the home of his friend Bonch-Bruevich in the nearby Finnish village of Naivol.

During June and July factory after factory went on strike in Petrograd. The proletariat, paying increasing heed to the Bolshevik siren song, grew ever less patient with the inadequacy of its wages and the refusal of a government, which carried on an "imperialist war" for "capitalist profits," to grant the eight-hour day. At the beginning of June the Bolsheviks had majorities in the factory committees and in the trade unions of Petrograd, though they held only one-third of the seats in the workers' section of the Soviet. By July 1, the Bolsheviks controlled the workers' section, and in mid-July they were able, in the workers' section, to put through a resolution in favor of the slogan "All Power to the Soviets." [78]

But the leftward progress of the factory workers was slow compared to that of the men in the regiments, to whom the Bolshevik hymn to peace was a direct justification for their unpatriotic but understandable desire for self-preservation. Among the soldiers the preparations for the offensive had aroused great bitterness. This was heightened by the offensive itself, as men, drafted from the hitherto idle regiments, were sent to the front. The rancor of the soldiers was intensified when delegates from the front told their comrades in the garrisons of soldiers driven into battle by armed Czech prisoners, by Cossacks using whips, and so forth. Actual casualties also were very heavy. On July 13 the Second Machine Gun Regiment adopted a resolution opposing the offensive and demanding a transfer of power to the Soviets. The Third Regiment at the same time resolved to refuse to select fourteen companies of frontline reinforcements.[79]

By July 16 the Bolshevik Central Committee was again faced with a dilemma similar to that which had confronted it in June. To the Second All-City Conference of Bolsheviks meeting that day came word that certain regiments were in the process of undertaking armed antigovernment demonstrations. Tomsky issued the party directive asking party members and sympathizers to "keep the masses from further demonstrations." The demonstrating regiments, the directive declared, had acted in uncomradely fashion. They had not asked a committee of the Bolshevik party to attend a discussion of the question. Therefore the party "could not take upon itself the responsibility for the demonstration." The Central Committee proposed that the Petrograd Party Conference issue a call to quiet the masses.[80]

As the day of July 16 progressed it became clear to the Central Committee that despite great Bolshevik efforts to restrain it,[81] the demonstration was rapidly attracting participants. By half-past eight in the evening four fully armed regiments—all of those stationed in the proletarian Viborg section of Petrograd—were on the streets; many factory workers were thronging about, shouting "All Power to the Soviets," and some blood had already been shed. The committee also had learned that other military groups, among these the Kronstadt sailors, had decided to march out on July 17. Late that night, therefore, the Bolshevik Committee departed from its earlier position. The party of the proletariat, it was decided, did not have the right to wash its hands of the demonstration. The party would take part in the movement with the purpose of "giving it a peaceable and organized character" so that it "should not be given the aim of an armed seizure of power."[82]

Lenin, though not present at the above discussions, had clearly managed to impress upon his followers the need for centralistic discipline around the program of "patient explanations." But by July 17 neither the Petrograd masses nor particularly the armed forces were in the mood for patient explanations. The milling hundreds of thousands utterly dwarfed in size and virulence the demonstrations of May. Ignoring the provisional government, portions of the mob swarmed to the Tauride Palace to demand that the Soviet declare itself the sole government of Russia. Instead, the Soviet, outraged and alarmed, passed a resolution stating that the demonstrators were acting treasonably to the war-ridden country.

Various regiments marched straight to Bolshevik headquarters for instructions, evidence enough that what they sought was the realization of Soviet power, if necessary by the most direct methods. Lenin knew this well enough when on the afternoon of the seventeenth he appeared on the balcony of Ksheshinskaya Palace to address the Kronstadt sailors, twenty thousand strong and ready for action. He also knew that power in Petrograd was his for the taking. Earlier that day when the courier Savelich had arrived at Naivol to tell Lenin of the crisis, Savelich had wondered aloud whether serious things had not begun. "That," Lenin had muttered in reply, "would be altogether untimely." [83] Caught in his own snare with a revolutionary force at hand that his grand strategy forbade the use of, Lenin gave a talk that let the sailors down badly. Explaining the brevity of his speech on the ground of illness, Lenin expressed the conviction that "our slogan 'All Power to the Soviets' must win and would win, despite all of the zigzags on the path of history."[84] At the moment the zigzags were mostly in Lenin's mind. Given no leadership, the soldiers and workers flocked aimlessly around Petrograd for another day or so, and finally, having no end in view, disintegrated as a political force.

Yet the July Days had not been waste motion in the arena of history. They had served to convince the moderate Socialists, by this time in control of the provisional government, that they had more to fear from Lenin than from the bourgeoisie. Making use of the advent of government-supporting troops, the moderates went on the political offensive, and with the help of forged documents denounced Lenin as a conspirator acting in the interests of Germany. Several Bolshevik leaders were seized and Lenin barely escaped to Finland. One-day leader of a growing pro-Bolshevik force and master of Petrograd, Lenin was the next day a "German spy," and, as he wrote to Kamenev, in danger of being "bumped off." [85] This in turn had the subsequently momentous effect of prodding Lenin from a political position, moderate, where Russian revolutionary developments were concerned, to the position of a man forced to think in terms of desperate adventurist action. [86]

THE SEIZURE OF POWER

To PRESERVE his life and that pre-eminence in Russian affairs through which he might win renown in Europe, Lenin, before July 17, had shrunk from preaching revolutionary violence. But the events of July had abruptly hurled him from the heights of political prestige. As the head of a defamed party and an outlaw hiding in Finland, he could no longer count upon the use of safe democratic devices through which he had hoped to go on channeling mass support behind the achievement of Soviet power. For the first time Lenin began to think of a revolutionary coup [1] as a means for lifting himself atop the Russian foothills of world revolution, thence to gain the Olympian summits of Europe.

The Decembrists and the Narodniks, revolutionary groups of the 1820's and 1870's respectively, had also dreamed of taking power by means of a conspiratorial *coup d'état.* In a country possessing few intellectuals and a vast population too backward to be organized into an army of revolution, such a tactic seemed the only one with a chance for success. Lenin too, as things had turned out, found himself compelled to enter upon the traditional road of Russian revolutionism. But the last thing Lenin would have wanted was an identification in European eyes of his plot, and whatever came out of it, with the revolutionary styles of nineteenth-century Russia. Whatever the number or quality of those participating in Lenin's conspiracy, the group taking power would have to be labeled "dictatorship of the proletariat," the only instrumentality of revolutionary power provided by Marx.

Up to July, Lenin had found it expedient to describe a future Soviet government as similar to the Paris Commune. However, he had not thought of dictatorship of the proletariat as properly applicable outside the industrial West. He had consistently denied that a Russian Soviet government would constitute a dictatorship of the

Notes begin on page 211.

proletariat,[2] and he had distinctly rejected that which the idea of proletarian dictatorship implied in terms of revolutionary action— the taking of power by violent means.[3]

By August, 1917, however, Lenin had been reduced to the hope of achieving power supported by a tiny proportion of the population, principally the proletariat. This explains his need at that time to convert his previously collected notes into the book *State and Revolution*. On the whole the book remained a tract devoted to European experience, but by writing it, Lenin was apparently trying to convince himself, with the hope of subsequently convincing Europe, that there was a dialectical justification for a minority seizure of power in Russia. In an obvious reference to the intended *coup d'état,* the book's preface described the revolution (in August, 1917) as "evidently completing the first stage of its development." The revolution in its entirety could be understood "only as a link in the chain of socialist proletarian revolutions called forth by the imperialist war." Therefore, since the masses of Europe as well as Russia would soon be overthrowing capitalism, "the question of the relation of a socialist proletarian revolution to the state" had acquired immediate practical political significance.[4]

In short, since Russia was a part of Europe, there was nothing unorthodox in the establishment of a preliminary or half-baked dictatorship of the proletariat in Russia. This would blend with the Continental dictatorship that would rise out of the impending European revolution. In his draft outline of the book Lenin wrote: "Shall I not add a chapter or paragraphs in a seventh chapter; concretizing the task of the proletarian revolution by the experience in the Russian revolution of 1917?" He answered: "Yes, this is necessary. Develop Chapter VII." [5] Lenin felt the need for describing the Russian experience upon which a Russian dictatorship would be based and also for outlining the specific form [6] it might take. The practical needs rising from a seizure of power, however short might be the time between its occurrence and the European revolution, would demand a scheme for the organization of power. Yet as his question to himself shows, Lenin was reluctant to make too much of Russia in a book intended for a European public. Probably he was unhappy about having to set down a concrete dictatorship design for Russia before he had had a chance to put one into effect in Europe. A scheme designed for Russia, he may have feared, would necessarily assume a form unsuited to Western conditions and might further hamper his ultimate plans by identifying both him and his dictatorship idea with Russia rather than with Europe.

It is significant that Lenin never found the time to write more than a few lines of the last chapter to *State and Revolution*. This, his post-script to the first edition, ascribes to the interference of "the political crisis; the eve of the [November] revolution": "Such 'interference' can only be cause for rejoicing. However, the second section of the pamphlet [regarding Russia] will probably have to be put off for a long time. It is more pleasant and useful to experience revolution than to write about it." [7]

But precisely on the eve of the November revolution Lenin did write two long articles which by and large foretold the form of the Soviet regime.[8] Slightly edited, these could easily have comprised the unwritten portion of a book not given to the publishers until December. If Lenin did not see fit to include this material in *State and Revolution*, it can only be because he did not want to do so. Still, to judge by the passage below, Lenin was unable to constrain himself from interpolating into this Europe-directed tract a strong hint of the reasoning he would subsequently employ to justify the establishment of a proletarian dictatorship in Russia.

In Chapter III of *State and Revolution* Lenin cited from a letter of Marx written to Kugelmann, April 12, 1871, the time of the Paris Commune. Marx wrote: [9]

> If you look at . . . my *Eighteenth Brumaire,* you will see that I declare the next attempt of the French Revolution to be: not merely to hand over, from one set of hands to another, the bureaucratic and military machine—as has occurred hitherto—but to *shatter* it; [the italics, Lenin points out, arc Marx's] and it is this that is the pre-condition of any real people's revolution on the Continent. This exactly constitutes the attempt of our heroic Parisian comrades.

After commenting on Marx's insistence upon violence and the distortion of this view by the "prevailing Kautskyan 'interpretation' of Marxism," Lenin went on to draw further and far less warranted conclusions from the citation.

> Secondly, . . . this extremely profound remark of Marx deserves particular attention in that it states that the destruction of the bureaucratic-military state machinery is "the pre-condition of any real *people's* revolution." [It is most important to note that the italics are Lenin's, not Marx's.] This concept of a "people's" revolution seems strange on

Marx's lips. And the Russian Plekhanovists and Mensheviks, . . .
who wish to be considered Marxists, would probably explain this expression as a slip of the tongue. To such a crippled program of liberal-
ism have they distorted Marxism. . . .

On the Continent of Europe, in 1871, the proletariat did not in a
single country constitute the majority of the people. A "people's"
revolution, actually drawing the majority into the movement, could be
such only if it included both the proletariat and the peasantry. Both
classes then constituted the "people." Both classes are united by the
circumstance that the "bureaucratic-military state machinery" perse-
cutes, oppresses, and exploits them.

To *shatter* this machinery, *to break it up*—this is the real interest of
the "people," of its majority—the workers, and most of the peasants—
this is the "pre-condition" of a voluntary union of the poorest peasants
with the proletarians; while, without such a union, democracy is shaky,
and socialist transformation is impossible.

Toward such a union, as is known, the Paris Commune was striving,
but it did not attain its end for reasons internal and external in nature.

Consequently, when he used the phrase "real people's revolution,"
Marx by no means forgot the peculiar character of the petty bourgeoisie
(he spoke of them much and often), and was very carefully taking
into account the actual relationship of classes in most of the Continental
European states in 1871. From another standpoint, also, he laid it
down that the "shattering" of the machinery of the state is demanded
by the interests both of the workers and of peasants, unites them, places
before them the common task of destroying the "parasite" and replacing
it by something new.

From the mere mention of the word "people" by Marx, in a letter
not intended for publication and hence certainly not carefully
checked for accuracy, Lenin drew the inference that Marx had meant
a union of proletarians and peasants. From the mere word "Continent," which Marx used in referring to events in France of 1848–
1851, and Paris of 1871, Lenin derived not merely France or Paris,
but all the countries of the Continent of Europe, Eastern Europe and
Russia, of course, included. Adding the two together, Lenin had
found a way of claiming Marxian approval for a violent seizure of
power in Russia and for the building of a revolutionary dictatorship
on the basis of a proletarian-supporting peasantry.

In the period following the July Days the functioning of the
Bolshevik Central Committee was seriously encumbered. Lenin,
Zinoviev, and other members had gone underground and such party

luminaries as Kamenev, Lunacharsky, and Trotsky sat in jail. Numerous rank and filers were quitting the party, and many of those who had been on the verge of joining were withdrawing their applications. With these defections, of course, went sources of funds so essential to continued agitational activity. Those remaining in the party suffered baiting and beatings. *Pravda* was wrecked by anti-Bolshevik elements and other party organs throughout Russia were also put out of existence. Regiments that had shown pro-Bolshevik tendencies in the July Days were either disarmed, as were many factory workers, or sent to the front.[10] Admittedly things looked very bleak for the Bolshevik cause for a few weeks in late July and early August. The July Days should have shown Lenin that the Russian masses were going his way whether he himself led them or lagged behind. Momentarily confused by the July defeat and the subsequent barrage of anti-Bolshevik clamorings, they soon resumed their instinctive march to the left down the trail marked by Bolshevik slogans. But Lenin did not anticipate this development. In general he expected that the "leaderless" proletariat would be carried along with the tide of reaction. Fed on Marxian writings and believing Russia to be in the throes of a "European" revolution, Lenin overestimated the strength of the Russian bourgeoisie and their "counterrevolutionary" fury. In Petrograd's July Days he saw the counterpart to the June Days in Paris of 1848. He envisaged the Cavaignacs swooping through the city to crack the skulls of workers and massacre Bolsheviks.[11] He made much of the fact that a single worker, Voinov, was killed.[12] Himself he thought in mortal danger if apprehended,[13] and he was sure that standing trial under the prevailing reactionary conditions would expose him to a "legal assassination."[14]

As a result then of conditions existing and imagined, Lenin had no hope of instituting early revolutionary action of the type that his pronouncements of this period seemed to call for. That he foresaw no immediate opportunity for launching the proletarian offensive is best shown by the way in which he accounted for his July Days' behavior in articles written during late July and the first weeks in August.

Above all, as Lenin emphasized, neither he himself nor his party had been responsible for the revolution-bordering nature of those explosive days.[15] His program, he recalled, had ever been peaceable in its striving for Soviet power.[16] If, since July 17, the peaceable solution was no longer possible, that was the fault of the SRs and the Mensheviks, who since May had involved themselves ever more with the bourgeoisie and on July 17 had "finally sunk into the cesspool of counterrevolution." That the Bolsheviks had not washed their hands of the July 17 movement, did not, Lenin maintained, indicate approval of the tone or purpose of the demonstrations. It had been the "unconditional duty" of the party of the proletariat to stand by the masses, even if there were excesses, "in an attempt to give their well-justified demonstrations a peaceable and organized character." [17]

Lenin had been accused of being a German agent and of having plotted in July to overthrow the government. The coupling of these two charges, of course, created, and was meant to create, the impression that the July Days had been engineered by Lenin for the purpose of aiding the German army. Naturally Lenin wanted to rid himself of a stigma suggesting that his revolutionary program had ulterior motives, for it might cause the masses to doubt the sincerity of their would-be leader. Also, since Lenin feared capture and possible legal lynching, he wanted to prepare his public opinion case as far as possible in advance.[18] The best way to discredit the slanderers was to disprove the charges made against him. To prove one is not a spy is always difficult. But there was at hand ample evidence to prove that the Bolsheviks, and Lenin especially, had made serious efforts to prevent the July demonstrators from resorting to forcible means. By proving himself guiltless of fomenting a revolutionary plot, he might also undermine the accusation of having been in the pay of Germany.

But by stressing so heavily his own peaceable intentions concerning the July Days, Lenin was not ingratiating himself with those sailors, soldiers, and workers, who had come out ready to fight for what they thought had been Lenin's battle slogans, only to see impending victory forfeited by their leader's irresolution.[19] Lenin kept reasserting his innocence of starting the July Days' demonstrations. He also lauded himself for not having abandoned the proletariat in the moment of crisis. But all this did not explain why Lenin, once the demonstration was under way, did not even try to take power. This question, so troubling to the fighters of July and some Bolsheviks too, Lenin at this time made no serious attempt to answer.[20] Instead, he chose to make his explanations to the court of Russian public opinion, thereby taking the risk of further demoralizing those upon whom he would have to depend for support in the event of a call for armed action. This shows that however much he might stress the need of a new tactic, he did not expect it to go into practical operation in anything like the near future. However, Bolshevik fortunes improved rapidly in the latter part of August; so much so that it became possible again for Lenin to reckon with the possibility of taking early militant action.

A real bid for power, Lenin knew, would have to be supported by the factory workers and would, above all, depend on substantial military assistance. But the only proletarians Lenin could rely upon were the Petrograd workers, and of course only the Kronstadt sailors and various Petrograd units were available to him on the military side. His potential forces being limited in number, his stroke would have to be swift and drastic—it would have to pierce the political heart of Russia, the government, at the first blow or fail entirely in its objective. The *coup d'état* therefore would have to take place in Petrograd and was bound to shape up as a re-enactment of the July Days—using the same cast of characters, particularly in the mob scenes. The only difference would be in the way the lead part would be played, thus bringing about a happier ending. But to sound the clarion for a storming of the fortress, and expect it to be answered by the very ones who regarded themselves as let down the previous time, involved certain necessary explanations to the party and to the Petrograd masses. Before the same army would be willing to follow Lenin on the battlefield of the first defeat, it would want clearly to understand why Lenin had not taken power in July and, assuming there was good reason for his not having done so, in what ways conditions had since changed to make another try more likely to be successful.

During September and October, Lenin made numerous attempts to answer these questions. In an article of September 1 he pointed out that the slogan of seizing power would have been "incorrect" in July because "even the Bolsheviks" were still indecisive about treating the Mensheviks and SRs in the government "as counterrevolutionaries." [21] After the May crisis, when Lenin strongly decried its immoderate behavior, the chastened party took pains to exercise the greatest possible cautiousness. The Bolshevik lack of decisiveness in July was therefore Lenin's lack.

In his September 16 "Draft Resolution on the Political Situation," Lenin stressed the thought that the masses previous to July 18 had "not yet actually experienced the counterrevolutionary policies" of the generals, the landowners, the capitalists and their SR and Menshevik collaborators, and would therefore not have supported the Bolsheviks in an attempt to seize power. This statement ignored the fact that it was the Bolsheviks who had restrained the violence-bent July demonstrators. On July 16–17 the leaders of the Soviet had been threatened with lynching unless they took power into their hands. SR leader Chernov was actually dragged away by the mob and only Trotsky's intercession saved his life. The "Draft Resolution" further stated that "not one organization" of the party, either central or local, had formulated the slogan of seizing power on July 16–17 or had even brought the "question up for discussion." Thus Lenin tried to explain his failure to act on the absurd ground that the leader of the Bolsheviks took orders from the party.

"Events have since revealed," the statement went on, "that the real error of our party in the days of July 16–17 was only that it considered the general situation to be *less* revolutionary than it actually was" and "*still* considered possible a peaceful development of political transformation by way of a change in the policies of the Soviet" when actually such a hope was futile because of the involvement of the moderate Socialists with the bourgeoisie. This erroneous view, "sustained only by the hope that events would not develop too fast," the party could not have "rid itself of other than through participation in the popular movement of July 16–17 with the slogan 'All Power to the Soviets' and with the aim of giving the movement a peaceful and organized character." [22]

The above statement becomes accurate enough if the word "party" is replaced with the name "Lenin." The key may be found in Lenin's mode of expression. For it was specifically Lenin who had hoped that "events [in Russia] would not develop too fast," lest they embroil him in struggles conceivably endangering his life or prestige and hence his aim of taking power in Europe. It had been this hope that had led Lenin to formulate the April Theses geared to the idea of a not too rapidly fermenting revolution and the illogical expectation that the moderate Socialists would be willing to collaborate with the Bolsheviks in the establishment of Soviet power.

In a letter captioned "Marxism and Revolt," written September 26–27, Lenin again blamed his refusal to take power in July on the political unreadiness of the masses and the Bolsheviks, and stated specifically that Bolsheviks were then not backed by the "majority of the workers and soldiers of Petrograd and Moscow." Since that time, he wrote, the masses not only of the capital cities but of the entire country had swung behind the Bolsheviks, thereby "assuring" a successful rising.[23]

The contention that the masses had not been behind the Bolsheviks in July justified Lenin's behavior of that moment. The same contention also underrated the significance of the spontaneous worker-soldier demonstrations during and before the July Days. But Lenin also wished to persuade his party and its followers that the Petrograd masses were again ready to rise, and what better proof of this than their volcanic impatience as manifested by past eruptions. Thus in an article of September 29, Lenin disputed his statements of September 26–27. He declared it to be a "fact" that the Bolshevik slogans had "actually won over the *majority* of the active revolutionary masses in Petrograd on May 3–4, July 1, and July 16–17," and observed that the "fault and error of the Bolsheviks," in the period from March 12 to September 11, "was the *insufficient* revolutionism of their tactics and in no way the immoderate revolutionism of which the Philistines accuse us." [24] However, he again neglected to note that the "insufficiency of revolutionism" had been derived from his own desire to avoid the personal risks involved in a Bolshevik-led coup, the only realistic way in which Soviet power could have been achieved.

As the time approached for the prospective coup, Lenin became ever more inclined to recall the fine opportunity for taking power which had existed in July.[25] On October 21 he argued pro and con with the same stroke of the pen, writing that "if we made a mistake on July 16–18, it was only in that we did not take power. I think that this was not a mistake at that time, for then we were still not in a majority." [26]

To admit clearly and unequivocally that power could and should have been taken in July would have been tantamount to declaring that his April program, based on the prospect of a peaceable achievement of Soviet power, had been wrong. As the leader of an impending critical struggle, Lenin may have feared that confessing to having used incorrect tactics would have the effect of undermining the morale of his forces. It should also be recalled that the April program had been irrationally pieced together and cemented by Lenin's self-delusionment. Thus the very mechanism that had enabled Lenin to devise the program, impossible of achievement, may well have made its flaws indiscernible to him, for who is as blind as he who will not see? But most important, Lenin, throughout September and part of October, was not yet certain, even while advocating a *coup d'état,* that some peaceable solution to the attainment of Soviet power was not still possible.[27]

Altogether the confused explanations of the July Days' tactic, or lack of tactic, probably grew out of a threefold combination (1) of Lenin's need to deny personal error, (2) a refusal to admit to himself the irrational nature of the April policy, and hence the egoistic motivation with respect to the course of Russian revolution which underlay it, and (3) his waverings as to whether or not the time had finally arrived to jettison the April program and to take recourse to violent measures. Particularly illustrative as to the last-mentioned point was Lenin's immediate response to the failure of the Kornilov coup and the events attendant upon that failure. The Kornilov incident, commonly reported to have opened the gates to the Bolshevik seizure of power, was by no means the factor that prompted Lenin to move in that direction. Instead, though it glaringly exposed the weakness of the groups opposing him, the incident, as Lenin first believed, had renewed the possibilities for a return to his April tactic.

As Minister of War in the provisional government, Kerensky was directly responsible for the rapid promotions awarded to General Lavr Kornilov in July, 1917. Kerensky had admired Kornilov for revitalizing military discipline, which the democratic innovations of the revolution [28] and Bolshevik propaganda had all but obliterated. On July 22, as newly appointed Commander of the Southwestern Front, Kornilov had reintroduced the death penalty for desertion. By the end of July, Kornilov had become Commander in Chief of the Russian Army. On August 7, Kerensky became Premier of the third provisional government, whose ministers, except for four members of the Kadet (Constitutional-Democratic) party, were drawn from the ranks of the Mensheviks and SRs. Kerensky soon realized that he had created a monster, for Kornilov, in line with his basic desire to strengthen the military situation of Russia, deemed it necessary not only to curb demoralization at the front but also to crush those forces in the rear—the Soviet as well as the "Bolshevik traitors"—which he thought were leading the country into chaos. During August, Kornilov became increasingly outspoken about the need for the establishment of martial law and so became the unofficial spokesman for all of the Rightist forces in Russia and the bête noir of the Left. On September 7, having gathered a military force for an attack upon Petrograd, Kornilov demanded that Kerensky turn over to him all military and civil authority. When on September 9 Kerensky dismissed Kornilov from his post as commander in chief, the latter decided nonetheless to chance a *coup d'état* and sent a cavalry division against the capital.

In the face of Kornilov's move Kerensky welcomed the aid of the Bolsheviks in the forming of a revolutionary Red Guard. In return, Trotsky, Kamenev, and others of the party's Central Committee were released from prison. Sentiment among the Petrograd masses took a sharp leftward turn, and on September 13, Kornilov's forces having by that time melted away, the Bolsheviks held the majority in the Petrograd Soviet. For the moment it appeared to Lenin that the SR and Menshevik leadership would no longer be able to participate in a coalition with the bourgeoisie who had become discredited by their association with Kornilov. To win the SRs and the Mensheviks to his objective of Soviet power, Lenin, on September 14, drew up a proposal for a compromise among the Socialist parties. Lenin wrote:

Our party, like every other political party, strives to win political domination *for itself*. Our goal is the dictatorship of the revolutionary proletariat. Half a year of revolution has proven . . . the correctness and inevitability of such a demand in the interests precisely of *this* revolution. . . .

There has now taken place such a sharp and original turn in the Russian revolution that we, as a party, can offer a voluntary compromise—true, not to the bourgeoisie, our direct and principal class enemy, but to our nearest adversaries, the "ruling" petty-bourgeois democratic parties, the SRs and Mensheviks. . . .

The compromise on our part is our return to the pre-July demand of all power to the Soviets, a government of SRs and Mensheviks responsible to the Soviets.

Now, and only now, perhaps *only for a few days* or for one or two weeks, such a government could be . . . established in a perfectly peaceful way. It could most probably secure a peaceful *forward* movement of the whole Russian revolution. . . .

Only for the sake of this peaceful development of the revolution . . . can and must the Bolsheviks, . . . partisans of revolutionary methods, enter upon such a compromise. . . .

The compromise would consist in this: that the Bolsheviks, seeking no participation in the government (which is impossible for an internationalist without an actual realization of the conditions of a dictatorship of the proletariat and the poorest peasantry) would refrain from immediately advancing demands for the transfer of power to the proletariat and the poorest peasants, from revolutionary methods of struggle for the realization of this demand. The condition which is self-evident and not new to the SRs and Mensheviks would be full freedom of propaganda and the convocation of the Constituent Assembly without any new procrastination or perhaps even convocation at an earlier date.

The Mensheviks and SRs, as the governmental bloc, would then agree (assuming that the compromise has been reached) to form a government fully and exclusively responsible to the Soviets, under conditions of giving all power to the Soviets also locally. This would constitute the "new" condition. No other condition would, I think, be advanced by the Bolsheviks, who would be confident that really full freedom of agitation and the immediate realization of a new democracy in the composition of the Soviets (new elections to them) and in their functioning would in themselves secure a peaceful forward movement of the revolution, a *peaceful outcome* of the party strife within the Soviets. . . .

What would both "contracting" parties gain by this "compromise"? . . .

The Bolsheviks would gain the possibility of freely agitating for their views and of trying to gain influence in the Soviets under conditions of really full democracy. . . . For the sake of such a possibility at such a difficult time, it would be worth while to enter into a compromise with the Soviet majority of today. *We* have nothing to fear under a real democracy, for the course of events is going our way. . . .

The Mensheviks and SRs would gain in that they would at once obtain the full possibility of achieving the program of *their* bloc, while basing themselves on the admitted overwhelming majority of the people and having secured for themselves the "peaceful" use of their majority in the Soviets.[29]

Though aware of the tremendous increase in his strength among the masses and the corresponding decline in the power of his "nearest adversaries," Lenin tried at this stage to cajole and subtly threaten the SRs and Mensheviks to coalesce into a government that would exclude both the bourgeoisie and the Bolsheviks, but permit the latter the freedom of propaganda. Granted that Lenin had few doubts but that the Bolsheviks would before long have come to control such a government; still, the method by which he preferred to gain his ends was clearly one designed to "secure a peaceful forward movement of the revolution, a *peaceful outcome* of the party strife within the Soviets." As in July, so in mid-September and even subsequently,[30] Lenin wished to avoid the use of force if there seemed a safer way of reaching his goal.

Various writers, among them W. H. Chamberlin, have written that Lenin's attitude toward seizing power at one or another point in 1917 was determined principally by what amount of support he could hope for from the various segments (army, provinces, and so forth) of the Russian population.[31] According to this conception, Lenin in July, considering his popular base too weak, did not wish to risk seizing power. In November, thinking himself more firmly based, he elected to make the move. Actually the intensity of Lenin's desire to seize power at any given moment in 1917 was not directly but inversely proportional to the amount of support he thought he could expect from the masses. That is, precisely when he regarded his popular following as greatest did he least think in terms of using violence.

In the midst of the July turbulence, when he felt strong, he spoke for peaceable transition of power to the Soviets. After the July Days, when he thought his party crushed and discredited, he began to hatch plans for the *coup d'état* and wrote *State and Revolution.* After the Kornilov fiasco, however, when he knew his strength among the masses to be greater than ever, Lenin drew up his compromise plan and offered to refrain from violence. Lenin's ultimate decision to seize power was not made from a feeling of puissance, but, in line with the above pattern, was the product of desperation and a belief that there was no other choice. The pace of Lenin's drive toward a *coup d'état* accelerated noticeably after the Kornilov affair, and this has helped to enhance the impression that Lenin predicated his decision, which led to the November revolution, upon the newly critical revolutionary situation. The Kornilov incident did affect his decision, but not in the manner commonly supposed.

On September 3 the German army had taken Riga and this meant that the Germans' road to Petrograd was open. Because of how and where the forces that would support the Bolsheviks were concentrated, Lenin believed that once Petrograd was lost, all, or almost all, would be lost. The Germans could have been expected to make short shrift of the Bolsheviks. The danger to Petrograd in Lenin's view became particularly intense after Kornilov's coup, for this he interpreted as the Right's last-gasp chance to take control of the situation. Lenin feared that the "landowners, the bourgeoisie . . . and the generals and officers on their side" would deliberately surrender Petrograd to the Germans rather than relinquish "their power over the people and their profits." [32] There was but one way Lenin could hope to stop the Germans short of Petrograd—to offer them a separate peace. In planning his September 16 compromise offer to the SRs and Mensheviks, Lenin had probably figured that once the bourgeoisie had been definitely ousted, the Bolsheviks, free to propagandize, could soon have created enough popular pressure on behalf of peace to force the Soviet coalition to sue the Germans for terms. However, Lenin's blueprint for compromise never left the drawing board. The SRs and Mensheviks failed to act as Lenin had hoped they would, and it soon became clear to him that another Kerensky-headed socialist-bourgeois government was in the offing.[33]

From a government that included "treason-minded" bourgeois ministers, Lenin could expect no offer of peace to the Germans. If red Petrograd was to be saved through a peace offer, power, Lenin reasoned, must be taken at the earliest possible moment. He wrote on September 16:

> The workers and peasants of Russia have absolutely no way out except through a victory over [the bourgeoisie and their associates].
> . . .
> The working class, when it acquires power, will alone be able to pursue a policy of peace, not in words, like the Mensheviks and SRs, who in fact support the bourgeoisie and its secret treaties, but in deeds. It will immediately and under any military situation whatever, even if the Kornilovist generals, having given up Riga, shall also give up Petrograd, offer to *all* peoples, open . . . *just* conditions of peace.[34]

Lenin's campaign to seize power, which went into high gear only after September 16, was aimed essentially at ending the war with Germany and saving Petrograd, his steppingstone to Europe. From September 16 to November 6, Lenin ran a frenzied race against the time unknown when one way or another the Germans might take Petrograd. Frustrated to the limit by his need to remain in hiding during the crucial seven weeks, Lenin wrote letter after letter, each demanding that the Bolshevik Central Committee call for an immediate rising. He wrote late in September:

> Why must the Bolsheviks take power right *now?*
> Because the impending surrender of Petrograd will make our chances a hundred times worse.
> But to prevent the surrender of Petrograd while the army is headed by Kerensky & Co. is not in our power.

Nor can we "wait" for the Constituent Assembly, for by the very surrender of Petrograd, Kerensky & Co. *can* always *destroy* the Constituent Assembly. . . .

It would be naïve to wait for a "formal" majority on the side of the Bolsheviks; no revolution ever waits for *this*. Kerensky & Co. are not waiting either, but are preparing the surrender of Petrograd.[35]

Suggesting that England might join Germany in an attack upon revolutionary Russia, Lenin warned that a "separate peace between the English and German imperialists" had to and could be prevented, but only by "acting quickly." [36] By "acting quickly" Lenin meant the taking of power followed by a separate peace offer to Germany, which, giving Germany an advantage in the war, would make the forming of an anti-Russian coalition unlikely.

Regarding the chances for a successful *coup d'état*, Lenin gave arguments of the type included in his September 27 letter to the Central Committee. Entitled "Marxism and Uprising," portions of this afore-cited document explained why power should not have been taken in July and explained further that conditions since had changed in that the Bolsheviks had back of them the majority not only of the workers but of the peasants. In addition, as Lenin pointed out, the Bolsheviks knew where they were going, whereas *"imperialism as a whole* and the entire bloc of SRs and Mensheviks [were evincing] extraordinary vacillation." [37]

But supposing the Germans did not accept the peace offer of a Bolshevik-headed government and continued to wage war upon Russia? Lenin wrote in answer to this hypothetical question:

Only our party, having won a victory in an uprising, *can* save Petrograd, for if our peace proposal is turned down, and we obtain not even an armistice, then *we* shall become "defensists," then we shall place ourselves *at the head of the war parties,* we shall be the *most "warring"* party, and we shall carry on a war in a truly revolutionary manner. We shall take away from the capitalists all the bread and all the shoes. We shall leave them crumbs. . . . We shall send all the bread and all the shoes to the front.

And then we shall save Petrograd.

The resources, both material and spiritual, of a truly revolutionary war are still infinitely great in Russia; there are ninety-nine chances in a hundred that the Germans will at least grant us an armistice. And to receive a truce at present means to conquer the *whole world.*[38]

In the last sentence lies the entire key to Lenin's thinking in this period.

To the argument that a Bolshevik seizure of power was sure to unleash a civil war from which would flow "rivers of blood," Lenin replied that no civil war could ever come close to killing the numbers of men sacrificed in the imperialist war since the beginning of the July offensive.[39] In the same article Lenin also denied the likelihood of and hence the dangers to Bolshevik power of foreign intervention, after an offer of a just peace should have been made, since "a uniting of the rival Anglo-French and German imperialisms *against* a proletarian socialist Russian republic would be *impossible* in practice, and a union of the English, Japanese and American imperialisms would be hard to accomplish and offers no danger [in view] of Russia's geographic position." The forward movement of the Russian revolution would have the salutary effect of advancing the inevitably maturing European revolution. This in turn would give the Russian proletariat "*every* chance of retaining" power "and of leading Russia until the time of a victorious revolution in the West." [40]

Aside from the menace of intervention to a proletarian-based Bolshevik government, would this small ruling minority be able to maintain itself in power? Upon what experience could it draw in the business of administering the apparatus of government?

In his lengthy article, "Will the Bolsheviks Hold State Power?" written October 7–14, Lenin denied that the proletariat was isolated. Behind it, as the only force that could satisfy their respective needs of land, self-determination, and peace, stood the peasantry, the national minorities, and the soldiers. Making light of the supposed complexities of administration, Lenin asserted that the Soviets constituted a device ready-made to take over and run the state's machinery. In this article's vividly portrayed dictatorship of the proletariat as applied to Russia, and also in the previously written "The Threatening Catastrophe" (September 23–27), are undoubtedly the conceptions which would have gone into the projected but never-written last chapter of *State and Revolution*.

To prove that 240,000 Bolsheviks would be able to govern Russia, Lenin emphasized that these would be "governing in the interests of the poor and against the rich." The 240,000, moreover, represented a million, for, as the experience of Europe and Russia had established, the number of votes a party drew in an election was always about one-fourth of its actual adult following. "So here we have already a 'state apparatus' of *one million* people devoted to the socialist state not for their monthly pay checks but out of idealism." [41] Behind this million Lenin perceived other tens of millions who seeing "that the proletarian power was not cringing before the rich, but was helping the poor . . . that it was taking surplus products from the parasites and giving them to the hungry . . . could also be called upon with full confidence for the most direct and daily participation in the administration of the state." [42]

Until about mid-October the Bolshevik Central Committee remained adamant to Lenin's pleas for action. Its membership by and large stood on the position of Lenin's April program, which, precisely after the Kornilov incident, seemed about to pay handsome dividends. Lenin's post-Kornilov compromise proposal was in itself an admission as to the existence of this probability. Most of the leading Bolsheviks saw no advantage in stirring up trouble when, as even their opponents were admitting, everything seemed to be going their way. The date for elections to the Constituent Assembly, moreover, had finally been set for November 25, and there was no chance that Socialists would win less than 90 per cent of the seats. The Assembly then would pretty well constitute the Socialist coalition government which Lenin as late as September 16 had approved of. To the other Bolshevik leaders the possible loss of Petrograd to the Germans was not as fearsome a prospect as it was to Lenin. Thinking primarily in terms of the revolution in Russia, they could not understand why the loss of one more Russian city to the Germans would be so disastrous. As in April, their views diverged from those of Lenin because he was mainly concerned not with the Russian scene but with his own position vis-à-vis world revolution. To Lenin the loss of Petrograd would be a serious blow, for it might, among other things, reduce his position to that of a fugitive in some remote part of Russia at the very moment when the volcano of European revolution was beginning to erupt.

Lenin perceived that his stress upon the danger to Petrograd was having little effect in arousing the party to take hasty action. Hence he proceeded to concoct other reasons, some quite absurd, which might convince the Central Committee that a *coup d'état* was an urgent necessity. The workers, Lenin argued, had given a majority to the Bolsheviks in the Soviets of Petrograd and Moscow. In the provinces too the Bolsheviks were registering victories; also the peasants were rising. This proved that the Bolshevik party had received a popular mandate to take power and to put its slogans into effect. The masses were impatient and expected action. Hesitancy might disillusion the masses as to the willingness of the Bolsheviks to act.[43] Delay might be fatal.[44]

The masses, it is true, were impatient that the demands voiced by the Bolsheviks be met, but they had been so at least since May, 1917. Yet whenever in the past the masses had actually exploded, Lenin himself had been the one to restrain their impetuosity.

Lenin attacked his party's flirtations with the other Socialist groups as manifested by Bolshevik participation in the State Conference and in the Council of the Republic.[45] Such behavior, he maintained, could only confuse the masses, already sick of eternal vacillations. To retain the allegiance of the workers it was necessary for the Bolsheviks to make a clean break with the SRs and the Mensheviks, and this could be done only by a seizure of power. To wait for a Congress of Soviets or for a Constituent Assembly, Lenin insisted, would also serve to confuse the masses.[46]

An increase in Bolshevik influence could only have served to bring the announced aims of the party closer to fulfillment. It was therefore illogical for Lenin to contend that rapid Bolshevik gains, even if made through a peaceable and democratic process, would confuse the masses.

Another Kerensky-Kornilovist plot, Lenin declared, was in the making, its purpose that of *"preventing* the Soviets *from obtaining power."* [47] "Why," Lenin asked in an October 10 letter to Smilga, "should we tolerate three more weeks of war and Kerensky's 'Kornilovist preparations?'" [48]

Not a shred of evidence has ever been produced to verify Kerensky's "plot."

On October 20 Lenin saw a similarly shadowy Russian-English conspiracy designed to prevent the establishment of Soviet power. In a letter to the Petrograd City Conference of Bolsheviks, Lenin wrote that the inaction of the English fleet during the occupation of Oesel by the Germans, "coupled with the government's plan to move from Petrograd to Moscow" proved "that a *conspiracy* ha[d] been formed between the Russian and English imperialists, between Kerensky and the Anglo-French capitalists, to surrender Petrograd to the Germans and *thereby* stifle the Russian revolution." [49]

Leaving no stone unturned, Lenin also sang the emotion-stirring song of revolutionary idealism to the members of the Central Committee. Citing the arrests of worker-heroes in Europe and mutinies in the German navy as evidence of Europe's impending revolution,[50] he asked in an October 12 article whether the Bolsheviks would refuse to do their share. Bolsheviks having "faith" in the Congress of Soviets and in the convocation of the Constituent Assembly, he wrote, "would prove traitors" to the proletarian cause. "The whole future of the Russian revolution is at stake. The whole honor of the Bolshevik party is in question. The whole future of the international workers' revolution for socialism is at stake. The crisis has matured." [51]

On October 10 a much-frustrated Lenin proffered his resignation to the Central Committee, which refused to accept it. At the same time he began to bypass that inert body, and sent exhortatory missives to local Bolshevik units in the armed forces in order to orient them toward readiness for insurrection. These units, Trotsky suggests, then exerted strong pressure upon the Central Committee, and on October 23 it voted, over the protests of Zinoviev and Kamenev, for the seizure of power. The date was set for October 28, but it was not until the night of November 6, on the eve of the long-delayed meeting of the All-Russian Congress of Soviets, that the plan actually went into operation.

5

TROTSKY AND LENIN

OUT OF THE EVENTS of October and November, Trotsky emerged as the coleader or, at worst, as the number two man in the Bolshevik party. In the months leading to November, Lenin had perforce been invisible to the party's rank and file. To newly recruited Bolsheviks he had been merely a name. By contrast, the ever-present Trotsky, exhorter of the garrison troops, president of the Soviet, and field general of the November triumph, loomed up as a giant among men. Also, among the old Bolsheviks Trotsky had gained immense stature. During the crucial weeks before the *coup d'état,* he, almost alone in the Central Committee, had sided with Lenin on the issue of seizing power. The very idea of the "workers' state," in addition, was linked in Bolshevik minds with Trotsky's theories. Since Lenin himself appeared to have accepted Trotskyism, Trotsky's prestige was further enhanced.

As never before in Bolshevik history, there existed after November, 1917, a second pole of power in the party. In the months following the *coup d'état* particularly, Trotsky was a factor with which Lenin had to reckon. The struggle between the two in that period is best understood in the light of the entire history of their relationship.

It was at the Russian Social Democratic Congress of 1903 that Trotsky initiated his long-enduring dispute with Lenin. Shocked by Lenin's expressed intention of dumping the revolutionary elders Axelrod and Zasulich from the editorial board of *Iskra,*[1] the youthful and yet unhardened Trotsky joined the Mensheviks in denouncing Lenin's centralistic scheme for the organization of the Russian Social Democratic party. Trotsky's autobiography, written in 1930, explains that his break with Lenin

occurred on what might be considered "moral" or even personal grounds. But this was merely on the surface. At bottom, the separation was of a

Notes begin on page 214.

political nature and merely expressed itself in the realm of organizational methods. I thought of myself as a centralist. But there is no doubt that at that time I did not fully realize what an intense and imperious centralism the revolutionary party would need to lead millions of people in a war against the old order. . . . At the time of the London Congress of 1903, revolution was still largely a theoretical abstraction to me. And the desire to see a problem independently, and to draw all the necessary conclusions from it, had always been my most imperious intellectual necessity.[2]

The above is a very confused statement. Trotsky attempts to draw a clear line between the personal and the political nature of his break with Lenin but is unable to do so. After describing the personal issue as being "merely on the surface," he still concludes his explanation for the difference in political outlook in terms of his basic personality need to see a problem independently. Trotsky, even in 1930, was unable to perceive or admit that his indignation of 1903 regarding Lenin's highhanded attitude toward the "older ones" and the party in general was political on the surface, but personal at bottom, and was an instinctive protest against subordinating to the will of some all-powerful central committee or person his own potent ego or individualism.

On this issue of party structure, then, actually on the issue of freedom to dissent,[3] Trotsky fought Lenin for fourteen years. This was particularly ironical since in matters relating to broad revolutionary theory, Trotsky, in the period 1903–1917, was always much closer to Lenin than to the revisionistic Mensheviks.[4]

The peculiar dilemma of Trotsky's position was especially apparent in 1914. Trotsky's *War and the International,* written in Zurich shortly after the war began, declared the war to be a prelude to Europe's proletarian revolution and expressed complete distrust of the Second International. In essence, then, Trotsky's work duplicated Lenin's views of the moment. If Trotsky, unlike Lenin, failed to carry his ideas through to their inescapable ends this may readily be ascribed to his awareness that the conclusions to be drawn from them would place him squarely on the side of Lenin.[5] The manifesto of the Zimmerwald Conference, composed by Trotsky, agreed completely with Lenin on the imperialist nature of the war and the treason of the Socialists. Missing was Lenin's call to civil war led by a Third International. Trotsky in 1915 still sailed unhappily between Scylla and Charybdis, unable seriously to fight Lenin, unwilling as yet to join him.

In the period 1904–1906, as previously mentioned, the views of
Lenin and Trotsky differed on the matter of the party's postrevolu-
tionary prospectus. So long of course as the tsar was not overthrown,
the question of whether the party would take the path of Trotsky's
"permanent revolution" or that of Lenin's "passive interim" remained
a mere exercise in polemics. Before 1917, then, this question could
never have become a matter of intense argumentation. Yet this difference in political views, like the dispute over party organization,
also reveals a basic variance in the personalities of the two men.

As indicated by the grandiose sweep of "permanent revolution,"
Trotsky painted his Marxism in broad, vivid strokes. Seize power in
Russia, start the march on Europe—and all would happen just as
the manifesto had prophesied. The young Trotsky had full faith in
the mechanism of history, whereby everything of importance was
predestined. Knowing what course it would take, Trotsky was ready
to plunge joyously into the current of events. Whether or not he
survived was to him a secondary matter. Of his fatalistic and vision-
ary qualities Trotsky himself was fully conscious. "In questions of
the inner development of the party," his autobiography states, "I
was guilty of a sort of *social-revolutionary* fatalism. This was a mistaken stand, but it was vastly superior to that *bureaucratic* fatalism,
devoid of ideas, which distinguishes the majority of my present-day
critics." [6] In another passage Trotsky declared that no great work
was "possible without intuition." Neither theoretical education, he
writes, "nor practical routine can replace the political insight which
enables one to apprehend a situation, weigh it as a whole, and for-
see the future. . . . The events of 1905 revealed in me, I believe,
this revolutionary intuition, and enabled me to rely on its support
during my later life." Trotsky goes on to say that whatever errors,
small or great, he had committed "always referred to questions that
were not fundamental or strategic, but dealt rather with such deriva-
tive matters as organization and policy." [7]

Lenin, though certainly not lacking in scope of vision, was, unlike
Trotsky, incessantly concerned with the detail of how "it was to be
done," of leaving nothing to chance. Above all, having drawn his
diagram, Lenin considered it vital that he personally guide the plan
to success. This made it essential that he preserve his person for the
leadership function. [8]

As the war progressed and world revolution appeared to Trotsky
to be imminent, his last remaining links to Menshevism finally rotted

away. Just before departing from New York on his return to Russia, Trotsky wrote an article in which, as he points out, he had arrived at conclusions identical with those then held by Lenin as to the directions which the revolutions in Russia and Europe would take. In Lenin's April Theses Trotsky was quick to perceive a prescription for "permanent revolution." If, as Trotsky saw it, Lenin had accepted his scheme, there could be little point in continuing the fourteen-year-old feud.[9] The matter of how the Russian workers' party was organized had ceased to be an obstacle to a union with Lenin, for the entire Russian revolutionary movement would soon become merged with that of Europe. Very soon after his arrival in Russia, and despite some lingering distrust on Lenin's part, Trotsky, though nominally not a Bolshevik, became an ardent and effective spokesman for Lenin's policy.

Trotsky's misconception as to the meaning of Lenin's April Theses led him to believe that Lenin, from April on, was moving directly though cautiously toward a Bolshevik seizure of power in Russia. In his *History of the Russian Revolution* [10] Trotsky praises the moderation of Lenin which had held the leftist Bolsheviks in check during the May riotings. He deplores the irresponsibility of Smilga and others of the Central Committee, who, before the June demonstrations, spoke of seizing post offices, telegraph agencies, arsenals, and so forth. Trotsky wrote:

> The existence of such moods is easily understandable. The whole course of the party was toward a seizure of power, and the question was merely of appraising the present situation. An obvious break in favor of the Bolsheviks was taking place in Petrograd, but in the provinces the same process was going slower. . . . Lenin, therefore, stood firm on his April position: "Patiently explain." [11]

The whole course of Lenin (it is Lenin that Trotsky means when he uses the term "party") was at that time exactly opposed to a seizure of power—for reasons already explained. Trotsky's belief that Lenin's course was guided by a day-to-day appraisal of the chances for a successful *coup d'état* caused him also to misread Lenin's motives in refusing to take power during the July Days. With the argument that the provinces and the army were not yet politically ready to support a Bolshevik coup in Petrograd,[12] Trotsky defends "the leadership of the party," that is, Lenin, as "*completely right in not taking the road of armed insurrection. It is not enough to seize power—you have to hold it.*" [13] Lenin did at one point explain his

July behavior on this ground. But he did so only ten weeks after the event, at a time when, for reasons previously explained, it became necessary for him to pretend that he had seriously contemplated taking power in July, when in fact such an idea had never entered his mind.

Trotsky did not officially join the Bolshevik party until after the July Days. Characteristic of the two men, Trotsky boldly presented himself for arrest and trial in July, whereas Lenin, "safeguarding the leadership," discreetly went into hiding. It was only after the July Days that Lenin began to plot his *coup d'état,* but even then he was not in theoretical coalescence with his new Bolshevik colleague. Lenin's thinking in August revolved about a minority-based adventurist uprising. Trotsky, whose ideas on the subject had undergone no change since his arrival in Russia, still thought in terms of a rising supported by a significantly great percentage of the masses. For the brief moment following the mid-September defeat of Kornilov, Lenin, considering his position strengthened, moved abruptly rightward and drafted his compromise offer to the moderate Socialists. Days later he was again calling for an armed overthrow of the government.

Between early July and late September, Lenin's conception of the pace of the revolution went through two complete pendulum swings, each beginning far to the political right of Trotsky's conception and ending well to its left. During that time Trotsky did not even perceive that he and Lenin were out of rhythm. Trotsky's *History* mentions Lenin's attempt to compromise with the moderates.[14] Apparently unable to understand the significance of Lenin's move, Trotsky makes no attempt to explain it. When shortly thereafter Lenin began to press the Central Committee for an immediate insurrection, Trotsky believed that Lenin always, as he points out, keenly evaluating international and Russian conditions, had decided on the basis of these considerations that the time for a rising was at hand. Trotsky reports on the shock which the Central Committee felt upon receiving Lenin's first letter calling for an insurrection. "The sharpness of Lenin's change of front," he writes, "took even the heads of his own party by surprise." "We all gasped," he quotes Bukharin as saying. "Nobody had yet posed the question so abruptly."[15]

Trotsky was of course all with Lenin on the matter of armed revolt. But since he regarded Lenin's attitude as based on an appraisal of the chances for success, he took it upon himself to make a slight corrective to Lenin's plan. Insurrection, yes; but Trotsky felt it would be better to wait—setting the time of the rising for the day when the All-Russian Congress of Soviets would meet. The turning over of power to that body would then give sanction to the insurrection and provide it with an aura of national support. The Bolsheviks, who hoped to take power in the Soviet, would be aided in not being nakedly exposed as the organizers of the uprising.

Over the resistance of the moderates in the Central Executive Committee of the Soviet, who feared that an All-Russian Congress might turn into an All-Russian government, the date for the convening of the congress had been set for November 7. But Lenin did not wish to wait that long. "The beginning of 'decisive action,'" Trotsky writes, "Lenin on October 23 presented to the Central Committee as the task of the next days. We must not wait [or] postpone. On the front—as we have heard from Sverdlov—they are preparing an overturn. Will the Congress of Soviets ever be held? We do not know. We must seize power immediately and not wait for any congresses." [16]

Trotsky ascribes Lenin's frantic haste to a correct evaluation of the situation in view of impending European revolution and the likelihood that the concerted revolutionary mood of the masses would, if not instantly channeled, have overflowed in anarchism and chaos.[17] But Trotsky, though his *History* understandably sloughs over it, favored at least a brief delay, and in this seemingly trivial difference of opinion lies a basic variance in the two men where the significance of the insurrection was concerned. For Trotsky, thinking in terms of the world revolutionary picture, in which Trotsky was but a tiny speck, could afford to wait until the more favorable moment for the achievement of Soviet power through a Bolshevik uprising. Lenin, however, had the telescope turned the other way. In this view Lenin came slightly ahead of world revolution. Therefore Petrograd must be saved from German attack or bourgeois treachery. Successful or not, and gamble though it was, this was Lenin's reason for insurrection and this the primary reason for haste, whether or not the best possible moment had arrived.

As it happened, the insurrection did occur at the time Trotsky thought right. But this was for reasons beyond Lenin's control, and it was Trotsky who was in immediate command of the fighting forces

of the insurrection. But each moment of delay after October 28, the
date originally set for the coup, was to Lenin an eternity. With success, of course, Lenin was not inclined to argue. The moment of triumph was at hand and it had clearly been brought about by Lenin's
control over the party and by Trotsky's leadership of the Military
Committee. For the moment these two shared the spotlight as the
Damon and Pythias of the revolution. However, though they had
reached the same point on the chart, they had arrived by different
routes, and what to Trotsky was the first step in the process of setting
off the European revolution, was to Lenin the means whereby he had
saved himself to head that revolution.

THE TREATY OF BREST-LITOVSK:

THE OPENING MOVES

LENIN'S PEACE PROGRAM, as enunciated at the May party conference, had, as shown earlier, been predicated not upon the thought of a sudden Bolshevik seizure of power but rather upon the expectation of a gradualistically established Soviet government in which the Bolsheviks would only later become predominant. This program had contained two basic points: (1) there would be no separate peace offer to Germany, and (2) there would be a quick and open offer of democratic peace to all peoples. That would bring about the full confidence of the workers of the warring countries toward one another and inevitably lead to uprisings of the proletariat against those imperialist governments that would oppose the proffered peace.[1]

By September, 1917, Lenin no longer thought of peace as something that could wait for Soviet power achieved gradually, followed by a hopeful proposal to the world at large. By September peace had seemed to Lenin so urgent a necessity that he meant to seize power specifically to the end of swiftly making peace. Lenin's new intention made sense only if linked with the idea of a Soviet government opening separate peace negotiations with the Germans. But such an action would mean a complete turning away from Lenin's earlier stated position on the separate peace; at the same time it implied the ditching of the democratic principles that he had proclaimed as the basis of peace proposals by a Soviet government.

Aware of the difficulties that might confront him in making so abrupt an about-face, Lenin, even while holding out to his adherents the bait of peace as an incentive to revolutionary action, had tried his best to reconcile his *Realpolitik* with the supposed high-mindedness of bolshevism. In a late September article, calling at-

Notes begin on page 216.

tention to the danger of a bourgeois betrayal of Petrograd, he used a trick of phrasing to gloss over the ugly phrase "separate peace." The situation, Lenin wrote, was such that *only our* victory in an uprising *will put an end* to the game of a separate peace against the revolution by openly offering a more complete, more just, more immediate peace *in favor* of the revolution." "If our peace proposal is turned down," Lenin went on, as though to prove that he had in no way gone back on his revolutionary democratic principles, "and we obtain not even an armistice, then we shall become 'defensists,' then we shall place ourselves *at the head of the war parties,* we shall be the *most 'warring'* party, and we shall carry on a war in a truly revolutionary manner. . . . And then we shall save Petrograd. . . . The resources, both material and spiritual, of a truly revolutionary war are still infinitely great in Russia." [2]

In another indirect approach to the problem, Lenin's article of October 9–10 contended that a future Soviet government would offer "*immediately* to *all* the belligerent peoples [and their governments] the conclusion of an immediate general peace on democratic conditions," and would publish and repudiate the secret treaties. He wrote:

> Such conditions of peace will not meet with the good will of the capitalists, but they will be met by all the peoples with such tremendous sympathy and will call forth such a great . . . outburst of enthusiasm and . . . indignation against the continuation of the predatory war that it is extremely probable that we shall at once obtain a truce and a consent to open peace negotiations. For the workers' revolution against the war is irresistibly growing everywhere, . . . but only a break with the capitalists and an offer of peace can hasten its progress.
>
> If the least probable thing happens, that is, if not a single belligerent state accepts even a truce, then the war on our part becomes truly forced upon us, it becomes a truly just and defensive [revolutionary] war.

But to this profession of idealism Lenin then attached a rider that was actually a thinly veiled argument in favor of a separate peace. After ridiculing the "absurd assumption" that a joint German-Entente intervention would take place against Russia following the offer of a "just peace," Lenin wrote that "England, America, and Japan, even were they to declare war against Russia, . . . would not cause Russia one hundredth part of the damage and misery which the war with Germany, Austria, and Turkey causes it." [3]

Bolshevik opinion in the years following the seizure of power generally accepted the notion that Lenin, immediately after the *coup d'état,* had been in favor of making a separate peace. Wrote Soviet scholar I. Volkovicher in 1928:

> In our literature of late there appears mention to the effect that Lenin "from the very beginning" was for immediate peace. From the very beginning—this apparently means from the beginning of the peace discussions. Nevertheless, such assertions rest on absolutely no foundations. In the first place, the authors of this version themselves give no evidence which would in any way strengthen this supposition. In the second place, there are various indications pointing to the contrary. At the beginning of the discussions, Lenin actually considered it necessary to delay negotiations.[4]

In my judgment Volkovicher's opinion was ill-founded. Lenin seized power in order to make a quick peace. But the ease of the Petrograd success coupled with the chain reaction of Bolshevik triumphs throughout the Russian Empire had produced in the party, and among its youthful left-wing elements especially, an exalted state of fanaticism.[5] To a group of crusaders eager to participate in the much-heralded overthrow of Europe's governments, a straightforward appeal by Lenin for a peace with imperial Germany would hardly have come as a welcome message. So Lenin had to pretend to be playing the game according to his earlier prescribed rules of procedure.

The seizure of power, having eliminated the possibility that the bourgeoisie would sell out Petrograd, enabled Lenin to breathe more easily. For a time he could allow the leftist trend to have its day in the sun. Lenin would certainly have preferred to be able to accept his party's optimism as warranted. It was, after all, highly questionable whether a minority-based Russian dictatorship could survive, except for early support from the European revolution. Also, as Lenin knew, a separate peace would strengthen the position of the militarists in Germany and possibly delay the German revolution.[6] The same peace, by releasing German troops fom the Russian front, would surely breed hatred for bolshevism in the Entente countries [7] and there too harm the cause of revolution. But all these were long-range considerations, which in Lenin's mind were far outweighed by more immediate dangers. If peace was not soon made, there threatened not only a sudden German offensive, possibly as the spearhead of a joint Allied-German interventionist move, but also a revolt of the peasant-soldiery, who had ranked themselves behind the Bolsheviks largely because of the peace promised by Lenin.[8]

In his November 8 "Report on Peace" [9] to the Congress of Soviets, Lenin read a "Declaration on Peace" which he thought should be adopted by the government about to be formed. Offering "democratic peace" to all belligerents, the declaration expressed the willingness of the "workers' and peasants' government" to negotiate with capitalist governments. At the same time it voiced a clear distrust of such governments and placed the real hope for peace in the revolutionary force of the people behind them. Less apparent in the text are ideas suggesting that Lenin, though unable to say so in specific terms, actually desired a separate peace.

Nine times in the brief declaration and supplementary comment Lenin used the term "immediate" in connection with the term "peace." Though clearly intended to satisfy the peace hunger of the Russian masses, the undue emphasis upon immediate peace, since such could be obtained only from Germany, must also be construed as a strong propagandistic nudge, preparatory to later moves, in the direction of a separate peace. Equally significant is a statement, made twice, to the effect that the conditions for a "democratic" peace, so greatly stressed in the declaration, were not to be considered "ultimative." As though to disguise the true meaning of this twice-mentioned point, Lenin expressed the belief that if the Soviet peace terms were too rigid, the capitalist governments would too easily be able to reject them, having the excuse, before their peoples, that the Soviet government had made impossible proposals. Covering up still further, Lenin remarked that listening to counterproposals was not yet the same as accepting them.

Despite these qualifications, Lenin's willingness to compromise with the previously much-advertised "democratic" terms is clear. Since neither a peace through revolution nor a general peace conference of all the warring powers would have made necessary a compromise with "democracy," such willingness can be construed only as Lenin's attempt to keep the door wide open for a separate peace with the Germans.

On the very occasion of delivering his report Lenin received a rather embarrassing challenge from the floor. "There is a contradiction here," an unidentified member of the audience charged. "First you offer peace without annexations and indemnities, and then you say you will consider all peace offers. To consider means to accept."[10]

Lenin rose, and John Reed reports his reply:

We want a just peace but we are not afraid of a revolutionary war. . . . Probably the imperialist governments will not answer our appeal —but we shall not issue an ultimatum to which it will be easy to say no. . . . If the German proletariat realizes that we are ready to consider all offers of peace, that will perhaps be the last drop which overflows the bowl—revolution will break out in Germany. . . .

We consent to examine all conditions of peace, but that doesn't mean we shall accept them. . . . For some of our terms we shall fight to the end—but possibly for others will find it impossible to continue the war. . . . Above all we want to finish the war.[11]

The above comments were delivered impromptu and at an extremely confusing moment in Lenin's life. They reveal him with his mental guard down and throw a piercing light upon the various unresolved cross currents chasing about in his mind in the period just before, during the time of, and immediately after the *coup d'état*.

"We are not afraid of a revolutionary war." This phrase was not directly a reply to the challenger but rather to the doubts in Bolshevik minds, which may have been raised by the challenger's question. Lenin's unpopular intent toward separate peace had suddenly been drawn into the light of day and he had needed quickly to assert that he was really in perfect Marxist harmony with what he knew to be the majority sentiment of his own party.

"Probably the imperialist governments will not answer our appeal." But the tone of the peace decree itself was by no means pessimistic on this score, conveying rather the notion, which remained the Bolshevik conviction for weeks thereafter, that most of the governments could be expected to respond to the peace appeal. This opinion had been clearly stated by Lenin on October 9–10: "If the least probable thing happens, that is, if not a single belligerent state accepts even an armistice. . . ."

At that time, of course, Lenin had been making propaganda to explain that the great likelihood of a truce would make it possible to retain power once it was taken. Having won power, however, Lenin was eager to consolidate his hold upon it by making a separate peace. He did not like the idea of leaving things to such indeterminable factors as proletarian pressures upon imperialist governments. Still, the peace decree itself had had to express the hopeful prospects contained in his earlier propaganda. It was Lenin's impromptu reply that voiced his real sentiments. Out came the impatience with the sop phrases of yesterday which were now impeding him. Blurting out the bald truth of the situation, he exposed his intention sooner or later to waken the happy dreamers in his party into the chilly dawn of the existing reality.

"If the German proletariat realizes . . . that will . . . be the last drop which overflows the bowl—revolution will break out in Germany." Here was sheer prestidigitation; Lenin was converting his invitation to the German high command to make a conqueror's peace into the drop that would fill to overflowing the bowl of German revolution.

The party membership in general took out of Lenin's message that which matched their own sentiments and no doubt quite overlooked the less apparent contents of both the peace address and Lenin's reply to the questioner. For a time, indeed, the hope for a democratic peace backed by the threat of European revolution appeared to their naïve eyes as in the process of fulfillment. The glistening bubbles blown entirely from their own pipes, the triumphant noises emanating from their own mouths, these blinded and deafened them to the realities of November and December, months which marked a series of sugar-coated but grim setbacks to the Bolshevik expectations of a democratic peace.

During November Foreign Affairs Commissar Trotsky received only rebuffs from the Entente governments, but from them the Bolsheviks had not expected too much in the very beginning. The impending revolution, they thought, would soon put the scoundrels on the right track. In the meantime the Bolsheviks could enjoy an illusion of strength derived from the arrogant manner of the Soviet overtures to the Allied governments. An added slap in the face was given the Allies by the publication on November 23 of the secret treaties. During this period Lenin had lost no time in establishing contact with the very receptive Germans. The German willingness to open discussions, the Bolsheviks misconstrued as a victory for the revolution.

What should have been a sign of things to come was the fact that of all the guests invited to the great peace party ending the imperialist war, the group to accept was that headed by Germany, the greatest imperialist of them all. As might have been suspected, the wolf had joined the party intending to consume a larger meal than his hosts had planned to serve. However, having begun to negotiate for an armistice with the Central Powers on December 13, the Bolsheviks put on a great show of confidence. Their pockets stuffed with currency redeemable only in case of Europe's early revolution, they confronted the Germans at Brest-Litovsk not as the representatives of a defeated nation but rather in the manner of the arbiters of a new order on the Continent. Lacking any authorization by Russia's erstwhile allies, the Russian delegation at Brest proposed terms that could have applied only to a conference of all warring powers. On December 17 Trotsky notified the Allied embassies that the armistice had been concluded and that peace negotiations would begin, and asked them to participate, or to state whether or not they wished peace.[12] He received no answer.

Despite the absence of the Allies, there were moments at Brest when the Bolsheviks, already believing they had seen the miracle, were given what to them seemed new proofs of its substance. The German acceptance of the Soviet stipulation that no fighting forces be moved during the period of the armistice (noon of December 17, 1917, to noon of January 14, 1918) from the Black Sea–Baltic Sea front, left the impression that the Germans were inclined to bargain rather than simply dictate their terms, and this promoted further Russian enthusiasm. On Christmas Day, three days after formal negotiations for a general peace were initiated, the Central Powers went so far as to acquiesce in the Bolshevik tenet of a nonannexationist peace, with the proviso, however, that this would apply only to a peace involving all the warring nations. Through Chairman A. Ioffe, the happy Russian delegation then expressed "its satisfaction that Germany and her Allies were as alien to plans for any sort of territorial seizures . . . as they were to any attempt to destroy or limit the political independence of any people whatsoever," [13] and proposed a recess in the negotiations (the date for resumption of plenary proceedings was set for January 9) so that "the peoples, whose governments have not yet joined in the discussions for a general peace may have the opportunity to become sufficiently acquainted with the now established bases for such a peace. Upon the expiration of the designated period, the discussions must be resumed, regardless of whether other warring powers . . . have joined them." [14] A wire relating the magnificent success of the Russian peace proposals to the Soviet government was enough to bring about a monster demonstration in Petrograd on December 30, "in honor," as Trotsky has it, "of the democratic peace." [15] But if the Russian delegates had dreams of returning home to be greeted by cheering throngs, they were destined to a rude awakening.

German diplomatism, to which that of Austria was necessarily appended, was intended largely as a form of world propaganda, its purpose being to dull the gleam though not the edge of the German annexationist carving knife. The transfers of territory, it was expected, would be arranged with the Russians whenever the discussions arrived at the down-to-earth level of separate peace talks, but even then a pretense of self-determination would be allowed to prevail. This, the Germans believed, would satisfy the Bolsheviks. The democratically phrased formulas might enable the latter to deceive the Russian masses into thinking that the Bolsheviks had somehow or other fulfilled their promises. If by some outside chance the Entente saw fit to join in the peace discussions, that still would have suited the Germans, for they, already half certain that the war was lost, were willing to settle for the *status quo ante bellum*.[16]

When the Russians behaved as though a nonannexationist peace even with Russia alone was in the making, the German and Austrian missions finally realized that they were playing their tricky game not with cynical sophisticates, traditional to diplomacy, but with a peculiar brand of zealots. Lest the entire peace talks collapse in an absurdity of confusion,[17] it became necessary at once to let the Russian delegation know the true nature of the German intentions toward Russia. At a noon breakfast on December 26[18] German General Hoffmann, who from the beginning had opposed the diplomats' tactic on the ground that it was "essentially a lie,"[19] brusquely told Ioffe that the territories then occupied by the German armies would remain in German hands. "Ioffe," reports Hoffmann, "acted as though struck over the head."[20] On December 27 Ioffe, Kamenev, and Pokrovsky remonstrated at length with von Kühlmann and Hoffmann of Germany and with Czernin of Austria. "Amid tears of rage," Pokrovsky demanded to know how one "could speak of peace without annexation when some eighteen gubernias were to be taken from Russia."[21]

It was the dogmatic faith in the fast-rising pressure of European revolution and not a belief in the good will of the German government that had led the Bolsheviks of the Brest delegation to think that German diplomacy was seriously considering some sort of a democratic yardstick in its contemplated treaty of peace.[22] This view also had given wings to the hopes of the party enthusiasts as they followed the course of the negotiations. When the German mask fell, the party's general reaction was equally doctrinaire. Democratic peace had been offered the imperialists; it had been rejected. The next move, as prescribed by the book, was the revolutionary war.

At this point Lenin decided that he could no longer go along with the revolutionary romanticism in the party. A revolutionary war, in view of the Russian army's disintegrated condition, could, as Lenin knew, mean only an unresisted German advance, leading to the fall of Petrograd and other centers of Bolshevik strength. Threatening Lenin was a danger similar to that which had faced him in the period from September to November. To prevent that, it will be recalled, he had undertaken the risk of what from his point of view had been the premature seizure of power. During the early January recess in the talks, Lenin suggested that Trotsky take charge of the Russian delegation in the discussions about to be resumed. "In order to delay the proceedings," said Lenin to Trotsky, "there must be some one to do the delaying." [23]

Whatever his earlier thoughts on the subject, Lenin by this time was quite pessimistic as to the likelihood of early German or European revolution.[24] He was more than ever convinced that the separate peace would provide the only chance that his and Bolshevik power would endure. Lenin's desire for delaying the Brest proceedings came about not as Trotsky believed, because Lenin wanted to give the European revolution more time to ferment, but because he needed time to prepare his case in opposition to the party's will for revolutionary war, which above all he wanted to prevent.

Once at Brest, Trotsky made it his business to drag out the discussions. In his involved disputations with von Kühlmann, who headed the German diplomatic mission, Trotsky at the same time attempted to expose before the world the "wolfish appetites" of the Germans, as concealed beneath the diplomats' talk of self-determination. He also lost no opportunity to spread Bolshevik propaganda among the German troops in the area and to broadcast inflammatory messages to the German people. On his way to Brest-Litovsk Trotsky had had the opportunity to observe the condition of Russia's fighting forces as illustrated by the troopless trenches facing the German lines. A renewal of a Russian military effort, he points out, was not even worth contemplating.[25] The signing of a peace treaty, however, Trotsky regarded as the improper tactic for two reasons. The March and November revolutions, he thought first, might have made such deep impressions upon the German masses that the German government, in attempting to carry on the war against the Russia of the revolution (as against that of the tsar), would find its hands tied by revolutions in the rear and in the army. "The January strike in Germany," as Trotsky recounted his reasoning, "showed that the break had begun. But how deep was it? Must we not try to put this alternative before the German workmen and the German army: on the one hand, the workmen's revolution declaring the war ended; on the other, the Hohenzollern government that orders an attack on this revolution?" [26] Trotsky notes in the second place that the Right Socialists of Germany and the Entente press were busily depicting the Bolsheviks as paid agents of the German government, the former portraying the negotiations at Brest-Litovsk as a comedy "with the roles allotted in advance." [27] This fiction, once accepted by the proletarians of the Entente countries, would "consequently facilitate the military intervention of the Entente against [the Soviet government]." Cost what it might, Trotsky writes,

before the signing of peace [the Bolsheviks] must give the workmen of Europe a clear proof of the deadly enmity between us and governmental Germany. It was these very considerations that on my arrival in Brest-Litovsk suggested the idea of that "pedagogical" demonstration, that was expressed in the form: We shall stop the war but without signing the peace treaty. I conferred with the other members of the delegation, found them in sympathy with the suggestion, and wrote about it to Vladimir Ilyich. His answer was: "If you come [to Petrograd] we will talk it over." [28]

"Possibly," Trotsky surmises, "this answer already showed that [Lenin] did not agree with my proposition." [29] Trotsky had correctly sensed the meaning of Lenin's equivocation.

7

THE TREATY OF BREST-LITOVSK:

THE END GAME

WHILE ON VACATION in Finland, January 6–10, Lenin had begun to outline the approach he would take in persuading the party to choose the separate peace over a revolutionary war.[1] Just before this time, at the renewed Brest sessions, the Germans had made their concept of self-determination more explicit. "For strategic reasons," as they explained on January 2 and 5, "their forces would remain" in all of Poland, Lithuania, and in the major parts of Latvia and Belo-Russia.[2] On January 10 the Moscow regional bureau of the party adopted a resolution demanding "the breaking off of peace negotiations with the imperialistic Germans, . . . the disruption of every form of . . . relations with all diplomatizing gangsters," and called for a party conference or meeting to discuss the question of peace.[3] On the same day the Petersburg Committee formulated a categorical protest against the possibility that an "imperialistic peace pact" be concluded with Germany.[4]

On January 20, having returned from Brest, Trotsky took up his "no war-no peace" scheme with Lenin. The latter wryly agreed that Trotsky's plan was "all very attractive," but was not likely to stop General Hoffmann from mounting an advance.

"You have said yourself," he told Trotsky, "that the trenches are empty. And suppose he begins the war again in spite of everything?"

"Then," replied Trotsky, "we would be forced to sign the peace treaty, and it would be clear to everyone that we had no other way out. By that alone we would strike a decisive blow at the legend that we are in league with the Hohenzollern behind the scenes."

"Naturally there is much to be said for that," was Lenin's answer, in effect a shrug of the shoulders, "but after all, it is too bold. For

Notes begin on page 218.

the moment our revolution is more important than everything else; we must make it sure, cost what it may." [5]

Trotsky had one more argument to offer. He pointed out that those in the party who favored a revolutionary war were the left Communists, the very ones who had most actively backed the November seizure of power. By signing a peace with the Germans, Lenin would not only be risking a split in the party, but would be siding with the right wing of the party, that is, with those who had opposed the revolution in November and had favored a bloc with the other socialist parties. Trotsky tried to frighten Lenin with the prospect of slipping toward the tainted Right, but failed to realize that Lenin could be left or right, as the moment suited him. Having swung leftward in the pre-November period only because he had been compelled to do so by motives which transcended matters of Russian party politics, Lenin was just as easily prepared to swing right if that would help him achieve the same ultimate purpose.

"That is all indisputable," Lenin said, granting Trotsky's contention, "but for the moment the question is the fate of the revolution. We can restore balance in the party. But before everything else we must save the revolution, and we can only save it by signing peace terms. Better a split than the danger of a military overthrow of the revolution. The Lefts will cease raging and then—even if it comes to a split, which is not inevitable—return to the Party. On the other hand, if the Germans conquer us, not one of us returns." [6] "Not one of us" would include Lenin, and he had no intention of disappearing from the hard-won limelight.

Sensing that he might not succeed in preventing Trotsky from selling his idea to the party, Lenin lost no time in preparing his ground for the resulting eventualities. Trotsky's plan, if it failed to touch off a German revolution and cause a paralysis in the German army, would most surely give rise to a renewed German offensive. In that event, having lost additional territory, Lenin and the party would still be faced with the same problem, that of making peace or of carrying on some sort of revolutionary guerrilla warfare. Anticipating that he would at such a moment still have Trotsky as well as the "revolutionary war" faction of the party to cope with, Lenin tried to pin Trotsky down to a favorable commitment.

"Very well," he said. "Let us admit your plan is accepted. We refuse to sign the peace treaty. And the Germans at once attack. What will you do then?"

"We will sign the peace terms under bayonets," was Trotsky's answer. "Then the picture will be clear to the workmen of the whole world."

"But you will not support the solution of a revolutionary war?" Lenin asked him.

"Under no circumstances," replied Trotsky.

"With this understanding," Lenin declared, "the experiment is probably not so dangerous. We risk the loss of Estonia and Latvia." Lenin then dug sharply at Trotsky's permanent revolutionism. "Some Estonian comrades came to see me recently," he went on, "and told me how splendidly the peasants had begun the socialist structure. It is a great pity if we must sacrifice socialist Estonia, but for the sake of a good peace [with Trotsky] it is worth agreeing to a compromise."

According to Trotsky, Lenin spoke the last sentence "jokingly." However, since the entire statement has a bitter flavor, it is hardly likely that Lenin was joking, except of course in a sardonic and gibing sense. And the fact that Trotsky knew he was being attacked is revealed in his defensive reply, in which he pointed out that even if an immediate peace was signed, the Germans might still take Estonia and Latvia. To which Lenin answered that this was a possibility, but "only a possibility, while [the loss of those regions by not signing a peace] is almost a certainty. In any case," Lenin concluded abruptly, "I stand for the immediate signing of peace, it is safer." [7]

On January 21 an assemblage of sixty-three leading Bolsheviks, in Petrograd as delegates to the Third Congress of Soviets, heard Lenin read his "Theses on the Question of Immediate Conclusion of a Separate and Annexationist Peace." Lenin's argument, essentially, was that the Soviet Republic was in itself worth preserving, despite the fact that "all our hopes of the *final* victory of socialism are based on" the conviction that "socialist revolution in Europe must and will come." But until the European flame went up, it was up to the Bolsheviks to keep aglow the world's sole socialist ember.

To the contention that separate peace would constitute a deal with German imperialism, Lenin retorted that a revolutionary war was tantamount to supporting Allied imperialism. "Thus," he declared, "whichever move we make, we cannot tear ourselves wholly free from a connection with one or the other imperialist side—and we shall never be wholly able to do so until world capitalism has been overthrown. The correct way forward then, since the time of the victory of a socialist government in one country, is not to decide the question from the point of view of preference to one or another imperialism, but exclusively from the point of view of the best conditions for development and strengthening of the already begun socialist revolution." [8]

To the contingent of Moscow Bolsheviks at the meeting, this proposition could have seemed only an affront. These mostly youthful zealots were scarcely in the frame of mind to view their projected "holy war" for European revolution in the light of an adjunct to British-French imperialism. This idea was particularly painful coming from the man to whom they looked for leadership in such a venture. "I stand on the old position of Lenin," [9] was the doleful plaint of one of the delegates, referring to Lenin's oft-reiterated mention of revolutionary war as applicable to circumstances exactly like those then prevailing. When it came to a vote on the path to follow, a majority of thirty-two, comprising mainly the younger group, demanded revolutionary war, sixteen followed Trotsky, and a mere fifteen votes were cast for an immediate signing of the peace.

Lenin, as he wrote soon thereafter, was reminded of the "analogous" situation in the party in the summer of 1907, when the

> vast majority of the Bolsheviks was for boycotting the Third Duma, while I defended participation in it . . . and for this I underwent furious attacks for my opportunism . . . as at that time, the majority of the party workers, motivated by the best revolutionary instincts and the best traditions of the party, were carried away by a "clear" slogan, *but failed to grasp the new* socio-economic and political situation, and failed to perceive the *changed conditions,* demanding a swift, abrupt change in tactics. And my entire argument, as [in 1907], was concentrated in explaining that Marxism demands taking into account objective conditions and their changes, that it was necessary to place the question concretely, . . . that the basic change now consisted in the creation of a republic of Soviet Russia, and that above everything, both for us *and from the international-socialist point of view* was the securing of this republic, . . . that at the present moment the slogan of revolutionary war could serve only as a meaningless gesture which, *in possibly the cheapest way,* would help the imperialists to *destroy* . . . the young republic.[10]

Lenin might also have been reminded of his own leftward swing in April, 1917, when, isolated from the party, he had attacked the "old Bolsheviks" such as Kalinin for clinging to the "outdated" Leninism of 1905. But it was not this time the "old," but rather the very young,[11] Bolsheviks who had failed to keep pace with the will-o'-the-wisp tactical path of Lenin.

On January 24 the sixteen-member Central Committee met to decide the issue. Proponents of revolutionary war had been contending that it was the Bolsheviks' duty to support the German revolutionary movement. Lenin, to whom the thankless role of revolutionary shock trooper had little appeal, argued that the Bolsheviks lacked a clear understanding of the state of affairs in Germany, and he made the colorful remark that the "already born—completely healthy child—the Russian socialist republic" was of greater immediate concern than a "Germany as yet but pregnant with revolution." [12]

But Lenin was careful at the same time to dissociate himself from any negation of the revolutionary movement in the West as advanced at the meeting by his supporters Stalin and Zinoviev. Stalin argued against the program of revolutionary war and that of "no war-no peace" on the ground that "there was no revolutionary movement in the West, but merely potential . . . and with potentials we cannot figure." In echoing a thought expressed by Lenin in thesis 6 of the Peace Theses, Stalin, citing out of context, had stuck his heavy foot through the delicate web of Lenin's spinning. Lenin quickly squelched Stalin. "Of course," he said, "[there is a mass movement in the West] though the revolution has not yet begun. But were we for this reason to change our tactic, we should be traitors to international socialism." Zinoviev made the point that the "ruin of the socialist republic," would be a greater evil than the likelihood that the signing of a peace "would strengthen chauvinism in Germany and, for a short time, weaken the [revolutionary] movement everywhere in the West." In thesis 19 of the Peace Theses Lenin had admitted that the signing of a peace would temporarily produce a chauvinistic reaction in Germany. But now, in answer to Zinoviev's contention, he forcefully denied that the conclusion of peace would for a time weaken the movement in the West.

"If," he declared in ringing terms, "we believe that the German movement could react quickly in the event of a breaking off of peace talks, then we should have to sacrifice ourselves, for the German revolution will be much more powerful than our own." [13] If for the moment it was expedient for Lenin to adopt a Russian-oriented position, this was only to preserve himself, not Russia, for world revolution. Whenever Europe should begin to undergo its real labor pains of revolution, Lenin, already father of the healthy

Russian baby, hoped to be standing outside the delivery room, flowers in hand.

In contrast to the broad party meeting of January 21, that of the Central Committee was dominated by older and cooler heads. Only Kossior and Dzerzhinsky spoke out for revolutionary war. Of the remaining fourteen, seven backed Lenin's stand for immediate peace, seven Trotsky's "no war-no peace" position. This, however, does not mean that either side constituted a solid phalanx. Both factions, as the discussions reveal, were actually made up of a variety of shadings; for example, the already-mentioned Stalin and Zinoviev variants from Lenin's position. "Trotsky's position," Stalin remarked bluntly at one point, "is no position at all." This of course had much truth in it and certainly those who supported the "no war-no peace" line did not do so out of strong convictions.

As individuals, most members of this faction would have favored revolutionary war. But among these there was not a single man courageous enough to assume the actual leadership of so daring an orientation. Trotsky's halfway formula therefore served them as a compromise between conscience and moral weakness.

Perhaps the most significant aspect of the occasion was the fact that it established Trotsky as a serious challenger for the leadership of the party. Central Committee majorities had opposed Lenin in the past, but there had never previously been an individual strong enough to spearhead such a force. For this reason the vote of 9 to 7 against Lenin, the two proponents of revolutionary war naturally joining the Trotsky-supporting faction, represented the most serious intraparty defeat ever suffered by Lenin on a crucial issue.

Lenin's Peace Theses had attacked as useless further procrastination in the talks with the Central Powers. But at this point, whether to win time in which to regroup his forces within the party or merely for the purpose of delaying the effectuation of the "no war-no peace" policy, Lenin proposed a resolution declaring that the Brest negotiations continue to be drawn out "by every means." The committee approved his resolution by 12 votes to 2, and this for the moment was all Lenin was able to save from what he considered a debacle.

On February 10, having for thirteen more days carried on the dreary debates with von Kühlmann, Trotsky delivered his since-famous "no war-no peace" proclamation. An offensive against Russia, to begin February 18, was announced by the German command on February 16. On the same day Russian Commander in Chief

Krylenko wired Lenin, asking how the Russian headquarters was to react to the imminent German attack. Lenin turned to Trotsky, who was in his office when Krylenko's message arrived. "There is nothing for us to do," Lenin declared, "but sign the old conditions if the Germans still agree to them." Trotsky retorted that he had promised to agree to offer peace only in the event of an actual offensive, not in the event merely of its announcement. "Naturally," he told Lenin, "it means new sacrifices. But they are necessary so that the German soldier enters Soviet territory in actual fighting. They are necessary so that the German workman on the one hand and the French and English workman on the other may understand." [14]

Worse yet from Lenin's point of view was the decision of the Central Committee which met the next day, February 17. Trotsky, Bukharin, Lomov, Uritsky, Ioffe, and Krestinsky outvoted Lenin, Stalin, Sverdlov, Sokolnikov, and Smilga in favor of delaying the reopening of peace discussions not only until the offensive had begun but even for a time longer, so that "the effect of the German offensive upon the workers' movement [in Europe]" might be observed.[15] Again picking up the pieces, Lenin, who arranged the voting,[16] managed at least to gain a majority, Bukharin, Lomov, Uritsky, and Krestinsky abstaining, on the proposition that "we conclude peace, having established for a fact the German offensive, as well as the absence in Germany and Austria of any revolutionary uprisings [resulting therefrom]." [17] Trotsky, alone of the above-designated anti-Lenin faction, voted with Lenin, and this was in accord with the deal which he and Lenin had made. However, this vote by Trotsky, as compared with his previous vote and the abstention or opposition [18] of his five erstwhile colleagues, clearly pinpoints the intermediacy of Trotsky's position between that of Lenin and that of an essentially prowar grouping. Also revealed is the absence of a firm bond between the anti-Lenin faction and the leader it had chosen to stand behind. Lenin's second proposition, that "all opposition be rendered [by the party] in the event of an attack on Germany's part," was agreed to unanimously.[19] To Bukharin, Ioffe, and the others, this of course had the pleasant tone of revolutionary war. To Lenin it signified the very last of all possible ditches from which he might attempt a defense of that which he had won through a lifetime of labor.

The next day brought the news that the German offensive had actually begun. Trotsky, reporting to the Central Committee the morning of February 18, mentioned German aircraft over Dvinsk and an expected attack upon Revel. But worst of all was the appearance of four German divisions from the Western front and a radio proclamation by Prince Leopold of Bavaria to the effect that Germany, according to her "historic mission," was in the process of saving the West from the dangers of the East, at this moment "the bolshevik infection." Did this mean that Germany was in collusion with the Entente? Was this the start of the long-dreaded joint imperialist anti-Bolshevik intervention? If so, this would have made any new Soviet peace offer useless, leaving only the alternative of revolutionary war. Lenin himself at this moment wavered somewhat from his former stand, appearing frustrated not so much by the fact that his Central Committee opposition refused to decide in favor of the peace offer, but that it seemed disinclined to take any decisive stand whatsoever.

"We face a situation in which it is necessary to act," he said. Indecision at such a time, he pointed out, would badly confuse the masses, if the situation subsequently became one in which it would be necessary to call upon them to rally for a revolutionary war.[20] Lenin still preferred making a peace offer to the Germans. Even if it were not accepted, it would indicate which way the wind was blowing, and would at least make it clear to all concerned that revolutionary war was indeed the last and only alternative. But the decision by a vote of 7 to 6 went Trotsky's way, that is, to allow time for a reaction to the offensive to develop among the proletarians of Germany.[21]

Since nothing at all stood in the way of the German advance, the news that day became increasingly disturbing. By evening, when the Central Committee again went into session, Trotsky gloomily reported the fall of Dvinsk and the likelihood of a German drive into the Ukraine. Still Trotsky maintained that the time had not yet come for peace negotiations, though he was willing to go so far as to "turn to Vienna and Berlin and ask what their [new] demands might be." Lenin was heartsick at this continuing procrastination and declared:

> One cannot joke with war. It is no longer possible to wait for the situation to become fully clear. The masses will not understand. If this means war then why are we demobilizing, . . . if the Germans demand destruction of the Bolshevik power, then, of course, we must fight. . . . Merely to question the Germans . . . is no policy. The only thing is to propose the resumption of negotiations, . . . While we

write notes, they will seize stores, railway cars. . . . History will say that we sold out the revolution. We could have signed a peace that would in no way have threatened the revolution. . . . To argue further against the partisans of revolutionary war is impossible, but one must fight the partisans of waiting. One must offer the Germans peace.

It was too late for peace, Ioffe contended. The German military party had evidently triumphed, and the Germans were intent upon seizing Livonia, Estonia, Finland, and the Ukraine. "If there is no revolution in their rear," Ioffe concluded, "they will get more. If there is, we will take everything back." Bukharin, for the first time openly taking a position favoring revolutionary war, also pointed to the hopelessness of peace offers because the Germans were this time going "*va banque*" and "united imperialism [was marching] against the revolution. . . . We are now left only our old tactic, the tactic of world revolution."

"If we give up Finland, Estonia and Livonia," Lenin answered, "the revolution is not yet lost . . . if [the Germans add to their former terms the demand that we do not] intervene in the affairs of the Ukraine, Finland, Livonia and Estonia, then this too we must accept unconditionally." [22]

"Suppose the Germans attack anyway? Suppose they march on Moscow?" This was the question which Trotsky cites Lenin's opponents as having baited him with.

"Then," Trotsky has Lenin answering, "we will withdraw to the east to the Urals, and declare anew that we are ready to sign the treaty. The Kuznetsky basin is rich in coal. We will form a Ural-Kuznetsky Republic, based on the industry of the Urals and the coal of the Kuznetsky basin, on the proletariat of the Urals and the Moscow and St. Petersburg workmen we can take with us. If need be we can go further east, beyond the Ural Mountains. We will go to Kamchatka but we will stand together. The international situation will change a dozen times, and we will enlarge the borders of the Ural-Kuznetsky Republic again and return to Moscow and Petersburg. But if we now thoughtlessly involve ourselves in a revolutionary war and lose the flower of the workmen and our party, naturally we can never return." [23] This statement reveals the extent to which Lenin was willing to go to avoid a military embroilment against great odds in which he would unavoidably have had to play a chief part. Lenin, no less than Bukharin and Ioffe, looked expectantly to Europe's revolution, but Lenin wanted to be alive, if in Kamchatka, when it happened. Bukharin and Ioffe, on the other hand, seemingly preferred to stand their ground and perish for the cause. But then, neither of the latter two regarded himself as essential to the triumph of international socialism.

Throughout the discussions of February 18 Trotsky maintained his first-stated position, and just before the vote was taken he posed his proposition "not to ask a truce, but to ask what the enemy's terms might be." His vote, however, went with Lenin and became the margin assuring victory for the notion to propose peace. On February 19 the peace message was dispatched to the Germans and stated that "the Soviet of People's Commissars considers itself forced to declare its willingness to sign [without delay] a peace treaty with the same conditions as were proposed by the delegation of the Quadruple Alliance at Brest-Litovsk." [24]

During the next anxious days the Soviet government, while hoping for peace, had to prepare for the contingency of war. A committee for revolutionary defense was set up, and Trotsky was designated as its head. On February 15, just before Hoffmann's actual redeclaration of war, Trotsky had taken it upon himself to tell British agent Bruce Lockhart that the Soviet government would welcome Allied military aid in the event of a renewed German attack. Once the Germans were on the march, Trotsky urgently importuned Allied embassies, military missions, and agents. "If the Allies would send a promise of support," Lockhart reports Trotsky as having told him, "[Trotsky] would sway the decision of [his] government in favor of war." [25]

An Allied offer of support did come forth, dispelling the notion of an anti-Bolshevik collusion between the rival imperialists. But Trotsky then had to weather a fierce storm in the Central Committee debate of February 22. Most of the committee members agreed that it was quite impermissible for a revolutionary government to accept support from imperialists. Even Sverdlov and Smilga, who were willing to conclude a peace with the German imperialists— that was justifiable since the Soviet Republic was defenseless—regarded Trotsky's tactic of expediency to be outside the bounds of revolutionary morality. [26] Trotsky threatened to resign as Commissar of Foreign Affairs and managed to win his point by a single vote. Lenin, determined by whatever means to hold the fort, sent a note to the meeting requesting that his vote be added to those "in favor of taking potatoes and weapons from the bandits of Anglo-French imperialism." [27]

On February 22 the German ultimatum with the expectedly worse peace conditions was received. The Soviet government was given but forty-eight hours in which to answer. When the Central Committtee met the night of February 23, Trotsky, after Sverdlov had read the German terms, announced that the time of the ultimatum would expire by seven the next morning.[28] The new German conditions, demanding that Russia relinquish Livonia, Estonia, Finland, and the Ukraine, had also released the opponents of peace from their Central Committee agreement of February 18. The harsh terms had fulfilled all their pessimistic prophecies and seemed more than ever answerable in their way only.[29] Lenin, expecting trouble anew and determined not to let this last new ray of hope escape him, took the floor at the outset and delivered an ultimatum. "The politics of revolutionary phraseology," he declared, "have come to an end where I am concerned. If such politics continue, I will resign both from the government and the Central Committee. For revolutionary war an army is needed. We have none. This means we must accept the conditions."

Trotsky delivered the two longest statements of the occasion. In the first he predicted that the Germans, having annexed the territories in question, would remain unsatisfied. Revolutionary war was therefore the preferable and feasible course, but only if the Bolsheviks stood unitedly behind it. If Lenin resigned, rather than yield to an opposing majority in the Central Committee, this action, bound to produce a split in the party's ranks, would make revolutionary war impossible.[30] Trotsky's second declaration further attacked the correctness of Lenin's position, which contained much "subjectivism" (a gentler word than "opportunism"). But being, as he said, unwilling to disrupt the party's unity,[31] Trotsky explicitly declined to take Lenin's place as leader.

Trotsky's arguments convinced Dzerzhinsky, Ioffe, and Krestinsky,[32] and on the final vote their abstention plus that of Trotsky provided Lenin with a victory in the Central Committee, his first on the issue of peace and coming just in the nick of time. Bukharin, Lomov, Bubnov, and Uritsky voted to reject the German terms and denounced the final "catastrophic" [33] decision as that of a minority. They declared that they would resign from all "responsible party and government posts," but would retain "full freedom for agitation within and outside the party for what they considered the only correct position." [34]

How is it to be explained that Trotsky repeatedly opposed Lenin in the debates on the question of peace or war only to yield to him in the final voting?   Permanent revolution was a notion Trotsky had conceived in his middle twenties, and it was an idea of romantic selflessness so typical of the *Sturm und Drang* of youth. Some eleven years later, when the Russian revolution occurred and the war had apparently prepared the way for Europe's revolution, the once-bright flame flared up anew to burn with a particular fury just before the seizure of power.

"You know," Lenin said to Trotsky, hours after the successful *coup d'état*, "from persecution and a life underground, to come so suddenly into power . . . *es schwindelt* [makes one dizzy]." Trotsky, who relates this, also felt more than a little shaky. "In spite of the experience of 1905 [as Head of the Soviet]," Trotsky was later to write, "there was never an occasion when I connected the question of my future with that of power. . . . And so it caught me unawares." [35]

It is extremely difficult to imagine the pre-November Trotsky, consciously on the defensive for being a Jew. His membership in a persecuted, semioutcast group must, if anything, have bolstered his uncompromising revolutionary orientation. But immediately after the seizure of power, Trotsky for this reason "tried to stay out of the government, and offered to undertake the direction of the Press. . . . Was it worthwhile to put into our enemies' hands such an additional weapon as my Jewish origin?" [36]

It would have been most unnatural had Trotsky, suddenly risen to a position of power, not begun to acquire a more cautious *Weltanschauung*.[37] At the same time he could not have wished to cease thinking himself the idealistic devotee of permanent revolution. As such, the new Commissar of Foreign Affairs spat verbal venom in equal measure at both the German and the Allied governments. In the first days of the Soviet regime, when he approached the Allied embassies with his insult-barbed invitations to a general peace conference, he made it clear enough that he was appealing to the revolutionary-minded peoples behind the despised governments. However, as weeks went by and only the Germans responded favorably to the peace overtures, Trotsky began to compromise with his "plague-on-both-your-houses" attitude and strove mightily to reach a friendly understanding with the governments, as distinct from the peoples, of the Allied Powers. This task was additionally difficult in that he had to overcome Allied suspicions that both he and Lenin were German agents, who, while sounding the call for a general peace, were really bent upon writing a separate peace pact with the Germans. Nonetheless Trotsky made persistent efforts to gain the confidence of the Allies and even after the actual talks with the Germans had begun, he missed no opportunity to assure them that the Soviet Republic wanted no peace with Germany and would be forced into such a peace only if the Allies remained adamant in their stand.[38]

Trotsky's revolutionary conscience could accept the idea of a general peace as a positive move toward the promotion of European revolution. On the side of expediency such a peace would be likely to save the Soviet government as well as his status therein. But the idea of a separate peace probably offended him both as a negative act toward European revolution and, more practically, because a pact with Germany would have provided no real guarantee that the Soviet Republic would survive. In a revolutionary war, as Trotsky's own argument against it (the troopless trenches on the Russian side) implied, lay the greatest danger that Russia might be overrun by the Germans. This of course would have led to an early decline in Trotsky's fortunes. As time passed and the Allies remained aloof, Trotsky realized ever more clearly that he was facing one of the dreaded alternatives, the peace with Germany or revolutionary war.

Having once taken the first small step toward opportunism, Trotsky soon permitted himself to move farther in that direction. As is evident from his actions, he managed ever more to convince himself that there would be nothing immoral in the establishment of normal relations between Soviet Russia and the Entente. Hence his proposition to Raymond Robins, made either late in December or early in January, that Allied officers be sent to stations along the entire chaotic Russian front in order, as he explained it, to keep the Germans from smuggling raw materials out of Russia and into Germany.

"I am not a diplomat or a general, and I can afford to be as ignorant as I am," the Colonel retorted, still catching his breath. "I don't understand you. Your proposition sounds good, but it sounds too

good. In America we would say there must be something on it. I
have to ask you frankly, why do you make it?" [39]

Trotsky, "visibly annoyed," explained to Robins that if the Soviet
government could keep the supplies in question out of German
hands, it might be able to use these as a bargaining point in subsequent negotiations at Brest-Litovsk. Trotsky anxiously stressed the
point that these raw materials were so vital to Germany that they
might win decisive concessions for Soviet Russia in the peace talks.[40]
By this Trotsky was also saying that these materials were crucial in
Germany's anti-Allied war effort, a point which Robins, eager to be
a hero, was quick to comprehend.[41]

Shortly thereafter Trotsky developed his "no war-no peace" concept, apparently an expression of his inability to face either the
separate peace or the revolutionary war. Trotsky defended his proposal in fine revolutionary phraseology, on the grounds that if put
into effect, it would offer proof to the Entente's proletarians that the
Soviet government was not bound to the German militarists. The
thought that such a Soviet policy would offer the same proof to the
Entente governments, he left unspoken.

On February 10 Trotsky was able to deliver his historic message.
As though seeking to profit from his spectacular performance, Trotsky, days later and before the German resumption of the war had
been announced, gave a two-hour interview to Bruce Lockhart. The
latter found Trotsky "full of belligerent fury against the Germans for
the humiliation to which they ha[d] exposed him at Brest. . . .
Trotsky *was* angry with the Germans." [42] Obviously Trotsky was
going all out to prove that the Allies had no need to fear his intentions. He allowed Lockhart to soothe his feelings, "injured" by the
treatment given him by the English at Nova Scotia in April, 1917.
By the time Lockhart left, he was at all events convinced [43] that the
"German danger was uppermost in [the mind of Trotsky]," whose
last words, as Lockhart left him, were: "Now is the big opportunity
for the Allied governments." [44]

During the hectic Central Committee meeting of February 18,
Trotsky was no doubt still waiting for the favorable Allied response
and hence was anxious for further delay in approaching the Germans.
If at the last moment he acceded to Lenin, this was most probably
because, in the absence of an Allied gesture of support, he, like
Lenin, not willing to risk revolutionary war, had to regard peace
with Germany as the only other alternative. However, he lost no

time, in the interim between the February 19 offer to the Germans and their acceptance of it on February 22, to renew his attempts to gain Allied support. This time he went much further than he had in his gambit by way of Robins and promised Lockhart that "if the Allies would send a promise of support," he "would sway the decision of [his] government in favor of war." [45] In effect, Trotsky had slipped so far afield that he was offering to bring about a restoration of the erstwhile Triple Entente military alliance. In the meantime Trotsky had succeeded in winning Lenin to his side, for the latter not knowing at what line, if any, the Germans would draw rein to their offensive, had perforce to accept Trotsky's pro-Allied position. This is evidenced by his message sent to the Central Committee meeting of February 22, approving the "taking of potatoes and weapons from [the Anglo-French] bandits."

At the February 23 meeting which considered the German ultimatum, Trotsky was still looking for the beginning of the Allied rescue operation, but again, since only promises were forthcoming, he reluctantly yielded to Lenin by his abstention from the vote.[46] Trotsky's explanation that, though favoring revolutionary war, he had not opposed Lenin because that would have meant splitting the party and heading it against Lenin, must be regarded as pure coverup. Trotsky, it is true, could temporarily have assumed leadership in the Central Committee, but only on terms of leading the country into revolutionary war, a policy he was as much afraid of as was Lenin.

The permanent revolutionists' struggle against the power-loving opportunist would seem to account for the pattern of Trotsky's behavior, beginning with the renewed German offensive and culminating shortly thereafter in what appears to have been a nervous breakdown. At the February 18 Central Committee meeting, before voting with Lenin against revolutionary war, Trotsky eased his conscience by muttering something about the party's "obligation to exert a moral influence." [47] Thus he was weakly accusing Lenin of opportunism, but very weakly, since he himself was at least dimly aware of his own guilt. At the February 23 meeting he again attacked Lenin's honesty of motive, but by influencing the decision against the only honest way of revolutionary war, a position which he verbally glorified, he again revealed an uneasy conscience.

That Trotsky abstained from voting on this occasion is evidence primarily of his inability to face himself. Apparently writhing from inner shame, Trotsky found it necessary after the vote had been taken to justify his abstention on the ground that he did "not wish to stand in the way of a majority being attained for a united [party] line." This statement added neither to what he had said before the vote nor to his stature in general. The submission of resignations by Bukharin, Bubnov, and others, Trotsky was quick to take as a reflection upon his honesty. Though admitting that he had abstained in the knowledge that his move would support Lenin, he made a sheepish attempt to prove himself better than he was by declaring that he would not have abstained from voting had he known that the war faction would resign.

Trotsky again abstained from voting the following day, when after stormy disputation the Central Executive Committee decided by a vote of 112 to 86, 25 abstaining, to accept the German ultimatum. Trotsky, who disdained even to participate in the debates, Bruce Lockhart found "skulking in his room" at the Smolny. "Have you any message from London?" was the first question of a greatly distraught Trotsky.[48] Receiving an indecisive reply from Lockhart, Trotsky flew into a rage. After a brief tirade on the subject of Allied interventionist plottings, he thrust a bundle of papers into Lockhart's hands. "Look at this," he shouted at the British agent. Lockhart immediately recognized the forged documents "proving" Trotsky's affiliation to the Germans, which had received such wide circulation among the Allied missions in Petrograd. Lockhart writes:

> I smiled but Trotsky was not to be placated. "So this is what your agents waste their time and money on," he hissed. "Your intrigues have only helped the Germans. I hope you are proud of your work. Your Foreign Office does not deserve to win a war. Your policy towards Russia right from the beginning has been indecisive and vacillating. Your Lloyd George is like a man playing roulette and scattering chips on every number. And now I have to put up with this. Do you know that while your fools of spies are trying to prove that I am a German agent, my friends down there"—he waved his arm airily towards the room below where the Central Executive Committee was sitting—"are calling me an Ententeophile." [49]

Trotsky, who kept himself in strict isolation for the next days,[50] was obviously a man sorely disappointed in his rather unreasonably harbored expectations that the Allies would come riding to his rescue. Also it can be assumed that the long period of schizoidal torment had worn him down emotionally. He had still not recovered his composure on February 27, though he did speak at the Tauride Palace, "bracing himself up," as Price writes, "for a supreme effort" in hurling "scorn against the imperialisms [of both sides], upon whose altar the Russian revolution was being sacrificed." So Trotsky, who had himself aided in the sacrificial ceremony, let out his frustration upon the Allies, at the same time perhaps trying to shake a heavy accumulation of guilt feelings from his own back. Thereupon he again went into retirement. "Rumor had it," writes Price, "that he was so overcome with mortification that he broke down and wept." [51]

The treaty of peace was signed on March 3. Shortly thereafter the Germans set up a puppet Rada in the Ukraine and then proceeded to harry the defenseless Soviet government with a series of demands, one being that Soviet Russia make peace with the "independent" Ukraine, that is, abandon all claims to Ukrainian territory. The obvious German aim to turn the former Russian Empire into a colonial hinterland, placed new arguments at the disposal of Bukharin's faction, which had warned Lenin against permanent ultimatums, and which, since its Central Committee defeat of February 23, had continued to agitate against the hitherto unratified treaty. On Bukharin's side too were the Left SRs, then members of the government coalition, who had refused even to sign the decree accepting the German terms, as drawn up February 25 by the Soviet Executive Committee.

At the Seventh Party Congress, which convened March 6 to debate the issue, even Lenin was in doubt that peace would come from the German scrap of paper. Though arguing for ratification, he was at the same time, along with Trotsky, making frenzied last-minute efforts to obtain pledges of Allied support, in which event he promised to resume the war. However, short of such support, he intended to exchange space for time and his government had already decided to move its seat from directly threatened Petrograd to Moscow. If war did become the last resort, he wanted at least a respite in which to build some semblance of an army. Therefore, he argued at the congress, the Soviet Republic must yield to the German ultimatum on the Ukraine. Adding emphasis to his point, he threatened to resign as head of the government unless his demand was met.

Trotsky, still up to his old tricks, spoke in fervent revolutionary terms, lashed out against the opportunism in Lenin's policy and defended his own stand of February 23 as "a great act of self-restraint"

and "a sacrifice of the Ego" for the sake of Bolshevik unity, whereupon he once again supported Lenin's position. At the Fourth Congress of Soviets, which met March 14–16, the vote went heavily in
favor of ratifying the Treaty of Brest-Litovsk.

During the spring of 1918, the Soviet Republic found itself in
a steadily closing vise. The Germans, disregarding the treaty, advanced persistently. In Russia the "treasonable" treaty brought
patriotic support to a growing anti-Bolshevik movement, headed by
a nucleus of officers from the former tsar's army. The Allies, hoping
to re-establish the eastern front against Germany, began to provide
the so-called Whites with military and economic assistance. During
1917 military stores sent to Russia by the Allies had piled up at
Archangel and at Vladivostok. Fearing that the supplies in Archangel
would be lost in the event of a German break-through, the British,
French, and Americans landed troops in North Russia. Against
the danger of war goods in the Far East falling to German and
Austrian war prisoners in Siberia, whom the Bolsheviks were re-
portedly releasing to fight against the Allies, a joint American-Japa-
nese force seized Russia's outlet to the Pacific. In the meantime
a Czechoslovak brigade, enraged by Bolshevik attempts to disarm
it, took control of the entire Trans-Siberian Railway.

By June the Reds had lost South Russia, the Murman region, and
all territory east of the Urals. Their lands reduced to an area roughly
equivalent to the sixteenth-century domain of Ivan the Terrible,
suffered further from critical shortages of food and other necessities,
chaotic conditions in the factories, and an almost total breakdown of
transportation. "There were moments," as Trotsky later wrote, describing the spring of 1918, "when one had the feeling that everything
was sliding away and crumbling, that there was nothing to hold on
to, to support oneself upon." [52] In this period Lenin's Brest-Litovsk
policy was bitterly attacked by Mensheviks and SRs, (Right and
Left), as well as by Bukharin's die-hards.

In his May 14 "Report on Foreign Policy," [53] delivered before a
combined session of the Central Executive Committee and the
Moscow Soviet, Lenin replied to his critics. He predicted that the
Soviet Republic, though only "an island within the stormy seas of
imperialist plunderings," would survive. The mutual hostilities within
world capitalism, he said, would make it impossible for the imperialists to unite against the Soviet Republic. When the "stormy

waves of imperialist reaction . . . hurl themselves upon the little island, ready it would seem to sink it, these waves will always beat each other off." Though slow in coming, the European revolution, which had to come out of a war that the imperialists were "incapable of terminating," would come to the rescue. These conclusions Lenin based entirely on economic analysis,[54] that is, on the Marxian dialectic.

Soviet Russia did survive the crisis, and Lenin's worshipers joyfully hail the brilliant Marxist analysis that prevailed against all doubters. However, the same panegyrists fail to note that European revolution, Lenin's second prediction, was not fulfilled. Since the second of two "scientifically" determined forecasts did not materialize, it is safe to conclude that the method used in making both prognostications was basically unsound, that if the Soviet Republic did survive the dilemma that Lenin placed it in, it was for reasons other than, or in addition to, those given by Lenin, or, in short, that it was perhaps in spite of, rather than because of, Lenin's policies.

As a matter of simple fact it was not a policy for Russia that Lenin had designed and imposed upon his party, but a policy for himself in terms of Russia. In the party debates over the treaty and later in justifying the signing of it, Lenin necessarily had to argue that the safety of the Soviet Republic was indispensable to world revolution. Primarily, however, it was the preservation of his own security with which he was concerned and this was guaranteed only by the continuing existence of the Soviet state. As soon as Lenin considered it expedient to his personal aim to gamble with the security of the Soviet state, and such a situation arose but a year after the Brest-Litovsk Treaty was signed, Lenin, as we shall see, was ready enough to do so.

"When you see a Council of Workmen's and Soldiers' Deputies at Berlin," Lenin remarked to Raymond Robins early in 1918, "you will know that the proletarian world revolution is born."[55] The same thought regarding the overwhelming importance of the German revolution he also stressed in his Peace Theses. The eventual German revolution, coupled with his expectancy of assuming control over it and whatever it might lead to, is the real key to Lenin's attitude in the period of the Brest negotiations. It was upon this belief in his own destiny that he staked the national existence of Russia and the destinies of a hundred million people.

In April, in October, 1917, and again in February–March, 1918,

Lenin had pitted himself against an initially hostile majority within the party leadership. The last of his battles had been the hardest fought, in part because in Trotsky, for a time at least, his opponents had found a leader of sorts. But, for the third time in a single year's span, Lenin had triumphed and had by so doing demolished the only figure of stature comparable to his own. That victory established Lenin as the unquestioned boss of the Bolshevik party. Until his health broke down he was completely free to utilize the party and, as this asserted its mastery over the country, the Russian masses to the furtherance of his ambitions.

From Brest-Litovsk on, in any event, whether in matters pertaining to affairs internal or foreign, Lenin's line was both that of the Bolshevik party and of the Russian people. This is why, essentially, an understanding of Lenin's personal ambitions is so vital a key in comprehending any facet of Soviet policy in the period after March, 1918.

AFTER GERMANY—THE WORLD!

IMMEDIATELY UPON ARRIVING in Russia in April, 1917, Lenin had sought, by advocating fraternization of Russian and German troops, to influence the revolutionary course of German events. Subsequently Bolsheviks made it their business to infiltrate the prisoner-of-war camps and began secretly to indoctrinate the captive audience of Germans, Austrians, Hungarians, Slavs, and Turks. After the Bolsheviks came to power the schooling became highly systematized. A "Federation of Foreign Groups of the Russian Communist Party" was formed and, in anticipation of their eventual repatriation, members of the various national groups were trained, among other things, to become teachers and organizers of bolshevism.

The Peace of Brest-Litovsk, however crushing its immediate impact upon Russia, gave Lenin the opportunity to make direct contact with the German masses. Article 2 of the Brest Treaty required both parties to refrain "from all agitation and propaganda against the government or the state or military institutions of the other party." That stipulation the Bolsheviks disregarded from the outset. Soviet Ambassador Ioffe arrived in Berlin in April, 1918, and immediately set about to use his post as a source of aid, financial and advisory, to the leftist press and parties. The Soviet Embassy also "bought information from officials in various German ministries," sent out "anti-war and anti-government literature . . . to all parts of the country and to the front," and spent one hundred thousand marks to buy arms for the revolutionists.[1] The German government was aware of these activities, but fearing, as military and economic conditions grew worse, to upset the relative stabilization of matters in the east, did little more than offer an occasional protest.

Late in June Lenin already spoke with conviction of hunger in Germany, of the disintegration of the German army, of the coming revolution in Austria-Hungary, the "exact day" being impossible

Notes begin on page 221.

to predict, and of European revolution in general.[2] In an address on August 23 Lenin declared that the German revolution was ripening, was "coming unconditionally and inevitably," but added that "only a fool can ask when the revolution in the West will come. One cannot count upon revolution, one cannot predict it, it happens spontaneously. And it is developing and must erupt." [3] By late September, with the German lines collapsing in the Balkans and giving ground in the west, it already became possible for Lenin to think in terms of days. Great headlines in *Izvestiya* triumphantly hailed the "Collapse of World Imperialism" and the imminence of social revolution.

"The crisis in Germany has only begun," Lenin wrote in a letter to a Moscow congress of October 3. "It will inevitably end with the transfer of political power to the hands of the German proletariat. The Russian proletariat follows these events with the utmost attention and rapture." [4] Lenin was clearly in a state of excitement similar to that which had possessed him in the fall and winter of 1916–1917. His desire for European revolution was so intense that even before the German revolution had occurred, Lenin "knew" that it would take place, and more, that power would fall to the proletariat, that is, to the proletarian dictatorship. From this the early spreading of revolution to all Europe had to follow.

At least some of Lenin's optimism seems to have risen from his need to overcome the gnawing fear that he would once again be disappointed.[5] However, having one way or another convinced himself that his predictions would be fulfilled and his policies would therefore be vindicated, Lenin indulged in the joy of roasting his doubters in and out of the party. "Now even the blindest of the workers of the different countries," he wrote, "will see how right the Bolsheviks [that is, Lenin] were in building their entire tactic on the support of a world-wide workers' revolution and in not fearing to make . . . the heaviest sacrifices." His Brest-Litovsk gamble having paid off, Lenin felt justified in asking further risks from the

> proletariat of Russia, which will not only follow the events [in Germany] with attention and rapture . . . [but will] strain all its forces *to help the German workers,* who face the heaviest trials, the most difficult transition from slavery to freedom [through dictatorship of the proletariat], the most tenacious *war against its own as well as English imperialism.* The defeat of German imperialism will signify for a certain time both the growth of boldness, bestiality, and reactionism as well as military aggressiveness on the part of Anglo-French imperialism.[6]

In view of the endless sacrifices that the Russian masses had been making ever since the beginning of World War I, it seems almost absurd that Lenin should at this point have been asking for strenuous efforts on behalf of the German proletarians who had suffered far less. It reveals how little Lenin really cared for the welfare of the Russian people when the great goal, which could be attained only through Germany, was in the offing. He felt no scruples in exhorting the battered Russian beast to drag its bleeding body into the final battle for Lenin's glory.

Lenin's letter continued:

The Bolshevik working class of Russia was always internationalist not in words, but in deeds, in distinction to those scoundrels, heroes, and leaders of the Second International. . . . The Russian proletariat will understand that from it soon will be required the greatest sacrifices on the battlefield of internationalism. The time is near when circumstances may demand of us help in liberating the German people from its own imperialism and in the struggle against the Anglo-French imperialism. Let us begin at once to prepare. Let us prove that the Russian workers can work much more energetically, fight and die much more unselfishly when the stakes are not Russian alone but also those of the international workers' revolution. . . . The Red Army of workers and poor peasants is ready for all sacrifices in the defense of socialism. . . . We planned to have an army of one million by spring, we now need an army of three millions. We can have it. And we will have it.[7]

The notion conceived in 1915 of a revolutionary Germany sending its troops into the struggle for Europe's revolution, Lenin was now applying to Russia.

When in August, 1917, he had written State and Revolution, Lenin, lest he become suspect of proposing a Russian model for Europe's proletarian dictatorship, had deliberately left unwritten the final chapter depicting the Russian form of revolutionary power. Nevertheless, and though it barely mentions Russia, State and Revolution describes a theoretical structure eminently suitable for Russia but having little, if any, application to Western society. The two basic ideas for a revolutionary government, as laid down in State and Revolution, are (1) the necessity for authority in the hands of a proletarian vanguard, and (2) the long period of transition in which the dictatorship of the vanguard would be necessary. Neither of these notions applied to the highly industrialized West, where there was no specific proletarian vanguard and where, once state power had been taken over by the proletariat, no long period of transition would have had to precede the establishment of socialism. But in Russia the small-numbered proletariat did constitute a vanguard as compared with the multitudinous peasantry. In Russia too a long transition would be required before the country could possibly have been made economically ready for socialism.

Even before the seizure of power, then, Lenin had been able to view the coming developments in Europe only through the eyes of a Russian. Once the Soviet form of power had actually come into existence, Lenin needed but a slight change in mental focus to perceive in the Russian revolutionary state a form suitable for transplantation into the West.

As the German collapse came near in the fall of 1918, certain elements in Germany, apparently unable to perceive the essentially Russian nature of the Soviet organizational form, began to call for the establishment of Soviet power. Among these elements were admirers of Lenin and Radek, as could be found in the small radical workers' groups of Bremen. The Spartacists, though alien to various aspects of bolshevism, were so disgusted with the bankruptcy which decades of moderation in the German Socialist movement had led to, that they also hailed the success of the Russian revolution. Further pro-Soviet talk was heard from returning soldiers who had been indoctrinated on the eastern front. The war-weary masses, eager to seize upon any message of hope, began to equate the word "Soviet" with the word "peace." The idea, in any event, was beginning to circulate, and to counteract this growingly vocal trend within German socialism,[8] Kautsky in August, 1918, wrote a pamphlet entitled *The Dictatorship of the Proletariat.*

In his scholarly, moderate, and by no means personally directed disputation, Kautsky attacked Lenin's theory of government, come to life in the Soviet Republic, as antidemocratic and hence opposed to socialism and to Marxism. Lenin, who wanted no "lackey of the bourgeoisie" to confuse the German and other European proletarians just as he could "feel the breath of the rising proletarian revolution—in England, Italy, Germany, and France,"[9] lost no time in writing his counterattacking pamphlet, *The Proletarian Revolution and the Renegade Kautsky.*

In this work Lenin many times reiterated the stress points of

State and Revolution: there could be no compromise with bourgeois governmental forms; the dictatorship of the bourgeoisie had to be forcibly removed and supplanted by an all-powerful dictatorship.[10] The intensity of Lenin's feelings is marked by the viciously personal tone of his attacks upon Kautsky. Lenin had many times in the past assailed Kautsky as one of the opportunists of the Second International. But this time the "blind puppy" is singled out for such a pen lashing as could have come only from a tremendously enraged heart. Lenin was grimly determined not to let Kautsky snatch from his arms the rich prize now within his grasp. Significant above all in this warning to the German working class not to let itself be deceived [11] is the thundering nature of Lenin's following proclamation:

> The tactic of the Bolsheviks was the right one, the *only* internationalist tactic, for it based itself not upon the cowardly fear of world revolution, not upon middle class "unbelief" in it, not upon narrowly nationalist desires to preserve the fatherland (fatherland of its bourgeoisie), but "spitting" upon all this—was based upon an *estimation,* correct (up to the war and before the renegadism of the social-chauvinists and social-pacifists) of the revolutionary situation existing in Europe. This tactic was the only internationalist one, for it produced the maximum possible in one country *for* the development, support, and incitement of revolution *in all countries.* This tactic has been justified by its enormous success, for bolshevism (by no means because of the merits of the Russian Bolsheviks, but because of the deepest sympathies of the *masses* everywhere for a tactic that is revolutionary in deeds) has become *world* bolshevism, with an idea, a theory, a program and a tactic that distinguish it completely from social-chauvinism and social-pacifism. . . . Bolshevism has created the ideological and tactical foundations of a . . . truly proletarian and Communist International that will utilize both the experience of the prerevolutionary and the presently *begun revolutionary era.*
>
> Bolshevism has popularized throughout the world the idea of the "dictatorship of the proletariat," has translated these words from the Latin, first into Russian, and then into *all* the languages of the world, and has shown by the example of the *Soviet power* that the workers and poorest peasants, *even* of a backward country, even with the least experience, education, and habits of organization, *have been able* for a whole year, amid gigantic difficulties and while struggling against the exploiters (whom the bourgeoisie of the *whole* world supported) to maintain the power of the toilers, to create a democracy immeasurably higher and broader than all previous democracies . . . and to *start*

the creative work of tens of millions toward the . . . achievement of socialism.

Bolshevism has . . . helped the development of the proletarian revolution in Europe and America more . . . than any party in any other country. . . . To the proletarian masses of [the world] it is every day becoming clearer that bolshevism has shown the way of escaping from . . . war and imperialism, that bolshevism *can serve as a model of tactics for all.*

Not only European but world revolution is maturing, and it has been aided and accelerated by the proletarian victory in Russia. . . . One country alone cannot do more. But this one country, thanks to Soviet power, has done so much that even were the Soviet power in Russia to be destroyed by world imperialism tomorrow, . . . even if worst came to worst, the Bolshevik tactic would still prove to have brought immense benefit to socialism and to have assisted the growth of the invincible world revolution.[12]

The foregoing should not be mistaken for an outburst of national pride. In his "Farewell Letter to the Swiss Workers," written in March, 1917, Lenin, expecting the outbreak of Europe's revolution, had made a special effort to dissociate himself ideologically from his native country to which he was about to return.[13] In 1918 Lenin, while boasting that Russian forms and tactics were applicable the world over, still deprecated Russia, as can be noted in his specific mention of the lack of any special merit in the Russian Bolsheviks and his emphasized comment on the backwardness and inexperience of the Russian masses. In praising bolshevism and the dictatorship of the proletariat as international phenomena, Lenin wanted to make it clear that he personally, as distinct from the Russian people, was the inventor of the successful forms and tactics worked out in Russia, and that he, though a Russian, could safely be accepted as the man to carry the same experiment to success the world over. Lenin, in attempting to introduce the Soviet dictatorship form into the West, appears like a talented and ambitious father trying to take his children into high society but abandoning the illiterate mother in the slums.

In attacking the supposedly false Marxism in Lenin's interpretation of "dictatorship of the proletariat," Kautsky, since Marx had left the meaning of his phrase so unclear, was on rather shaky ground.[14] But when Kautsky turned his fire upon the agrarian foundations of "proletarian" dictatorship in Russia,[15] he was sending an effective dialectical broadside into the theoretical house of cards that Lenin had built out of the Soviets. Kautsky's argument was so likely to convince Germany's proletarians that Lenin's state system was not applicable to their industrial homeland that Lenin devoted almost the entire final fourth of his long pamphlet to refuting the point raised in a few paragraphs by the "imbecile Kautsky." [16]

Lenin's argument in essence was nothing more than a restatement of his 1905 formula which justified the overthrow of the Russian bourgeoisie by the proletarian-led peasantry. This tactic, he pointed out, had been proved correct by the events of 1917–1918, and, having proven successful, had by that token presumably evinced itself a true Marxist tactic. Lenin wrote:

> Things have come out just as we predicted. The course of the revolution has confirmed the correctness of our reasoning. *First* with the "whole" of the peasantry against the monarchy, against the land-lords, against medievalism (and to that extent, the revolution remains bourgeois, bourgeois-democratic). *Then* with the poorest peasants, with the semiproletarians, with all the exploited [notice the manner in which Lenin shades the peasants into proletarians] *against capitalism,* including the rural rich, the kulaks, the profiteers, and to that extent the revolution becomes a socialist one.[17] To attempt to raise an artificial Chinese Wall between the first and second, to separate them by anything else *than* the degree of preparedness of the proletariat and the degree of its unity with the rural poor, is grossly to distort Marxism, to vulgarize it, to replace it with liberalism.[18]

To find a Marxian justification for his lumping together of industrial workers and landless peasants, Lenin again took recourse in Marx's single reference to a "people's" revolution,[19] which in *State and Revolution* he had so freely interpreted to mean proletarians plus peasants. As further proof of the socialist nature of the Russian revolution, Lenin wrote of the rapidly growing numbers of workers in high military posts,[20] the abolition of "*all* privately owned landed property," [21] the modest beginnings of collectivized farming,[22] and the nationalization of factories.[23]

Whatever the weaknesses in the case presented by his pamphlet, Lenin was at least able to conclude it with a triumphant postscript:

> The above lines were written on November 9, 1918. On the night of the ninth-tenth came news from Germany of the beginning of a victorious revolution, starting in Kiel and other northern towns and ports, where the power passed into the hands of Soviets of Workers' and

Soldiers' Deputies, then in Berlin, where, power also passed into the hands of a Soviet.

The conclusion which I still had to write to my pamphlet on Kautsky and on the proletarian revolution is now superfluous.

November, 10, 1918.[24]

With power in Germany falling into the hands of Soviets, what more had to be said? The German proletariat itself had refuted Kautsky in tones of thunder. Russia's November revolution had provided the happy ending to its theoretical justification, *State and Revolution*. Germany's November revolution was apparently doing the same for *The Proletarian Revolution and the Renegade Kautsky*, the justification for the extension of Lenin's Soviet system into Germany and thence into the rest of Western Europe.

This at any rate was the distorted prism through which Lenin was to view the European scene in the year and a half to follow. Through this same glass he had seen the starving and exhausted Russian masses as eager to work, fight, and die for socialism, and he had also envisioned a Red Army powerful enough to carry Lenin from the dictator's seat of Russia to that of Germany and Europe. For many months after November 9, 1918, Lenin was to exaggerate out of all proportion to its significance any occurrence in Germany or elsewhere that appeared to be bearing out his dreams. For those events that went counter to his anticipations he readily found favorable interpretations.

9

THE THIRD INTERNATIONAL

MEETING IN BERLIN, December 17–25, 1918, the first All-German Congress of Workers' and Soldiers' Councils voted itself out of power in favor of a National Assembly to be elected the following January 19. This event was clearly a signpost to the anti-Soviet way in which things German were headed. The socialist betrayers, as Lenin saw it, were still luring the proletariat away from its "true representatives"[1] to the support of the bourgeoisie and its parliamentary cover-up for the bourgeois dictatorship.[2] But the issue of Soviet power (Lenin's creation) versus parliamentary power, he continued to regard as the crucial one in the German revolution.[3] When on December 30 the Spartacus League constituted itself as the German Communist party, or KPD, Lenin delightedly hailed this first European offspring of the Bolshevik party as the "sincere and only representatives of the proletariat [in the struggle] against the alliance of the traitorous [leaders of the German socialist movement] and the bourgeoisie."[4]

In fact, the splintering off of the Spartacists from the Independent Socialist party of Germany, or USPD, represented the impatience of a "crazy fringe" with the "opportunism" of the broad masses. The move was actually testimony to the weakness of the leftist revolutionary trend in Germany.[5] But Lenin, writing on January 12, 1919, did not see it that way.

When the Spartacus League, headed by such world-important leaders [and] true partisans of the working class as Liebknecht, Rosa Luxemburg, Klara Zetkin, Franz Mehring, decisively broke . . . with the Socialists of the Scheidemann and Südekum type . . . and called itself "the Communist party of Germany"—then the *basis* of an actually proletarian, actually internationalist, actually revolutionary Third International, a *Communist International*, became a *fact*. Formally this

Notes begin on page 222.

basis is still not in force, but for practical purposes the Third International is now already in existence.[6]

In the small German Communist party Lenin perceived an exact parallel to his own tiny Bolshevik party of April, 1917, which he had led to a break both with the Mensheviks and with the Second International. Days after Lenin had written the above-cited tribute to the Spartacus-Communists, Liebknecht and Luxemburg were lynched by police forces and the KPD was outlawed by the Socialist-dominated German government.[7]

In those events Lenin saw a repetition of the July Days of 1917, "when the Russian Scheidemanns, the Mensheviks and SRs, also 'by official means' concealed 'the victory' of the White guards over the Bolsheviks, when on the streets of Petrograd the Cossacks lynched the worker Voinov for distributing Bolshevik leaflets." As in the case of the Bolsheviks, Lenin prophesied, the German Communists would survive their July Days' ordeal and go on to victory.[8]

It was not only in Germany that Lenin was then envisioning a rapidly growing movement toward bolshevistic Sovietism. In his "Letter to the Workers of Europe and America" he favorably contrasted the situation in Europe to that of five months earlier when he had written his "Letter to the American Workers."

> Now, January 12, 1919, we see a whole series of communist proletarian parties, not only in the border areas of the former tsarist empire . . . but also in Western Europe . . . in the countries of the Entente there are growing numbers of people who are going the Communist way, the way of MacLean, Debs, Loriot, Lazzari, Serrati. . . . Then, August 20, the proletarian revolution limited itself to Russia, and "Soviet power" . . . seemed still (and was in fact) only a Russian institution. Now, January 12, 1919, we see the powerful "Soviet" movement not only in parts of the former empire . . . but also in Western European countries and in the neutral countries [Switzerland, Holland, and Norway]. . . . The revolution in Germany . . . which is particularly important and characteristic as one of the most advanced capitalist countries, at once took on "Soviet" forms.[9]

There was no basis upon which Lenin could claim the laurels for the alleged progress of the Communist movement in the West. So making the maximum use of whatever was to hand, he tried to enhance the impression that Russian events, directed by him, were meaningful to the course of revolutionary developments abroad.

After the armistice of November, 1918, the German armies rapidly withdrew from Lithuania, Latvia, and Estonia, as well as from other lands of the former Russian Empire. It would have been normal enough, historically speaking, for Russian forces to have retaken the territories thus evacuated. But note the significance ascribed to these campaigns by the Soviet press. *Izvestiya* commented on December 25, 1918:

> Estonia, Latvia, and Lithuania are directly on the road from Russia to Western Europe and are therefore a hindrance to our revolution because they separate Soviet Russia from revolutionary Germany. . . . This separating wall has to be destroyed. The Russian Red Proletariat should find an opportunity to influence the revolution in Germany. The conquest of the Baltic Sea would make it possible for Soviet Russia to agitate in the Scandinavian countries so that the Baltic Sea would be transformed into the Sea of Social Revolution.

Under the heading "Three Capitals," *Izvestiya*, on January 10, 1919, was proud to announce that the working class within one week had taken Riga, Vilna, and Kharkov, "three new centers of the fraternal Soviet republics." Bolshevik dictatorships were set up in whatever portions of the former empire the Red Army was able to assert its control. This was justified by Lenin's conception of national self-determination, which held that the proletariat of any nation (the upper classes did not count) would inevitably wish to link itself in fraternal bonds with the "workers'" republic, that is, Soviet Russia.

Of particular interest in this connection is the role that Latvia was given to play. In Estonia and Lithuania the militarily feeble Red offensive encountered strong nationalistic resistance and failed to establish enduring Soviet regimes. But in Latvia, where the popular vote in the November, 1917, elections to the Russian Constituent Assembly had been 72 per cent pro-Bolshevik, a revolutionary government, lasting almost five months, was set up.[10] Despite the consistent interpretation that Lenin had previously given the term "self-determination," Latvia's government immediately declared itself sovereign, and more, made a great display of Soviet Latvia's supposed independence. On January 30, for instance, Soviet Latvia's President Stučka sent a note to Berlin informing the German government that its protest regarding the arrest of a German diplomatic representative in Riga should have been made to the Latvian and not to the Russian government.[11] Stučka freely admits that the Latvian

Bolsheviks "agreed to the proposal of the Russian comrades to announce the independence of Latvia [only] for the reason that otherwise the German social betrayers, like their bourgeois bosses, would
cry that Soviet Russia was not the bearer of freedom for small
peoples but was imperialistic in its plans. . . . Nowhere [in] the
history of our party . . . do we find the slogan of 'Independent
Latvia.' We have always scoffed at this slogan." [12]

The first Congress of Latvian Soviets, which met January 13,
1919, was attended by high-ranking Bolsheviks Sverdlov and
Kamenev, signalizing the special nature of the occasion. To Lenin,
Red Latvia was of great importance. Representing the farthest westward extent of Bolshevik power, Latvia was also the first clearly
non-Russian part of Europe which had accepted Sovietism. Latvia, it
was hoped, would serve as an advertisement to the world proving
that bolshevism was not merely a Russian but an international phenomenon, and was suitable to the West as well as to the East. At
the same time, lest the Western pro-Soviet elements be frightened
off by a too-early and too-obvious application of Lenin's international dictatorship principle, Soviet Latvia, actually a perfect mani-
festation in practice of Lenin's theory of self-determination, was
required to masquerade as a sovereign state.

At Zimmerwald in September, 1915, Lenin had been ready to
proclaim as the Third International a handful of dissidents from
Europe's Socialist parties. A little over a year later he was already
in the process of blueprinting the plans for a Lenin-dominated home
for the European revolution due, as he then thought, at any moment.
In his Theses of April, 1917, Lenin had made the demand, fantastic
to his Russian comrades, that the Bolsheviks break with the Zimmerwald bloc and themselves proclaim the Third International. Having
politely turned down Lenin's demand,[13] the Bolsheviks sent delegates to the Third Zimmerwald Conference, held in Stockholm,
September, 1917. Early in 1918 Lenin tried again, through delegates
from Soviet Russia, to transmit the stimulus of the Bolshevik revolution to Europe at large. But the missionaries assigned by the Central
Executive Committee of the Soviet regime to the task of arranging
contacts preliminary to a conference of left-wingers failed to get
through the blockade.[14] At the end of January, 1918, there took place
in Petrograd a meeting of so-called "representatives of left-socialist
parties" (attended only by revolutionaries then residing in Russia)
and they elected an "International Bureau." [15]

From the foregoing two things are obvious. First, Lenin tried at every possible opportunity to bring the Third International into existence, and second, he made his attempts without any reference whatsoever to the wishes of the European proletariat. From this it may be deduced that Lenin had a strong personal interest in fathering the new International. Why this was so is not difficult to imagine. While in Switzerland in 1915–1917, he had decided to take the leadership in what he considered the impending European revolution. But having ties with no European (that is, Western) revolutionary group, his only hope of asserting such leadership could have come through an international or supranational organization, over which, by the process of having given it life, he should have become the unchallenged head. Back in Russia after April, 1917, his attempts to form the new International became almost frenzied. The overthrow of the tsar, he thought, had definitely set the revolutionary fuse agoing. But still lacking in European affiliations, he was also, to make matters worse, isolated by distance from the proletarian powder kegs of the West. If a revolution ensued, as might happen any day, he would probably be unable to arrive at once upon the scene of the great explosion. Other persons specifically identifiable with the first shots, the barricades, and so forth, might acquire the heroic coloration and win the idolatry of the masses. Founding the new International previous to the day of revolution must have seemed to him the only means through which he might exercise control, necessarily remote, over a suddenly developing situation which was unpredictable as to time and place of occurrence.

In the German revolution Lenin perceived the shower of sparks preliminary to the final blowup. Desperate as he thus became to secure his future place as field marshal *in absentia,* his impatience was further goaded at the time by the fact that various European socialist groups had set about to revive the war-eclipsed Second International.

In December, 1918, the English Labour party proposed the convocation of an international socialist conference at Lausanne the following January 6. The Lausanne conference never materialized, but there did take place at Bern, February 3–10, a conference of ninety-six delegates, mostly of centrist persuasions. If such moves succeeded of their aim, the revolutionary will of the proletariat might be diverted into channels of compromise. At the same time it would become more difficult to convince all concerned that there was a need for another international organization. Using the Labour

party's proposal as his springboard,[16] Lenin late in December had
the Bolshevik Central Committee send a radio-telegram to "all
those standing on the position of a Third International," inviting
Communists of all countries to rally around the "already practically
existing International" in order to counterbalance "the International
of betrayers which is being formed with the obvious aim of creating
a stronghold against the rapidly developing world proletarian revolution." [17]

The phrase "already practically existing International" is worthy of
note. A similarly ambiguous form of expression was used by Lenin
on January 12 when he interpreted the formation of the German
Communist party to mean that the "revolutionary Third International, a *Communist International,* became a *fact.* Formally [it was]
still not in force, but for practical purposes [it was] already in existence." Lenin's political aims required that he bring into being that
for which there was little, if any, European demand. So by double
talk he tried to create an impression that there was in fact a mass
basis upon which the new International could be erected.

Later in January the Bolsheviks sent to various socialist parties
and left-wing groups abroad a lengthy appeal asking them to take
part in a congress of a *"now well-defined and existing revolutionary
International whose contours were already sketched out."* The message spoke of "the tremendously swift pace of world revolution,"
which, however, might be halted by the antirevolutionary league of
capitalist states then being organized under the "hypocritical title of
'League of Nations.'" The revolution's course was also in danger
of being diverted by "the attempts of [socialist-betrayers] . . . to
help their governments and their bourgeoisie again to deceive the
working class." The invitation justified the convoking by the Russians
of an international congress of revolutionary parties by citing the
"accumulated great revolutionary experience [of the Bolsheviks]."

Under the heading of "Aims and Tactics" the proclamation proposed a platform for the new International based "on the programs
of the 'Spartacus League' in Germany and the Communist party in
Russia." The declared aims and tactics added up to a call for seizures
of power and the establishment of proletarian dictatorships based on
the power of Soviets "or similar organizations." On the subject of
"Relations to Socialist Parties," it was stated that the war "had split
the old 'International' three ways, into openly social-chauvinists, the
vacillating 'Center,' headed by Kautsky, and the left wing. With the

social-chauvinists there could be only merciless struggle." The "Center" must be dealt with by using propaganda to separate the sincere revolutionary elements from the corrupt leadership. It was necessary, the appeal declared, to form a bloc with those elements of the working class movement, the syndicalists, for instance, who never having entered the Socialist party, "now stand in general and wholly on the point of view of the proletarian dictatorship in the form of Soviet power." Under the heading "Organizational Question and Name of the Party" the announcement discerned the "basis of a Third International" in the existence of groups "in various parts of Europe" which had "already consolidated themselves" and "which thought alike in terms of a general platform and tactical methods. These in the first instance were the Spartacists in Germany and the Communist parties in a series of other countries."

Noteworthy, for reasons to be made clear later, is the manner in which this document depicted Germany as the solar center of the new workers' universe and thereby implied that Russia would fill the function of an orbital planet.

The coming congress, the appeal went on to say, should create "a universal fighting organ of permanent connections and systematic leadership . . . which would subordinate the interests of the movement in each country to the interests of the revolution in its international framework. Concrete forms of organization, government, and the like, will be worked out by the congress." Finally, that it be distinct from the ruined Social Democratic International, the appeal asked that the new International be designated as "Communist International." [18]

Having boldly extended the invitation to what he hoped would become the founding congress of the Third International, Lenin had reason enough to wonder what, if any, response there would be from abroad. Aside from all other considerations, the blockade around Russia made it almost impossible to enter the country.[19] A reasonably internationally appearing congress could, of course, always be drummed-up out of the Bolshevik party alone, drawn together, as it had been, from the multinational empire. There were in Russia too such admirers of bolshevism as the Englishman Fineberg, Sadoul [20] of France, Americans Reinstein and Reed, and former prisoners of war such as the Hungarians Kun and Rudnyanszky, who had been converted to bolshevism. Thus there was no shortage of individuals who could, for appearances' sake at least, be accredited to

non-Russian nations. When indeed the conference opened in Moscow
on March 2, it was made up mainly of such elements,[21] only a few
of the thirty-nine "delegates" then at hand having done any traveling
to get there.[22] Luckily for Lenin, one German, Eberlein (Albert by
pseudonym), of the two dispatched by the German Communist
party, had managed to sneak through. This was of vital importance
since the German proletariat was the acknowledged bellwether of the
Western revolutionary movement. A handful of subsequent arrivals
added badly needed European coloration to an otherwise overwhelmingly Russian, or at best eastern-dominated, occasion.

The German, whose mere presence conveyed the exciting thought
of Western Europe in revolt, was in fact the bearer of a sobering
mandate. Rosa Luxemburg on January 12 had told Eberlein that
she preferred to see some time elapse before a Third International
was founded. She and Liebknecht were killed three days later, but
the remaining Central Committee of the German party had instructed the two Moscow-bound delegates to oppose the immediate
founding of the new International.[23] In her famous tract on the
Russian Revolution, written in Breslau Prison during 1918, Luxemburg had scathingly criticized the Bolshevik stifling of mass initiative, the rule of the "Jacobins," and the occasional meetings of "an
elite of the working class" for the purpose of applauding the leaders
and of voicing unanimous approval for proposed resolutions.[24] She
did not consider the authors of these methods to be malevolent by
nature. As a Marxist, she was prone to interpret the thoughts or
actions of any individual as shaped predominantly by socio-economic
forces. In 1904, when attacking Lenin's leader-centralized ideas on
party organization,[25] she had explained that these had been forced
upon the Russian socialist movement by peculiarly Russian conditions.[26] In 1918 she expressed the belief that "the Bolsheviks would
[not have] instituted a dictatorship of a leading minority in the
name of a class [except for the fact] that they suffered under the
frightful compulsion of the . . . war, the German occupation and all
the abnormal difficulties . . . which were inevitably bound to distort any socialist policy, however [good] its intentions and [fine its]
principles." [27]

Whatever her qualms about bolshevism, Luxemburg clearly considered its vitality an indispensable factor in the European revolution.[28] But she hoped that the proletarian movement in the West,
given time in which to develop its natural Western form,[29] would

be able to resist the Russian-made strait jacket in which she feared
Lenin would attempt to confine it.

The stand taken by the German delegate to Moscow, in conformity with his party's decision, was most disappointing to Lenin. All
the other delegates were, so to speak, in his pocket. But without
German participation, what meaning could a Third International
have to the West? [30] At a preliminary meeting held March 1 for the
purposes of determining the time of opening and the order of proceedings at the conference, Lenin personally cornered Eberlein and
tried several times to bring him around.[31] However, the German
remained adamant and for the moment this seemed to have settled
the issue. Zinoviev, taking the floor March 2, declared in the name
of the Central Committee of the Russian Communist party that
though his party deemed it to be "the highest time to found the Third
International . . . since our German friends insist that this meeting
constitute itself only as a conference [not a founding congress], we
consider it necessary to associate ourselves temporarily with this proposal of the German Communists. However, we declare it our intention to continue our agitation for the formal founding, at the earliest,
of the Third International." [32]

But heavy pressure continued to be put upon the German delegate,
and the following day, when he, together with Bukharin, delivered
the report on "Guidelines of the International Communist Congress," Eberlein felt it necessary to explain his position in apologetic
and rather appeasing terms. The German party's desire for delay, he
explained to his "worthy comrades," was based on the German respect for what "all would admit" was the "justifiable" distrust toward
any such organizations which the Western proletariat had acquired
"in the course of time." After commenting upon the disillusionment
wrought by the failure of the Second International, Eberlein declared that the workers

> did not again this time wish to see a pompous founding ceremony and
> hear of paper resolutions. They want to know first who . . . stands
> behind these . . . upon whom they can rely in the coming struggles.
> . . . Today the struggle is one of life and death, and the workers
> want to know whether the aborning Third International possesses the
> strength to support the fight of the workers, or if it is in the position
> to create this strength. For this reason the workers [actually the German
> party speaking for the workers] believe that it is first necessary to say
> what we intend to do, to explain what foundations there are for carry-

ing on the struggle, and then they will declare whether or not they are ready to found the new International and join it. This way will be both the most correct and the simplest. . . . I can say emphatically that the German workers are not against the founding of a Third International, but they want this International, from the outset, to be armed with the strength necessary to support the proletarian struggle in all lands.[33]

Unwilling, apparently, to offend Lenin, Eberlein had made no mention of the German Communist distrust of the Bolsheviks. In the suggestion that it was the working class as a whole, rather than a numerically insignificant group, which should decide upon the time for officially instituting the new International, he had contented himself with conveying Luxemburg's democratic viewpoint. Bukharin also stressed the theme of cautious advance. Our guidelines, he said at the conclusion of his address, "have accepted the thought that the international proletariat is not on the offensive but on the defensive." [34]

In the discussion that followed, Kuusinen of Finland took sharp issue with that contention. "We in Finland," he declared, "went through one defensive revolution and want never again to repeat that experience." Arguing vehemently in favor of an immediate founding of the Third International, Kuusinen described the "doubts expressed by the German comrade against such a decision [as] unconvincing." [35] As a sort of climax ending the day's proceedings, an Austrian, Steinhardt, just arrived in Moscow after an arduous journey,[36] delivered a rousing speech "on the events that had led to the formation of a Communist party in Austria," and concluded by expressing the hope that "the federated world republic of Communists" would be attained, "in the not too distant future." [37] It was this speech, according to subsequent reports,[38] that turned the delegates against acquiescing in the German appeal for delay and moved them in favor of an immediate establishment of the Third International.

In the sense that all but Eberlein were inclined from the outset toward an immediate founding of the International,[39] the persuasive effects of the Austrian's rhetoric can easily be discounted. Steinhardt's highly emotional address,[40] however, did provide an opening [41] through which the hostility [42] toward the German's appeal to moderation could be vented. The real significance of the incident lies not in the Austrian's having altered the views of his listeners but that Lenin made no effort to dampen the ardency incited by Steinhardt, who, by the way, was known to be a man given to exaggerated and hysterical outbursts.[43] Even before Steinhardt's appearance, Lenin, had he wished to exercise his commanding influence, could have directed the assemblage to override the German veto and found the Third International. But such an action would have seemed a brazen slighting of the delegate sent from the very heart land of the revolution. Steinhardt's speech, then, came as a *deus ex machina*. Lenin could gracefully accept it and whatever enthusiasm it aroused, as the voice of Europe, compelling him, as it were, to permit the German position to be flouted.

At the following day's session the tide of discussion flowed strongly in the new direction. After some brief comment on the "Guidelines," during which the Swiss Kascher voiced his opposition toward "delaying the founding of the Third International," [44] the "Guidelines" were accepted by unanimous vote. Then Lenin, in accordance with the day's agenda, read twenty-two theses on the need for replacing bourgeois parliamentary democracy with Soviet organizational forms. Following this, Lenin expressed the opinion that in view of reports on the rapid success of the Soviets in Germany and "even in England," the victory of the proletarian revolution "could be delayed only for a short while." [45] Then, though his twenty-two theses had hailed Germany as "the first European state—and one can say without exaggeration the first in the entire world," [46] he obliquely and quite unrealistically criticized the German Communist leadership by pointing out that it, unlike the Bolsheviks in Russia, had neglected to form Soviets in the rural regions.[47] Shortly after Lenin's rendition, Chairman Platten read off a four-point proposal submitted jointly by Steinhardt, Grimlund, Rudnyanszky, and Rakovsky, to the effect that the Third International be immediately constituted, and that discussion on the question be reopened.[48]

Stung by the critical concert directed against him, Eberlein, quite disdaining the tactful tone of his earlier comments, delivered himself of a sharp counterthrust. "Party comrades!" he addressed his no-longer "worthy" comrades,

> at the beginning of this conference we already took up much time in lengthy disputes over the question [of whether this was to be a mere conference or a founding congress]. We had agreed upon the proposal of the German representation, which considered itself bound by its mandate, not to vote for the immediate founding [of a Third Interna-

tional]. Since today again, despite the previous decision, some comrades are attempting nevertheless to bring about an immediate founding of a Third International, I am constrained to give you briefly the reasons that brought us to advise you [against such a move].[49]

Eberlein first restated in general terms his earlier argument to the effect that a Third International should be formed from below, by the masses, rather than from above, adding that a Third International

> must not only be a spiritual center, not only an institution in which the theoreticians engage in heated debate; it must also be the foundation of an organizational power.
>
> I always have the feeling that those comrades who so ardently press for a founding are allowing themselves to be very much influenced by the course of events in the Second International, that they wish to offer a competing enterprise to the convening of the Bern Conference. This to [the German party] seems less important, and when it is said that enlightenment is necessary, that otherwise all doubtful elements will go to the yellow [International], then I say that the Third International would not deter those elements who, even [at this late date] still go to that side, for those elements belong there.[50]

Lenin's haste in wishing to establish the International had, to be sure, been prompted in part by the prospect of a revived Second International. But unlike the Germans, he had no faith that the proletariat at the crossroads would take the "correct" turn unless guided by Lenin-made signposts. It had never been Lenin's way to wait for the freewill decisions of the masses to determine the course of his or their actions, and it was specifically his intent to project the image of himself as their leader into the minds of the Western proletarians. Whatever their merits, Eberlein's arguments ran directly counter to Lenin's designs.

Speaking further in the Luxemburg spirit, Eberlein contended that

> when the delegates from individual countries came [to Moscow] they could not come with the decision to take part in the founding of a Third International. It must be their task first to inform their memberships, and even the invitations indicate this, as it says on the first page: "All of these circumstances force us to take the initiative, in order to place the question of discussing the convocation of an international congress . . . on the order of the day." The invitation itself then says that we must first examine the question as to whether it is possible to convoke the comrades to a founding congress.[51]

Eberlein granted that the conference had exhibited a harmony
of views unanticipated by him upon leaving Germany, but that there
would be such a degree of conformity on this question "we did not
know in advance." But this conformity at Moscow, Eberlein maintained, still did not correspond to the realities of the proletarian
movement in Europe. Eberlein asked:

> Just what is the situation? Genuine Communist parties exist only in
> a few countries, in most cases these were fashioned only in the last few
> weeks, and in several countries in which there are Communists, these
> have no organizations. I am amazed when the delegate from Sweden
> demands a founding of a Third International and at the same time
> admits that there still exists no purely Communist party in Sweden,
> but only a large Communist group within the Social Democratic party.
> We know that in Switzerland and in other countries actual parties do
> not yet exist, must yet be created, so that the comrades who are here
> can speak only in the name of groups. Can they really say who stands
> in back of them? Finland, Russia, Sweden, Austria and Hungary, from
> the Balkans not even the entire federation—the representatives of
> Greece and Serbia do not regard Rakovsky as their delegate. [Eberlein
> was here referring to the above-mentioned proposal of Steinhardt,
> Grimlund, and others that the International be founded immediately.]
> What is missing is all of Western Europe; Belgium and Italy are not
> represented, the Swiss delegate cannot speak in the name of a party,
> missing are France, England, Spain, Portugal, and America is also not
> able to state which parties would back us. There are so few organiza-
> tions participating in the founding of the Third International that it is
> difficult to appear in public. . . .
> I beg you to consider carefully whether it is advisable on such
> flimsy foundations to proceed to the founding.[52]

To most of those present Eberlein's remarks must have seemed
akin to heresy. Alone amid a Bolshevik-minded clique, he had dared
to oppose the outdated and provedly futile concept that proletarian
leaders should follow the masses, to the tenets of Lenin so amply
justified by their success. The "European" barrage against Eberlein
having provided the smoke screen, the Russians could now swing
their own artillery into line.

"You want first to see the formal founding of Communist parties
in all countries?" Zinoviev asked bitingly of Eberlein. "You have a
victorious revolution [in Russia], which is more than a formal founding. You have in Germany a party which is striding to power and will

establish a proletarian regime in Germany inside a few months. And now we should hesitate? . . . Upon mature consideration, our party proposes the immediate founding of the Third International. That will show the whole world that we are spiritually as well as organizationally armed." [53] With this declaration, which signified the death of the brave attempt to make a democratic Third International, Grimlund of Sweden and Rahja of Finland quickly associated themselves.

In everything that occurred at the founding congress, including the steam-rolling of Eberlein's filibuster, the mastermind of Lenin was everywhere at work. The addresses of all the speakers but Eberlein, repeated with machinelike constancy the Lenin themes: the immediacy of the International's founding and the replacement of bourgeois democracy by the Soviet system, each speaker justifying this position in terms of his version of the state of affairs in his particular country. In the major reports of the congress, except for the Eberlein-Bukharin "Guidelines," which recommended delay in forming the International, the above themes were stressed along with all Lenin's other principal ideas. The report summarizing Lenin's *Imperialism* announced that the "new epoch [had] arrived. The epoch of capitalism's disruption . . . of the Communist revolution of the proletariat." [54] The joint report of Zinoviev and Platten castigated the attempt made at the February Bern Conference to "galvanize the corpse of the Second International," [55] and concluded by describing the conference as a "strikebreakers' conference—to be fought by the workers of all lands." [56] In the organizational setup that was arranged, an Executive Committee, headed by Zinoviev, and except for Eberlein, who could scarcely have been omitted, was composed entirely of "delegates" who would eagerly parrot Lenin's every word.

On March 5 the conference, unanimously but for a single abstention, converted itself into the First Congress of the Communist International. "Won and Recorded" was the gloating title of Lenin's March 6 article in *Pravda*, which celebrated the event. From the result of a vote, foreordained by a handpicked electorate, Lenin professed to conclude that the "ice [had] been broken," the "Soviets [had] triumphed throughout the world." Presumably, then, the "delegates" in Moscow had actually carried out the will of the world proletariat. Lenin wrote:

> We have inscribed on paper what has already taken firm hold in the minds of the masses. All [the delegates] knew—and what is more—all saw, felt, sensed, each from the experience of his own country, that

a new proletarian movement has been set in full swing, unprecedented in the world for its strength and depth, that it cannot be confined within any of the old [bourgeois] frameworks . . . The new movement is heading toward the dictatorship of the proletariat, . . . is heading toward *Soviet power* with the torrential might of . . . tens of millions of proletarians which is sweeping everything from its path. This we have recorded. We have reflected in our resolutions, theses, reports, and speeches what has already been won. . . . The foundation of the Third Communist International is the forerunner of the international republic of Soviets, of the international victory of communism.

In 1902–1903 Lenin had formulated an ingenious pattern of organization whereby his own compulsions became those of a small centralized party, and through this, supposedly, the will of the revolution-bent masses of the Russian Empire. So from the outset the Third International was not a response to a proletarian thronging to Sovietism, but the instrumentality through which Lenin, by means of an organization which he controlled, expected to impose his will upon the revolutionary masses of Europe and thence of the world.

10

VIOLENCE WHEN NECESSARY

LENIN, A MARXIST BY FAITH, was convinced that he—the faith's truest prophet—and history were moving in the same direction. Previous to 1915 he regarded a Russian revolution as due within his lifetime; after 1915, world revolution. Desiring as fervently to lead these revolutions as he wished to see them occur, the preservation of his own person and prestige was almost always foremost in his plans. In Russia before November, 1917, he headed the tiny Bolshevik party. Thereafter he regarded himself as leading the Soviet movement against the unawakened rest of the world. Since his cause was always backed by a minority, he was in general opposed to taking the risks that violent action entailed and preferred the tactic of the strategic alliance, a kind of divide and conquer from below.

In the early stages of his career Lenin pitted bolshevism against the Russian autocratic machinery, the Russian bourgeoisie, and the propertied peasantry. His party, though small, he conceived of as the single-willed spearhead of the proletariat, whose antagonists were disunited. The disgruntled peasant majority, he planned to incite against the upper classes, hence his notion of the temporary proletarian-peasant alliance. After 1915 Lenin foresaw Europe's proletariat united under his dictatorship and fighting against world imperialism. But each national bourgeois camp fought the others for the wealth of the world. Also, within each nation the bourgeoisie was split into factions and of course had to contend with its national labor force. In the colonial parts of the world, imperialism was awakening the peoples to nationalism and arming them to fight against their foreign exploiters. Lenin hoped to utilize these "contradictions within capitalism" in the coming struggle.

Upon returning to Russia in 1917, Lenin had preached the April Theses program of temporary Bolshevik collaboration with Mensheviks and SRs against a Russian capitalism linked to world capitalism.

Notes begin on page 229.

134

This plan had not worked out and he had found himself obliged to undertake an adventurist coup. But after the coup's success, when his small faction stood alone against world imperialism, he had been quick to resort to his basic tactic, as manifested by the Soviet concessions made at Brest-Litovsk. By November, 1918, in Lenin's view, the Brest-Litovsk policy had thoroughly proved its worth; it had kept the rival imperialist camps from joining to crush the emaciated Soviet Republic and had thus preserved Lenin and given him time to consolidate his power. Nor had the separate peace, as Lenin's party opponents had prophesied, stayed the coming of revolution in Germany. The German collapse, however welcome to Lenin, had also cleared the road for a major Entente offensive against bolshevism. But, as Lenin believed, the masses of Europe, disillusioned by the war's horrors, distrustful of their "traitorous" leaders, and spurred on by the example of Russia, were on the verge of rising. However, he was not sure whether the European revolution would come in time to save Soviet Russia. To be personally ready in case revolution came, he had organized the Third International. But he had no intention of staking all on a single card. In December, 1918, even as the blueprint for the Comintern was being drawn, Lenin, anxious to gain time and to utilize to the fullest the "contradictions within capitalism," had begun to extend the olive branch to the West, largely in the shape of Soviet economic lures to capitalists in the Allied countries.

Within the Allied leadership, then in Paris conferring about the peace of Europe, there was disagreement over the way in which the Russian situation ought to be handled. Clemenceau and Churchill favored an extension of anti-Bolshevik intervention. As a result of their efforts, a French division was landed at Odessa and British troops were sent into Transcaucasia. Further military and financial aid was granted the White forces under General Denikin in South Russia and General Yudenich in Estonia. Thanks to British support, Admiral Kolchak had become the dictator over all anti-Bolshevik forces in Siberia and also the commander in chief of the White military effort, which operated from four widely separated centers. Kolchak's own offensive began early in March, 1919, and moved rapidly across the Urals to take Ufa.

Woodrow Wilson and Lloyd George meanwhile were generally averse to the policy of intervention. Upon Wilson's prompting, the Supreme Allied Council in January, 1919, proposed that Russians,

White and Red, meet on Prinkipo Island and try to settle their differences. This proposal the Whites turned down, but Lenin was immediately amenable to the idea. Discussing the matter with William
C. Bullitt, Wilson's special emissary, who arrived in Moscow on
March 10, 1919, Lenin offered not only to acknowledge White sov-
ereignty over all territories then occupied by their forces,[1] but also
to repay tsarist loans with interest and to permit the exploitation by
foreigners of Russia's natural wealth. Just a few days earlier the
founding congress of the Third International had issued an appeal
"To the Workers of All Countries" to thwart "by revolutionary means,
if necessary," the interventionist efforts of their respective governments.[2] This token expression of the revolutionary faith was quite
eclipsed by the far larger portion of the same message "to the
workers." Directed to the industrialists and professional men of the
Western world, it told of the great mercenary benefits they could
obtain if peaceable relations were established between their countries and the Soviet Republic.[3]

On March 13 and again five days later, at the opening session of
the Eighth Party Congress, Lenin equated current Soviet foreign
policy to that pursued by Russia in the Brest-Litovsk period. This
simple statement of fact merits little comment, but much of significance can be deduced from its timing. The Soviet government had
for three months been offering concessions to capitalism, but not
once in that time had Lenin deemed it necessary to defend this
policy before the Russian people or the Bolshevik party. Red Russia,
encircled by White and foreign forces and facing the dread of continuing war and economic ruin, had clearly no choice other than a
peace at almost any price short of complete capitulation. The party's
leftists, who a year earlier had opposed Lenin's deal with German
imperialism, had long since been disarmed by the "proved" efficacy
of the Brest-Litovsk tactic of temporary appeasement.[4]

Obviously it was not to his own people or party but to Europeans
that Lenin in March explained his policy, and the necessity for this
had come about because of the founding of the Third International
earlier that month. To the delegates from abroad who were still in
Russia and who attended the Eighth Party Congress, Lenin had
apparently felt the need to justify the nationally oriented policy of
his country at a time so soon after he had openly assumed the leadership of the world revolution. Lenin too, perhaps by way of the
foreign delegates, was attempting to deliver a further message to

Europe at large. What was to be done, he asked in his March 13 address,[5] now that the Soviets had become the organizational form for the Third International? "Having achieved Soviet power . . . in one country—what is the role of the proletarian state amid capitalist states?"

Do not, said Lenin's statement in essence, expect the Soviet Union to send Red crusaders marching into Europe in order to hasten the advent of revolution. "The yellow Socialists love to throw around such phrases as 'the Bolsheviks believe in the almightiness of violence.' These phrases show only that the people who use them . . . are unable to teach their proletarians the tactic of *violence when necessary*." Violent means, Lenin pointed out, were not always the best in achieving revolutionary success.[6] The Bolsheviks, he admitted, had seized power in Russia through the force of arms. But this had been expedient at the time, first, because the Russian "masses had been organized in Soviets" (the implication here was that Western Europe's proletarians were not yet so organized and were therefore not ready for a rising), and second, because the Kerensky government had been too feeble to offer effective resistance. Where the foe was still powerful it was better to play a waiting game, à la Brest-Litovsk. This tactic the Soviet government had employed against the now-fallen German Empire and was using once more against the Entente imperialists whose governments were steadily growing weaker through the "natural" process of internal disintegration.

Lenin's comment, besides "explaining" the survival-oriented Soviet policy, also served to set down for the adherents of the Third International, for use in their European countries, a tactic of revolutionary gradualism similar to that which he had preached to the Bolsheviks in his April Theses. However, the Third International bore the stamp "Made in Russia," and might convey to Europe the idea of violence, through which, much as Lenin had hoped to avoid it, the Bolsheviks had taken power. This notion Lenin was anxious to efface not only because he was opposed to premature violence as poor strategy but because, as he feared, the proletarians of the West might be frightened away from Sovietism if they associated it with revolution by violent means.

The rise of a Soviet government in Hungary on March 21 caused Lenin for a time to alter his views regarding the purely defensive function of Soviet Russia. If contrary to his previous estimates the

Soviet movement was in the process of branching out rapidly through all Europe, he could not well afford to sit back on his Brest-Litovsk mentality. "The working class of Russia," Lenin wired Béla Kun on March 22, "will come to your aid with all its means." [7] "We are coming to you as soon as possible," a radio message added. "Constant radio contact between Budapest and Moscow is absolutely essential." [8] Soon thereafter the Germans hastily withdrew their troops from the Ukraine, leaving it open to easy Soviet conquest. The road to the West seemed open, and Lenin, despite the four-front civil war, began to set into motion a plan (which a number of White break-throughs toward Moscow and Petrograd soon made impractible), for sending Red forces through East Galicia and Bukovina to make "direct and intimate contact with the Soviet armies of Hungary." [9] The wish, above all, to lead the European revolution had suddenly made violence expedient whatever the risk to the Soviet Republic. But at the same time Lenin remained concerned that his image and that of bolshevism, as cast upon Europe, be associated with revolution through gradualistic peaceable means.

Again and again in his comments on the Hungarian revolution Lenin stressed the fact that Soviet power in Hungary had been achieved through a voluntary relinquishing of power by the bourgeoisie to the proletariat. "They used to say we were robbers," he told the Eighth Party Congress, ". . . that we hold power through violence. . . . Now the example of Hungary will quiet such talk." [10] Lenin went on to say that where the bourgeoisie do not offer fierce resistance, there is not necessarily brutality. "Granted that more victims fell in Russia than in other countries. This is not surprising when to us, as inheritance, was left the old chaos. Other countries can approach by other paths, more humanely, to the same Soviet power. This is why the example of Hungary will have decisive influence." [11]

In addition to serving as an example of humane revolution, Hungary, as Lenin saw it, might also advertise the Soviet way as even more suitable to Europe than it was to Russia. On March 23 he cautioned Kun by radio that "in view of the peculiar conditions of the Hungarian revolution, a mere and detailed imitation of our Russian tactic [in Hungary] would be a mistake." [12] Later Lenin was pleased to note that "unlike us (who are gradually socializing industry) [the Hungarian Reds had] at once legalized the transfer to social ownership of all industrial enterprises." [13] "In comparison with

Russia," Lenin said on April 17, "Hungary is a *small country*, but the Hungarian revolution will play perhaps a greater role in history than the Russian revolution." [14]

Lenin wrote on May 27 in his "Greetings to the Hungarian Workers":

> The Soviet power has been in existence in Hungary for only a little over two months, yet, as regards organization, the Hungarian prole-tariat already seems to have excelled us. That is understandable, for in Hungary the general cultural level of the population is higher; fur-thermore, the proportion of industrial workers to the total population is immeasurably greater, . . . and lastly, in Hungary the transition to the Soviet system, to the dictatorship of the proletariat, was incompara-bly easier and more peaceful. This last circumstance is particularly important.

Lenin blamed the European Socialist leaders, "fostered by decades of relatively 'peaceful' capitalism," for spreading "bourgeois lies about the Soviet regime in Russia" and for confusing "certain pe-culiarities of Russian Soviet government, of Russian history and its development, with Soviet government as an international category." But the Hungarian revolution was "helping even the blind to see . . . the essence of proletarian dictatorship does not lie in force alone, or even mainly in force."

"Comrades, Hungarian workers," he concluded, "you have set the world an even better example than Soviet Russia by having been able at once to unite all Socialists on the platform of genuine proletarian dictatorship." [15]

Hungary, Lenin wished the West to believe, had achieved the program of the April Theses which he had tried to put across in Russia. It was this, not the violent path to revolution, that he offered Europe.

Communications from Lenin to the Hungarian and Bavarian Soviet governments, the latter's ephemeral existence having begun April 9, are greatly relevant of his desire to direct from afar, to whatever extent this was possible, the policies of the newly estab-lished regimes. "What guarantees have you," he asked Béla Kun in his March 23 radio message, "that your new government is really Communist and not simply socialist—that is, betrayer-socialist? Do you have a Communist majority in the government? When will the Congress of Soviets convene?" [16] Kun, who knew his master's voice, replied some weeks [17] later in a fashion that for the moment at least "removed all [Lenin's] doubts." [18]

Even more detailed answers were demanded of the Bavarian Reds. What, Lenin wished to know, had they done in the struggle with bourgeois lackeys? Had they created Soviets of workers and servants by city sections in Munich? Had they armed the workers, disarmed the bourgeoisie? Had they made use of stores of clothes, and so forth, for immediate aid to the workers, and especially the field workers and the small peasants? Had they expropriated the factories and wealth of Munich capitalists as well as the capitalist farms in the environs? Had they abolished rent for small peasants, doubled or trebled the pay of field workers and miners, introduced the six-hour working day, and allowed the workers two or three hours daily in which to carry on governmental activities? Had the Munich bourgeoisie been dispossessed from their homes and had the workers immediately been transferred into rich homes? Had they taken control of all banks, taken hostages among the bourgeoisie, mobilized the workers both for defense and for ideological propaganda in the surrounding villages, and so forth? [19]

Point for point, it seems, Lenin was attempting to transpose to Germany the political process whereby his revolutionary regime had consolidated itself in Russia.

11

LENIN AND THE EAST

As BEFITTED ONE WHO had found in a Marxian revolutionary scheme of 1905 a place for the Russian peasantry, Lenin, long before any other Marxist, had been aware of the revolutionary potential of the Asian masses. If Russia, having but few proletarians, could be thought of as a land with world revolutionary significance, then why not Asia? [1] Previous to 1919 Lenin was certain that world revolution would begin in the West. At times, however, when the West failed to react to what he thought were revolutionary stimuli, Lenin, as indicated by his May, 1913, article, "Backward Europe and Progressive Asia," [2] tended to seek reassurance in the East. Its failure in 1914 to rise against the warmaking governments tended to shake Lenin's confidence in the Western proletariat, but the fact of war itself cushioned the shock. More powerful than any previous stimulus, the war's monstrosity, he thought, would surely arouse the West to revolution. But as the war years went by, the revolutionary sluggishness of the West continued to disturb him. In Western countries, his *Imperialism* explained, there existed a labor aristocracy. Bribed by the superprofits derived by the capitalists from colonialism, this aristocracy had deluded the proletariat into taking a patriotic instead of revolutionary position toward the war.

Imperialism, however, also contained a barely noticeable reference to Asiatic revolution. This passage, taken from Rudolf Hilferding's *Finanzkapital,* suggested that imperialism contained the seeds of its own destruction. In addition to arousing the xenophobia of the colonial world, imperialism was providing the colonial peoples with the resources and training for the achievement of the national state as a means to economic and cultural freedom and hence anti-imperialist struggle.

In the sense that it implied a rather long-range demise for imperialism, Hilferding's idea as used by Lenin constituted an element

Notes begin on page 232.

of contradiction to the main point of his book, written to prove that revolution would come out of the war-made disillusionment of the European masses. As shown by the little space devoted to it in *Imperialism,* Lenin had no intention of stressing Asian revolution as a great hope for the world proletariat. But the fact that he so much as touched upon the prospects for revolution in Asia indicates that there was at least some doubt in his mind that revolution would come directly out of the European war. During the two years after the March, 1917, revolution, when Lenin's belief in early European revolution was sharply in the ascendant, this doubt remained dormant. But Asia was not forgotten.

In the year following the November *coup d'état,* Soviet declarations of policy concerning the rights and revolutionary functions of the Moslems of the former Russian Empire were linked, as though through these Moslems, to the East in general.[3] In November, 1918, on the occasion of a congress of Moslem Communists in Moscow, Stalin wrote in *Pravda* of a bridge which the Russian revolution had constructed between the "Socialist West and the enslaved East," the building of a "new revolutionary front against world imperialism." "Nobody," Stalin declared, addressing the delegates directly, could "bridge the gap between West and East as quickly as [they could], since to [them were] open the doors of Persia and India, Afghanistan and China."[4] In this period Lenin regarded Asia mainly as an auxiliary force which, by exerting pressure against imperialism in the East, might help the Soviet state to survive in its struggle with the Western tentacles of the octopus. By 1919, when Soviet forces came into virtually direct conflict with those of Britain in the Near and Middle East, the anti-imperialistic appeals to Asia acquired immediate military significance, and throughout that year the Soviet government made numerous gestures of good will to the governments of Afghanistan, Persia, and Turkey.

In March and early April, 1919, a time of grave troubles for the besieged Soviet Republic, Lenin's hopes for early European revolution reached their heights. But soon thereafter, though the Soviet military situation improved, Lenin saw much in Europe that disturbed him. The Bavarian Soviet regime came to an inglorious end after a mere three weeks. On top of that and contrary to his predictions, the Allies by the end of April had been able to agree on the peace terms for Germany. Worse yet, the Treaty of Versailles, signed June 28, 1919, had failed to affect France and England (as

the Treaty of Brest-Litovsk, in Lenin's view, had affected Germany)
and had not led to the great proletarian revulsion in the West
which Lenin had looked for.[5] In July a trade union international was
set up at Amsterdam. This successor to the prewar International,
with headquarters at Brussels, Lenin linked with the Second International. In August came the ignominious downfall of the Hungarian Soviet regime. Somewhat later an idea of the Swiss Socialist
Grimm, to create a new International based on the fusion of the
dying Second and the embryonic Third, met with considerable
response in Western Europe. A similar position taken at the March
Congress of the USPD, to the effect that the German Constituent
Assembly might coexist with or unite with the German Soviets,[6]
had caused Lenin to castigate the "thrice-accursed German Menshevik Independents" for bemuddling the Soviet idea.[7]

All told, it was becoming increasingly clear that the revolutionary
tide was fast receding in Western Europe. But Marxism could not
be wrong, and since all the economic preconditions for revolution
were at hand, Lenin could permit himself to find but one explanation for its nonoccurrence. The masses, as in 1914–1916, had again
been deluded. The labor aristocracy, although forced to make certain verbal concessions to the revolutionary spirit, had by dint of
its flexibility managed to maintain control over the proletariat and
restrain it from overthrowing the bourgeois fortresses. Now appearing in the guise of centrism, this "aristocracy" was, as ever, linked
to the bourgeoisie by bribes derived from imperialist profits.

Sometime during the period of late summer and fall of 1919
Lenin arrived at a concept regarding the course of world revolution
differing radically from that which he had hitherto held. Though
continuing to regard the West as the eventual heartland of socialism,
he became convinced that revolution in the West would have to
be preceded by revolution in Asia. Undoubtedly contributing to
his new outlook was the fact that Russian contact with Communist-
controlled Turkestan, broken off early in 1918, was re-established
in September, 1919, as a result of the collapse of Kolchak's forces.
Having at this timely juncture recaptured the gateway to the East,
Lenin at once set in feverish motion a campaign to undo the
damages done the Soviet eastward face by the Russian Communists
who had run the Turkmen Soviets during their period of isolation
from Moscow. These Communists had fallen into the ways of the
old tsarist bureaucracy. Together with the local magnates they had

looted and terrorized the poor, turning them into implacable enemies of the revolution. This situation was duly noted by a commission of Russian Bolsheviks [8] arriving in Tashkent in November.[9]

A decree drawn up by Lenin in October and defining the task of
that commission had specified that self-determination of the peoples
of Turkestan, "and the abolition of all national inequality and privi-
lege of one national group at the cost of another" was the basis of
the entire policy of the Soviet government of Russia. Only such a
policy, Lenin had written, could "finally overcome the mistrust of
the native working masses of Turkestan, created by the many-yeared
domination of Russian tsarism, to the workers and peasants of
Russia." [10]

Quite contrary to the spirit expressed in the decree was the letter
Lenin wrote to the Turkmen Communists in which he directed
them to co-operate with the commission. He explained that the
establishment of "correct relations" with the peoples of Turkestan
had an immediate significance for the Soviet Republic, which "without exaggeration" could "be described as gigantic and world historical. For all of Asia and for all of the colonies of the world, for a
thousand million people, the relations of the Soviet worker-peasant
republic to the weak, hitherto oppressed peoples, will have a practical significance." Lenin "very much" begged the Turkmen Communists to "show by deeds the sincerity of our desire to root out all
traces of Great Russian imperialism for the supreme struggle with
world imperialism headed by that of Britain." [11] The cleanup of
Turkestan was aimed primarily to serve as a display advertising
Bolshevik egalitarianism throughout the colonial world.

Highly significant at this time was the appearance of a series of
articles by Stalin's protégé Mirza Sultan-Galiyev (a Volga-Tatar
Communist) in *Zhizn' Natsional 'nostei*, official organ of the Commissariat of Nationalities. These articles, which could scarcely have
appeared without Lenin's explicit approval if not encouragement,
maintained that Communist leaders had "committed a great strategic blunder by placing the main emphasis in their revolutionary
activity in Western Europe. The weakest link in the capitalist chain
was not the West but the East, and the failure of communist revolutions abroad was directly attributable to the inadequacy of Soviet
efforts in the Eastern borderlands." [12]

On November 22, 1919, Lenin addressed the eighty-two delegates
attending the opening session of the Second All-Russian Congress

of Communist Organizations of the Peoples of the East. The time had come, he declared, for all the awakening peoples of the East to take part in "deciding the fate of the entire world" and no longer to be "mere objects of [imperialist] enrichment." To develop rapidly, he said, the revolutionary movement of the East would have to tie itself directly to "the revolutionary struggle of our Soviet Republic," whose backwardness, immense extent, and position of link between Europe and Asia gave it the "entire burden" and "great honor" of serving as "the leader of the world struggle against imperialism."

The events of the Russian revolution, Lenin pointed out, could well provide inspiration for the Asiatics. The Red Army's victory proved that a revolutionary war waged by oppressed peoples could be won against "all the wonders of [European] technology and military art." Just as Russia had united its proletariat and peasantry in the struggle against capitalism and the survivals of feudalism, so could an even more backward Asia bring its peasant masses into the struggle "not against capital but against the survivals of feudalism." The unique task facing the Communists of Asia, said Lenin, was that which had faced the Russians, of applying to peculiar conditions, "nonexistent in European countries," the universal Communist theory and practice.

Lenin's speech concluded on the note that only the proletarians of the West could achieve the transition to communism, but that they could not achieve this without the help of the vanguard of Russians plus Asians.

The task is to awaken the toiling masses to revolutionary activity, to conscious action and organization, independent of what level they stand upon; to carry the genuine Communist teaching, intended for the Communists of the more advanced lands, over to the languages of each of the peoples, to achieve the practical tasks which need be achieved quickly and to join in the universal struggle with the proletariat of other countries.

Here are the tasks, whose solutions you will not find in a single Communist pamphlet, but whose solution you will find in the universal struggle which began in Russia. . . . You must base yourselves upon that bourgeois nationalism which is awakening in these peoples. . . . Along with this you must tell [the masses] in language they can understand that the sole hope for freedom lies in the victory of the international revolution and that the international proletariat is the only ally of all the workers and of the exploited hundreds of millions of the peoples of the East.[13]

Even before seeking the Russia-through-Asia-to-West chain reaction of revolutionary explosion, Lenin had hoped to guide the revolution in Europe to success through gradualistic and preferably nonviolent channels. Having decided to take the long way around, he naturally became all the more concerned that a moderate revolutionary pace should be maintained in the West. A premature attempt to take power would have to use violent means and was inevitably doomed to failure. Such a move therefore would serve only to frighten the proletariat from communism and impede the growth of Communist parties. So long as the fall of imperialism's Western bastions could not precede the toppling of their Eastern buttresses, then the interim could best be used to prepare the Western proletarians for their eventual day of decision. Some European Communists were ready to accept Lenin's views. Others, however, considered the revolutionary crisis so near at hand as to place the plotting for the overthrow upon the order of the day. Thus at its very inception the Communist movement of Western Europe was rent by a sharp difference of opinion.

In the summer of 1919 the forming of a British Communist party out of four existing grouplets [14] floundered chiefly on the issue of whether or not a proletarian party might run candidates for Parliament. On the same issue, as well as on the related one of whether or not to work within the old established "reactionary" trade unions, the German party seemed in danger of splitting into two factions. In the case of England, Lenin was consulted in a letter from Sylvia Pankhurst, leader of the Workers' Socialist Federation, a small East London group of pro-Soviet revolutionaries. In reply he expressed his admiration for the spirit of those, such as Pankhurst, who wanted no contact with the bourgeois Parliament. But the refusal to participate in Parliament he described as rising from a "lack of revolutionary experience."

In England, Lenin wrote, as in all imperialist countries where the bourgeois and imperialist-minded workers' aristocracy had been actively participating in the working class movement, it was especially necessary for the Communist party to maintain "an unbroken connection with the working masses." Only by agitating among the workers, joining in every strike and answering "every question of the masses" could the authority of the labor aristocracy be destroyed and the workers be "systematically" prepared for revolution. The workers must be educated "in advance" about the significance of "Soviet power, and propaganda and agitation for it." Hence it was necessary to act in bourgeois parliaments and "from within them carry on Soviet propaganda." There was no danger that workers in Parliament would be corrupted to "ministerialism" as long as the workers' party was "actually *revolutionary, . . .* actually *a party,* that is, a strongly . . . joined organization of the *revolutionary vanguard* [which, in the way the Bolsheviks had done with respect to their men in the Duma] would know how to control *its* parliamentarians and make of them genuine revolutionary propagandists such as Karl Liebknecht, and not . . . betrayers of the proletariat."

The entire question, Lenin wrote, was secondary and unessential as against the major one of unity of effort to gain, what both sides agreed was the goal—Soviet power. But realizing at the same time that in England the "secondary" problem might not so easily be brushed aside, he advised that if

no unity [was] possible in England among those favoring Soviet power precisely because of discord over parliamentarism and only for this reason, then [he] would consider as a useful step forward the immediate founding of *two* Communist parties, . . . both standing for transfer from bourgeois parliamentarism to Soviet power. Let one of these parties permit participation in Parliament, the other deny it, for this disagreement is now so unessential that it would be foolish to [quibble over it].

But even the simultaneous existence of two such parties would be great progress in comparison with the present state of affairs, and would in all probability be a transition to full unity and to a quick victory of communism.[15]

To the danger of schism in the German party Lenin devoted the vastly predominant portion of his "Greetings to the Italian, French, and German Communists," which appeared October 10 in *Kommunistichesky Internatsional*. Lenin employed all the arts of cajolery in order to convince the German Communist party that the disagreement within its ranks, being one merely of tactics, should not be allowed to obscure the common aim. Within the "decaying, dying" Socialist parties of Scheidemann and the Kautskyite Independents, Lenin explained, there was a fundamental "disagreement" in that the aims of the leaders were different from those of the masses. Already, Lenin wrote, the masses were abandoning the Scheidemanns (right-wing Socialists) and going over to the centrist Kautskyites, whose left wing had "in cowardly fashion" united the old bourgeois concepts of parliamentary democracy with those of the proletarian revolution, dictatorship of the proletariat and Soviet power. But in the next crisis the masses would move toward Soviet power, while "the leaders," in the face of revolutionary struggle, would remain "counterrevolutionaries . . . occupied with reconciling the unreconcilables [i.e., parliament and Soviet power]."

The disagreement among the Communists was of another kind. The Communists rested upon a single "rocklike" base—"the fight against bourgeois democratic illusions and bourgeois parliamentarism, the acceptance of the dictatorship of the proletariat and Soviet power." However, there was "nothing frightening" about such a disagreement; it was "a disease of growth," not "one of senility." Lenin diagnosed the German problem as exactly the type of "minor split" that bolshevism in its younger days had "more than once" experienced. "But at the decisive moment . . . of the conquest of power and the creation of the Soviet Republic, bolshevism was united . . . and united about itself all of the vanguard of the proletariat and the *gigantic majority* of the toiling masses." So too, wrote Lenin reassuringly, "will it be with the German Communists." [16]

Lenin went on to cite instances in Russia's revolutionary history of the successful Bolshevik use of the tactics of compromise. He mentioned the Bolsheviks' participation in the "reactionary and directly counterrevolutionary Duma of 1907," their participation in the elections to the "bourgeois Constituent Assembly in 1917 and 1918," their minority role "in reactionary . . . Menshevik trade unions [as bad as any in Germany]," and in the Soviets.[17]

The Bolsheviks of course had not gained power through a gradual process of winning over the majority (whose sympathy for the success of a revolution and overthrow of the bourgeoisie Lenin described as "*absolutely necessary*"),[18] but by a *coup d'état*. Though not in line with Lenin's original plan, the coup had nonetheless been the most spectacular event of Bolshevik history and had made the most significant impression upon Western revolutionaries. Lenin could neither deny the November seizure of power; nor was he then or ever in a position to explain how and why he had been forced into the adventurist tactic. The best he could do was to slide over it and try to reduce its significance by stressing the "long labors" and the "long struggle *before* and *after* the conquest of power" in gaining "the majority in *all* workers' organizations, and then in those of the nonworkers and of the small peasants." [19]

The "rather unimportant" conflict among the German Communists, coming as it did on top of the "secondary" problem that had snaffled the formation of a Communist party in England, was obviously a matter of utmost concern to Lenin. He praised the sincerity of the "most heroic [though inexperienced] revolutionaries of the [German] working classes," [20] but also charged this youthful movement with errors of syndicalism and with retreating from the ideas of Marxism. The German Communists, he wrote, must participate in parliaments and unions to fight the betrayers of socialism on every possible front and must form a strong centralized party uniting illegal with legal work "by hook or crook," in order "systematically and steadily" to achieve "the strictest control by the illegal party and its *workers'* organizations over the legal authority." [21]

Despite Lenin's sentiments in the matter (the word of the International was conveyed directly to the German party's Heidelberg conference by Radek, who was then in a German prison), the party split into two factions. The minority group labeled itself Communist Workers' Party of Germany, or KAPD. Lenin received the news late in October and immediately wrote a letter in which he suggested that the factions reunite. He described the faction of the minority as "like our own Leftists of 1918," and expressed the hope that the two sides would submit their reasons for the split to the Third International.[22] The following day, October 29, Lenin sent a message to "Comrade Serrati and the Italian Communists." In it he expressed gratification over the fact that the Italian Socialists' congress at Bologna had voted to participate in the election to "the bourgeois parliament . . . [and he hoped] that this [would] have the effect of doing away with the disagreement arising at this time among the German Communists on this question." [23] Lenin also expressed the suspicion that England and France, together with the Italian bourgeoisie, would try to push the Italian proletariat into a pretimely rising, thereby easier to crush it. But they would not succeed. The Italian Communists would "[win] the entire industrial and rural proletariat to communism as well as the small peasants, and if beforehand there occur[red] a favorable moment for

action, as the international situation would indicate, then the victory
of the dictatorship of the proletariat [would] be consummated." [24]

Lenin was preaching a tactic that had succeeded in 1917 in a
country in which the masses had had neither a share in their country's wealth, nor a conscious attachment to one or another political
party, nor a feeling of devotion to their government. Hence it had
been possible for the Bolsheviks to use the existing public institutions as forums from which to sway the multitude and at the same
time carry on large-scale conspiratorial activity for the purpose of
overthrowing the government.[25] But in the West the proletariat,
urban and rural, was attached to the traditions of democracy and
legalism, and the "betrayer" socialists, as Lenin conceded, were
strong and ubiquitous in workers' organizations. Also, in the West
governments were stable and could move effectively against illegal
groups. Why then did Lenin insist that the Bolshevik way of com-
bining underground parties with legal fronts was the only possible
formula usable in Western Europe?

Whatever Lenin's new ideas about the importance of the East
in initiating revolution, it was the West in which he foresaw the
real blossoming of socialism, and in the West ultimately where he
hoped to assume the leadership. This, it would seem, made it
necessary for him to accept the belief that his own arena of experience had been similar to that of the West and that his tactics, successful in Russia, were universally applicable.

From the fall of 1919 on, Lenin's preoccupation with the problem
of "leftism" grew ever more intense. The Lefts, he thought, were
isolating the Communist movement from the masses—might institute premature action and in general might impede the rise of mass
parties. Worse yet, they rejected the tactics which Lenin had, so
to speak, trade-marked and thereby denied Lenin's claim to leadership over their parties. By creating factions within the parties the
Lefts were also making it difficult for a single person to take command of the European movement. This last particularly would
explain why Lenin had suggested the forming of two parties in
England, which might conceivably unite, but had so strongly
opposed the splitting of the German party. As he well knew, factionalism, once begun within a party, was a never-ending process. As
"leftism" cropped up anew in various countries of the West, Lenin
became increasingly bitter, if not despondent, over the trend. Commenting in May, 1920, on the "fact" of the split in the German party,

and an "apparently . . . imminent" split in the Italian Communist movement, Lenin expressed the fear "that the split with the Lefts . . . [would] become an international phenomenon like the split within the 'Centrists'. . . . Be it so. A split, in any event, is better than confusion that impedes the ideological, theoretical, and revolutionary growth . . . of the party and its harmonious, really organized practical work which actually paves the way for the dictatorship of the proletariat." After challenging the Lefts to try to succeed in their erroneous ways and suggesting that "practical experience" would "soon teach them," Lenin urged that "every effort . . . be made to prevent the split with the Lefts from impeding, or to see that it impeded as little as possible, the necessary amalgamation in the early future into a single party."

"Certain individuals," Lenin then wrote, striking out against would-be rivals, "especially among the unsuccessful pretenders to leadership, may (if they lack proletarian discipline and are not honest with themselves) persist in their errors for a long time; but when the moment is at hand, the working masses will easily and quickly unite themselves and unite all sincere Communists into a single party capable of accomplishing the Soviet order and the dictatorship of the proletariat." [26]

If, as time passed, the Asia orientation became ever more palatable to Lenin, this may well have been because of Europe's growing "leftism." To one so desirous of wielding absolute control, Asia must indeed have seemed a promised land. Asia was eager for guidance from "advanced" Russia in a way of course that the West was not. Asia had no Marxian tradition and therefore no false prophets to confuse the masses. Lenin then might unobstructedly implant his views as orthodoxy, obviating the deviationism that was making it so hard for him to keep Europe's proletarians in line.

In compensating himself with Asia for a Europe which was for the moment eluding his grasp, Lenin was bound to acquire an entirely new perspective on Russia. Hitherto but a convenient base for his own Western-directed operations, Russia all at once became the hub about which the wheel of world revolution revolved; the bridge, as Stalin had written, between East and West. At the time of Brest-Litovsk and during the subsequent year, Russia had been important to Lenin mainly in that her vast expanse had enabled him to gain time and preserve his existence. But by 1920 Russia had in Lenin's eyes acquired a new significance. If socialism, raised by

Lenin out of a peasant society, could prove nothing to Europe, it could yet provide an excellent model for Asia. But to serve this end Russia would first and foremost have to rebuild her ruined economy and import whatever would be necessary for the task of reconstruction. This need more than ever demanded the establishment of peaceable relations between Russia and Europe and provided an added reason why Lenin, while trying to retain and strengthen his grip upon the incipient Communist movement of Europe, would at the same time be content to have the European proletariat take a slow zigzag course toward communism, which in any event could not be achieved in Europe before the overthrow of imperialist rule in the East.

With Europe in 1920 Lenin made every effort to re-establish normal relations. The treaty of peace contracted with Estonia in January, he hailed as "a window to the West," a channel through which goods might enter into otherwise still-blockaded Russia. His attitude toward the revolutionary movement in the West, Lenin set down in his book *Left Wing Communism, An Infantile Disease*. The book, completed by May, was intended to provide an ideological guideline for those in the West who were scheduled to convene in Russia on July 15 to attend the Comintern's Second Congress. *Left Wing Communism* was for the most part a more carefully worked out restatement of the tactical directives contained in the afore-cited letters to the English and German Communists. Otherwise the book developed the following thesis.

Revolution in the West, still a long way off,[27] would have a more difficult time getting started than had been the case in Russia.[28] This was so because the working masses of the West, the peasantry in particular, were more subject than their Russian brethren to deeply rooted "bourgeois democratic and parliamentary prejudices."[29] Therefore bolshevism (Marxism come to life for the first time in Russia),[30] which meant absolute centralization of the party[31] coupled with the tactic of gradualism and compromise,[32] was even more applicable in the West than had been the case in Russia.

Implicit, though never so stated in the book, was the notion that Western communism should subordinate itself to Lenin's control. Implicit further, if only in Lenin's thinking, was the idea that communism could not triumph in the West until Asiatic revolutions should have prepared the way for such a development.

In June, 1920, Fusse, a Japanese journalist, interviewed Lenin.

"Where," he asked, "does communism have the best chances for success—in the West or in the East?"

"Genuine communism," Lenin answered, "can thus far succeed only in the West. However, the West lives on account of the East. European imperialist powers support themselves mainly from Eastern colonies. But at the same time they are arming their colonials and teaching them to fight. Thereby the West is digging its grave in the East."

12

THE SECOND CONGRESS OF THE COMINTERN

WHEN IN MARCH, 1919, the Third International was founded, there was outside Russia no revolutionary party that could have been described as significantly representative of its country's working class. At that time too Russia was effectively isolated from Europe. The heart of bolshevism, therefore, was having a difficult time of it trying to pump blood into the arteries of the movement's feeble extremities. "At the First Congress of the Comintern," Lenin was later to declare, "we were in essence only propagandists. We only threw out to the proletariat of the world the basic ideas. We only gave out a call to battle and asked where the people were who were capable of going our way." [1] Under such conditions Lenin could not even have contemplated the setting up of an organization which would possess the machinery for co-ordinated international action.

In the year following the founding congress the picture changed. Existing Communist grouplets acquired larger memberships. New Communist parties were formed; the Bulgarian out of a left-wing faction in that country's socialist movement, the American out of syndicalist elements in the United States labor movement. Certain syndicalist groups,[2] though not yet ready to constitute themselves as political parties, affiliated themselves with the Third International. Others [3] expressed their intention of so doing. The Socialist party of Italy joined the Comintern, as did the Norwegian Labor party. The German Independent Socialists, convinced that the Second International was no more, were beginning to look upon the Third International as the future center of socialism. There were in addition groups of nationalist revolutionaries in Asia who were attracted to Lenin's International because the Soviet government had taken so consistent an anti-imperialist line. Therefore with the Second Congress of the Comintern scheduled for convention in mid-July, 1920, the erstwhile propaganda association seemed ready for conversion into an effective propellant of world Communist activity, and, as Lenin wished, into an enlarged Bolshevik party completely under his control.

Lenin intended to leave none of the decisions of the congress to the chance outcome of free interchange of opinion. Well in advance of its meeting, therefore, he drew up or supervised the drawing up of a series of guiding resolutions. These were designed to formulate the organizational structure of the Third International, on one hand, and, on the other, the tactics which the International was to pursue with regard to parliaments and trade unions, the national and colonial questions, and the problems presented by the small and middle peasantry. Soon after the congress convened, committees were set up to discuss each of the problems dealt with in the draft resolutions. Each committee was dominated either by Lenin himself or by Zinoviev or Bukharin.[4] Barring minor changes in terminology, therefore, the spirit of the original drafts remained unaffected by committee discussions except in such instances when Lenin, for one or another reason, considered a change necessary or desirable.

Lively floor discussions marked all the congress sessions. The apparent design of the Russians to seize control of the Third International met with considerable challenge, as did Lenin's notion that tactics derived from Russian revolutionary experience could be applied in countries of the West. But the Russian position at the congress was far too powerfully based to be seriously shaken. The mere fact that Europeans had seen fit to come to Russia indicated how exalted was the status of the provedly successful Bolshevik party as compared with the minor-merited revolutionary force which any Western delegation represented. Such delegates, already awed,[5] were further confounded by the fact that they knew only of conditions in their own countries and generally spoke only their own languages. The Russians, by contrast, were informed about conditions the world over and spoke many European languages. A given delegate was therefore unprepared to engage in dispute with the Bolsheviks on any issues except those that concerned him directly.[6] Delegates assigned to a committee were often unable to follow its proceedings. In the debates on the congress floor, which took place mostly in the German language, points of a discussion that might excite the Italians left the English unmoved and vice versa. Thus except in one notable instance the opposition to Lenin was unable to unite its forces.

Most of the Western delegations were further weakened by disagreements within their ranks. The Bolshevik contingent, needless to say, acted as one person. Lenin and Zinoviev, each a member of the five-man presidium of the congress,[7] and Radek did virtually all the talking for the Soviet bloc.[8] The 86 decisive votes of this bloc constituted a majority of about 169 decisive votes that might be cast on any issue.[9] Unequivocally in support of the Soviet bloc also were the delegates of European Communist parties [10] and the Asiatic delegations.[11] Thus the Russians, confident that any measure approved by them would automatically be assured of passage, could afford to be arrogant in their treatment of any overvociferous opponents. Zinoviev and more particularly Radek often spiced their comments with sarcasm and personally directed vituperation. If necessary, Lenin himself would take the floor to thunder down some critic. Whenever matters appeared to be getting quite out of hand, a hasty time limit would be called on discussion. An irate delegate might then find meager relief from his frustration either by abstaining from the voting that followed or in casting a futile negative ballot.

The first obstacle confronting Lenin at the congress was the syndicalist conviction that organized political activity was unnecessary. Lenin conceived of a Communist party in each nation as serving two vital purposes. The party would direct the activities of Communists in parliaments, in trade unions, and within other parties during the "April Theses" period of the European revolution. The party would also enable Lenin to exercise international control over Communist activities. The English Shop Stewards' delegates, however, disputed the contention made by Zinoviev that a party was essential, and they expressed particular resentment over his further insistence that such a party, when formed, should do altogether as the International bade.

Tanner of the Shop Stewards argued that Zinoviev had not "clearly proved . . . the absolute necessity for a rigidly disciplined highly centralized Communist party" and had not proved "that the dictatorship of the proletariat [was] synonymous with the dictatorship of the Communist party." Tanner did not agree that the Russian experience past and present should serve as a model for all other countries. He declared:

In England we are sure that things will be quite different. The situation there differs altogether from that of prerevolutionary Russia. To us, the Shop Stewards, the dictatorship of the proletariat means something entirely different from that which Zinoviev understands by the term. In our view the dictatorship of the proletariat must be accomplished by a minority—by the revolutionary minority of the English proletariat as represented by the Shop Stewards' movement. Members of political parties do not agree with this, but they must understand that we in England have a much greater number of class conscious proletarians than there were in Russia—proletarians who are ready and able to achieve the dictatorship [which has] a very definite meaning to . . . the English revolutionary workers.[12]

Tanner caustically asked

the Russian and other comrades if there [was] nothing more for them to learn from the struggles and revolutionary movements of other countries. [Had the Russians] come [to the congress] not to learn but only to teach? We will make the revolution in England; our Russian comrades cannot do it. They can help us, but we shall have to perform the act, and we are learning and preparing for that end.

Tanner granted that the Second International had gone under because of its looseness of structure and vagueness of aims, but he warned at the same time against the Third International's going to the other extreme and becoming "too dogmatic." Tanner concluded his statement by declaring that

every organization [should have] sufficient freedom of movement within the limits of its country to deal with, and adjust itself to, any special condition. The International must be founded upon a basis permitting the various parties to unite on the most important principles and methods. Everything else must be left at the discretion of each separate party.[13]

Such freedom of decision as Tanner described was precisely the antithesis to the kind of Communist movement that Lenin had in mind for England or for any other country. His reply to Tanner was flattering enough to the Shop Stewards,[14] but yielded no ground to their demand for independence of action. If such comrades as Tanner, Lenin declared, "stand for the existence of a minority which struggles decisively for dictatorship and educates the masses in this direction, then this minority is, in essence, the party." The difference between the Bolsheviks and the Shop Stewards, Lenin maintained, was merely that the Englishmen, because of their antiparty prejudices, were reluctant to use the word "party." Rejecting Tanner's charge against him of dogmatism as "altogether out of place here," Lenin demanded to know what sort of an International could exist if every member group could decide each question for itself.[15]

Lenin argued that it was tactically as well as morally correct for the Communist party to affiliate with the British Labour party, if only for purposes of criticizing that party and conducting its own political propaganda. On this point the delegates from the British Socialist party, which had joined the Labour party in 1916 to act as its left-wing conscience,[16] naturally sided with Lenin; the Shop Stewards and other British delegates opposed him.[17] Lenin declared himself willing to have the matter put before a special committee for further examination, but made it clear that the congress as a whole would render the final and unconditional decision. "We cannot say: this concerns only English Communists. We must declare in general which is the correct tactic."[18] To the Shop Stewards' contention that the majority of English Communists would refuse to join the Labour party, no matter what the International decided, Lenin retorted that "even the parallel existence of two parties for a certain period of time" was preferable to a refusal to follow the International's determination as to the correct tactic.

> If the majority is against [the given instruction] then it is necessary to organize the minority separately. This will have an educational value. If the majority of English workers continue to believe in the former tactic, then we shall draw our conclusions at the next congress. But we cannot permit it to be said that the [question of tactics in England] is a purely English problem—this would constitute an imitation of the worst aspect of the Second International.[19]

By far the stormiest controversy at the congress arose over the issue of the conditions for admission to the Comintern. The question of what groups to exclude was an extremely delicate matter at this point of the International's existence. If conditions of admission were made too lax, many reformist elements might enter. The revolutionary essence of the Comintern might thus become diluted and the organization might become another Second International. If on the other hand conditions for admission were made too rigid, broad masses of workers then adhering to various socialist organizations, notably the strong USPD, or attached to syndicalist groups, which Lenin viewed as well intentioned but misguided, might be excluded at the outset. If this occurred, Lenin would in effect be committing the very sin with which he had charged the "left Communists" of various countries—that of isolating communism from the masses. Lenin's *Left Wing Communism* had laid down for Europe's Communists the policy of temporary accommodation for the purposes of infiltration. To the Second Congress, as to a miniature replica of Europe's revolutionary movement, Lenin naturally intended to apply the same policy. At the inception of the congress, then, Lenin had no desire to anathematize those who, temporarily deluded, were nonetheless essential for providing the movement with a mass base.

Lenin's original nineteen theses on conditions for admission drew a line considerably to the right of center. Beneath an all-covering series of conditions demanding absolute obedience to a centralized body, the theses gave the Lefts the very specific directives to join parliaments and trade unions. For the Rights, who had begun to nibble at the bait, the conditions were far vaguer. Each organization wishing to join the Comintern was obliged by thesis 2 "to *remove* in planned and systematic manner from all posts in the workers' movement [party organization, press, parliamentary faction, union, and so forth] any reformists and partisans of the 'Center' and replace these with convinced Communists." Thesis 7 demanded that "each party" make "a full and absolute break with reformism" and such reformists "as Turati, Modigliani, and so forth," and do this "unconditionally and ultimatively in the shortest possible time." [20] Each group was left its own basis for judging how "convinced" a Communist a person might be and what constituted "the shortest possible time." Thus a mere verbal acceptance of the conditions for admission by centrist parties would admit them to the Third International, yet in fact leave them free to interpret these conditions almost as they pleased.

So intent apparently had Lenin been to win the large centrist parties to the Comintern that delegates from the USPD and the French Socialist party were not only invited to attend the Second Congress and given consultative votes but, more important, were seated on the committee whose task it was to decide upon the final drafting of conditions for admission. This could only have meant that their approval would be sought as to the final wording of the conditions. At the July 24 session of the congress the Lefts raised a clamor of protest against the "opportunist" manner in which the centrist delegates were being treated. The Russian clique did its utmost to protect the centrists from abuse, fearing apparently that otherwise they would be frightened out of joining the Comintern.

It was the Dutch Communist Wijnkoop who first raised objection to the fact that delegates from the USPD, "a government party," and the "somewhat but little better" French Socialists had been given access to the congress and, worse, were participating in the committee which was determining the rules of admission to the International. Radek took up the cudgels against this "illogical" proposition. He first mentioned the size of the USPD, as if winking at Wijnkoop to hold his tongue, then went on to speak of "behaving correctly" toward invited delegates and the masses they represented, and eventually, as Van Leeven, Wijnkoop's compatriot, and others began to join in the attack on the centrists, proposed that the discussion be closed and the vote be taken. Finally Radek lost his reserve and labeled Wijnkoop's comments "a sorry indication of verbal radicalism." Thereupon Däumig of the USPD took the floor to object to Wijnkoop's calling his party governmental and non-revolutionary.

"Comrades," declaimed Wijnkoop, in reply, "I consider it shameful that people such as Däumig try to take advantage of their demagogic acceptance at this congress. I consider it my duty to declare that . . . this same Däumig, at the very time of the Kapp Putsch, told the workers that they must not arm themselves. And now he appears here in Russia, where everyone knows thoroughly that victories can be won only through civil war. But Comrade Radek says here that we reveal verbal radicalism."

"Madman!" interjected Radek.

"In the opinion of Comrade Radek," answered Wijnkoop, "I am insane. . . . Aha, . . . he takes his words back. But I call the attention of the comrades to the sort of unworthy character, who, thanks to Radek, has already taken part in the discussion. Comrades, you don't know how bad it looks in the West to have such as Däumig . . . here at the same table with the representatives of genuine communism and revolutionary parties. I warn you of the consequences."

Zinoviev, after describing Wijnkoop as "positively ridiculous," made the point that 800,000 badly led USPD members were worth more than 2,000 to 3,000 Dutch "Tribunists." Predicting that within two months most of the workers of the USPD would be morally, formally, and organizationally joined to the Third International,

Zinoviev expressed the willingness of the Third International "to conduct discussions and seek unity with any mass party, which, however confused, wishes to fight with us in the proletarian cause."

The session ended in an orgy of name calling. Levi, of the German Communist party, accused the Dutch of having, the summer past, refused even to send the journalists Pannekoek and Gorter to aid the cause of the embattled German proletariat. "While . . . hundreds and thousands of workers of the USPD fell in battle, you sat peacefully about your sacks of coffee. And now you are—revolutionaries." [21] To top it off, Radek called Van Leeven a "stockbroker."

The course of relative conciliation toward Däumig & Co., charted by Lenin before the congress opened, failed to endure. By July 29, when the congress agenda called for a discussion of conditions for admission, the committee had already altered Lenin's original theses. To the two Italians previously cited in thesis 7 as examples of reformists with whom no compromise was possible, were added Kautsky, Longuet, MacDonald, and Hillquit.[22] Thesis 19 had also been changed. It specified that a party wishing to belong to the Comintern was allowed but four months from the end of the Second Congress to call a special session to decide upon the acceptance of the conditions for admission.[23]

The altered conditions strongly suggested an early purging of parties, yet fell short of demanding explicitly the ouster of any but the most notorious reformists. In committee Lenin had proposed the addition of a condition requiring that "all central committees and all the most important central institutions" of parties wishing to enter the Third International be composed of "not less than two-thirds of such comrades who, even before the Second Congress, had publicly and unequivocally expressed themselves in favor of entering the Third International." This proposal, which would undoubtedly have gone far to please the leftist sentiment, the committee had accepted by a vote of five to three, two abstaining. At the start of the July 29 session, however, Zinoviev announced that the Russian delegation had decided to regard this proposal as a wish rather than as a condition or a directive.[24]

Then, as though with some noisy barking to cover up the Russian reluctance to bite, Zinoviev held up to severe political scrutiny the records of various parties represented at the congress.[25] At the same time he continued to defend, but in terms far less positive than he had done five days earlier, the value of carrying on discussions with those whose position was in error. "We do not propose the immediate acceptance of the French party or the [USPD]," Zinoviev explained, obviously addressing himself to the Left elements, "but to authorize the Executive Committee of the Comintern to continue discussions, to ascertain that they have fulfilled the conditions presented to them, and to follow their press from day to day and after a time come to one or another decision. In committee the French [and German] comrades told us that they were in general agreed to our conditions." [26] The acceptance of conditions, Zinoviev hastened to add, meant nothing if the nature of the party "remained Kautskyite. We established these conditions in order to have criteria, so that there should be objective standards as to what the congress desires. I hope, in any event, that the congress will create clarity . . . so that each worker should understand what the Third International wants." [27]

This still-indeterminate position failed to satisfy the Lefts. As long as the terms of admission remained vague and discussions continued, there remained the possibility that undesired persons would enter into and defile the Third International. Goldenberg of the French Youth League recalled the slanderous campaign carried on against those in France who stood for the Third International by "these very people [whom] we intend to invite into the Third International simply because they . . . demonstrate verbal solidarity with [its] principles." In the name of his "comrades languishing in prisons, in the name of the real interests of the French proletariat," Goldenberg protested against "this artificial means of introducing unsuitable elements into the Comintern." [28]

The morning session of July 29 concluded on the stern note of a proposal by the Italian Bordiga. Thesis 16 of the original "conditions" demanded that a party wishing to join the Comintern replace, at the earliest, its old program by a new Communist program in the spirit of provisions laid down by the Communist International.[29] Bordiga voiced the desire to amend this thesis with the stipulation that the "minority of each party, which would oppose [the Communist] program, be for this reason ejected from the ranks of the party's organization." Bordiga further proposed that Lenin's earlier withdrawn proposal—that two-thirds of the members of the central institutions of parties wishing to enter the Comintern be Communists—go into effect. "Personally," said Bordiga, "I would prefer that [the central institutions] be entirely Communist in composition." [30]

The evening session of July 29 saw the leftist attack mount in fury. Wijnkoop, again violating the unwritten code, did not stop with attacking the centrists, but also charged the Russians with opportunist compromising. The Communist party of Germany, he complained, had been permitted to criticize the USPD. But there were present no representatives from the KAPD, who might have directed words of criticism against the KPD. "Is it true," he asked, "that the Communist party of Germany always goes in front of the masses? This question should be asked here, and we should receive an answer. But now," he taunted, "in the presence of the USPD this would be inconvenient. We are not among ourselves, we are here together with the Messrs. government Socialists. But it is necessary for us to be among ourselves and speak the truth to each other. But this was prevented by the Executive Committee." [31]

The German Münzenberg, following Wijnkoop, sounded so vehement an alarm against the dangers of a premature extension of the International's membership rolls, of "diluting and weakening revolutionary propaganda and action," that even Lenin began to feel uncomfortable.

"And whoever wants to admit the USPD?" Lenin interjected defensively.

"The discussions in the Executive Committee proved this," was Münzenberg's snappish retort. "The fact that comrades who only weeks or days ago were fighting the Third International by every means, declare that they are now ready without any reservations to sign the proposed conditions—is undoubted proof that these conditions were not formulated rigidly enough." [32]

Crispien of the USPD, who opposed his party's joining the Comintern, subsequently took the floor to explain his position. The Third International, he argued, was premature because workers who did not as yet comprehend where they were going in their own countries, were not yet ready to play a role on the international scene. "Who, by the way," he asked dramatically, "is suitable to be in the Communist International? Only the Russian Communists have not been criticized. . . . Otherwise none of the parties who have joined have not been criticized—and now those who have been criticized are breaking their sticks over the wicked Independents of Germany." Crispien suggested caution in the advocacy of party schism. "It is much easier to split the workers in Germany than it is to win them over and hold them together for revolution." [33] He went on to attack

Lenin's theses on the agrarian question. "Do you really believe," he asked, "that it is revolutionary for Germany to give land to the small peasants?"

"To bring them on our side," retorted Walcher, a member of the German Communist party.

"With such opportunistic methods you don't bring them to our side," [34] was Crispien's reply. Crispien and his colleague Dittman, who also took the floor, were frequently interrupted by jeers and catcalls. The "correct behavior" that Radek had earlier insisted upon had vanished completely from the floor of the congress.

The following day, July 30, the Russians, headed by Lenin, finally threw their full weight against the centrists. Serrati of Italy first made an attempt to pour oil upon the waters. He paid tribute to the great power of the Russian party as compared to the minute parties of the European countries, and "yet," he said, "you English comrades have the same voting right as Comrade Lenin." He pleaded that the various parties, apart for years because of the war, stop judging one another, but try rather to evaluate objectively the difficulty of conditions in each country. France, he thought, was not yet ready for revolution. However, the socialist leaders there had called a general strike in behalf of Russia and may have been sincere in their intentions.

"They were not sincere," Goldenberg interjected.

"But my dear friend," said Serrati, "we have no sincerity barometer in our pockets."

"We shall have to find this sincerity barometer," was the cold reply of Lenin, who went on to say that the French party had gone back on its word and had not proclaimed the general strike.

"Despite your criticism, my dear Russian friends," the Italian continued, "we all love each other very much. True, from time to time we attack one another, but then—well, that's how love is." (Laughter.) Deploring the attacks at the congress upon individual Italians, Serrati thought it was more important to achieve the revolution in Italy than to worry so much about men such as Turati remaining in the Italian party. Turati, Serrati declared, had been generally helpful to the revolutionary cause in Italy, had spoken out against the war, and had not permitted the police to fire into crowds. Besides, said Serrati, the Italian workers liked Turati because he was courageous and expressed himself clearly. "It is not our fault," he concluded, "that we are Italians and you are Russians. . . . I hold no personal grudge against anyone." [35]

"Please, no sentimentality," cried the obviously annoyed Lenin, who then took the floor to refute point for point Crispien's stand of the day before. "All methods of the Crispien argument," he said summing up, "are thoroughly Kautskyan. But Crispien says: 'Kautsky no longer has any influence in our party.' [Kautsky] may have no influence upon the revolutionary worker who joined later . . . [but] he has an enormous influence upon Crispien. . . . One needs no sincerity barometer to say that the direction of Crispien is not that of the Third International. If we say this, then we have determined the basic line of the entire Comintern." Lenin was careful, however, not to close the door entirely to whatever opportunity for compromise might yet be necessary.

> If Wijnkoop and Münzenberg expressed dissatisfaction with our inviting the USPD and our speaking with their representatives, I consider this incorrect. If Kautsky writes against us, we polemicize with him as with a classic foe. But if the USPD, which rose as a result of an influx of revolutionary workers, is here for discussion, then we are obliged to speak to its representatives, for they represent part of the revolutionary workers. We cannot collide all at once with the Germans, the French, and the English on the question of the International. Comrade Wijnkoop proves with each of his speeches that he shares the errors of [Dutch Communist] Pannekoek. . . . In this lies the basic error of the left group. But this is generally an error of a proletarian movement which is growing. [36]

Turning once again to Serrati, Lenin charged him with speaking in the tone of the Second International in his remarks on the French situation and particularly in his defense of Turati.

Subsequently, after Däumig and Stoecker of the USPD had made apologetic speeches to explain the difficult position of the revolutionary movement in Germany, Zinoviev, as though their words had been so much air, coldly assured the congress that the USPD and the French Socialist party as then constituted were not acceptable to the Comintern. "Did we actually lose anything," he asked, "in discussing our views in such detail and so clearly with their delegates?" As though this alone had been the reason for asking the centrist delegates to attend the congress and sit on the committee of admissions, Zinoviev asked, "Would it be bad to have the [Western] proletarians read the stenogram of the [July 29–30 sessions]? On the contrary. It is good that these disputes will become clear to the entire world." Zinoviev described the situation in Italy as "unbearable." He declared:

> The whole trade union movement is in the hands of reformists. For this the party is to blame. . . . For seven years already the Italian unions have had no congress, and this is tolerated by a party which belongs to the Third International. People such as D'Aragona know that the workers would chase them out if they called a congress. Such conditions— such a scandal. . . . So comrades, you see the matter is not as harmless and *gemütlich* as Serrati presents it in his speech. This, the Third International cannot tolerate. If the leaders of the Italian party continue to stand for it, we will appeal over their heads directly to the Italian workers. [Zinoviev turned his scorn upon the USPD delegates.] So far we have been proud of the fact that our party was a factor in history, that we hastened the process of history. . . . In Germany it is possible that the working class will move to the decisive struggles within the next months.[37]

Concluding the session, Radek characterized the USPD leadership as "hopeless." "I personally," he said, "after hearing Däumig and Stoecker, have lost hope that even if their kind made up nine-tenths of the Central Committee, they would really be able to bring a change into the party tactic." [38] The committee, soon after this, decided to include in the conditions for admission not only Lenin's two-thirds provision, but also the more drastic proposal of Bordiga. The latter became thesis 21 of the final revision of the conditions for admission. "Members of parties," it read, "who in the main reject the conditions and theses established by the Communist International, must be excluded from the party. This applies also to delegates to the special party congresses [which, according to the new thesis 19, were to be convoked within four months after the second congress of the Comintern]." [39] At the session of August 6, the twenty-one conditions were accepted, only two negative votes being cast.[40]

In the course of the congress, it is clear, Lenin's stand on "admissions" moved from a position very moderate, toward those still on the fence, to a position extremely rigid. In the process of this change of stand two phases can be detected. The first phase, extending from the outset of the congress, July 19 through July 29, may be described as a period during which Lenin and the Russian contingent in general yielded to the pressure of the European leftists. In the second phase, beginning on July 30, Lenin & Co. had already acknowledged the leftward trend to be the correct one and had moved to the front of the leftist pack in the business of haranguing the centrists. The first phase, that in which Lenin reluctantly gave ground, may be explained in the following manner.

Previous to the congress and during its earlier stages Lenin, as shown, had been intent upon pursuing a gradualistic tactic with regard to Europe, which was as yet unready for revolution. This is borne out by the principal theme of *Left Wing Communism* and other writings, and above all by the keynote address [41] to the congress made on July 19. Therein, as the most important proof of impending revolution, Lenin, playing down the European economic crisis, directed attention to the war-wrought rearrangement in the imperialist domination of the world. Describing a prewar condition in which 33 per cent of the world's people exploited 66 per cent, Lenin, lumping the victims of Versailles with the colonial peoples of the world, announced that since the war a mere 30 per cent (the upper classes of this 30 per cent, that is) exploited the remaining 70 per cent. Here was an interesting world-based parallel to the *Communist Manifesto* of prerevolutionary society grown preponderantly proletarian. Lenin did not fail to stress the gravity of economic conditions in postwar Europe, the quarrels among European capitalists, and the unbearable conditions of the European working class. But all this, he pointed out, did not make the situation of European capitalism hopeless. European capitalism was not yet confronted by properly organized revolutionary forces, whose formation, "our worst foe," the labor aristocrat opportunists, were frustrating, their efforts abetted by the misguided leftists.

Lenin's closing remarks inextricably linked the fate of Europe with that of the colonial world, principally with Asia. Referring to the Asiatic delegates at the congress, Lenin admitted the initial weakness of their movement, but declared the fact of its having begun to be important.

The union of the revolutionary proletariat of the leading capitalistic countries with the [oppressed] masses of the [proletariatless] . . .

colonial eastern lands is happening at the present congress. And it depends upon us—I am convinced that we will do this—to strengthen this unity. World-wide imperialism must fall when the revolutionary onslaught of the exploited and oppressed workers within each country, conquering the opposition of the Philistine elements and the influence of the contemptible leaders of the labor aristocracy, unites itself with the revolutionary attack of hundreds of millions of humans, who thus far have remained outside of history.

In making his moderate proposals with regard to admissions to the Comintern, Lenin had apparently anticipated that Europe's revolutionaries would understand and accept the view that Europe's masses still had a long way to go before they would be ready for drastic action. In the face of the unexpected storm of protest evoked by the admissions question,[42] Lenin apparently began to fear that his subtle tactic would be conveyed to Europe in distorted form. He may well have foreseen the disappointed delegates returning home to report to their organizations that Lenin was no better than Kautsky, that the Third International was little different from the Second. This would explain why he was willing, however reluctantly, to yield some ground from his position that victory should be pursued through the slow cautious building up of mass Communist parties.

Lenin's analysis of the European situation, though correct, was by no means in harmony with the feelings of many of the zealots who had journeyed to the Second Congress. These men were still charged with the revolutionary enthusiasm generated in the period from November, 1918, to April, 1919. They had come to Russia as to the vital center of world revolution not to hear about tactics of moderation but to learn how revolution in their own countries was to be hastened.[43] Most of these men had at least perused *Left Wing Communism*, and they had all sat through Lenin's above-cited opening address. But the basic ideas contained in these messages did not register with them. In part this may be explained on the ground that they were emotionally out of accord with the spirit of Lenin's words. Further eclipsing the moderate tenor of Lenin's theme was the fact that just at the time the Congress sat, July 19–August 7, there was taking place the Red invasion of Poland—to European eyes the most spectacular revolutionary event since the Bolshevik seizure of power. From ringside seats, as it were, the delegates in Moscow were able to watch as the Red Army advanced westward in pursuit of the

Poles, to note the proclamation of a provisional revolutionary government in Poland and the setting up of Soviets in every conquered Polish region. It would scarcely have been human, under the circumstances, had the grail-seeking Galahads in Moscow paid serious attention to Lenin's words about long-range policies in the achievement of European revolution.[44] As they excitedly observed the day-to-day progress of the Red Army, as marked on a huge map that hung before the congress,[45] they were convinced that this advance could have had no other purpose than that of inciting the proletariat of the West to immediate revolutionary action.

At the beginning of 1920, as indicated above, it was Lenin's most fervent and most frequently expressed desire that the people of Russia proceed to the task of rehabilitating their country at the earliest possible moment. Toward the accomplishment of this goal he counted upon the reopening of trade with Europe and naturally upon an enduring period of peace. But as the year advanced it became increasingly evident to Lenin that peace was not in the offing. Pilsudski, prodded, as Lenin thought, by the Entente, threatened to invade the Ukraine, and in the Crimea, Baron Wrangel, another "tool of the Entente," was reconstituting the remnants of Denikin's forces into an anti-Soviet army. During February–March, 1920, the Soviet regime made frantic efforts to come to terms with the Polish government,[46] even offering some territory east of the so-called Curzon line,[47] the boundary between Poland and Russia proposed by the Allied Supreme Council in December, 1919. This attempt at appeasement was to no avail. The Poles began their invasion on April 25, and five weeks later, Wrangel, acting in conjunction with them, commenced moving his forces northward into the Ukraine. "The two hands of French imperialism," [48] in Lenin's words, had gone into action.

On July 12, by the time the Poles were in full retreat from Russia, Lord Curzon notified the Soviet government of a Polish request that England mediate in bringing about a peace. The note suggested a territorial settlement along the Curzon line and indicated Britain's willingness to convoke a conference in London. At this conference the Baltic countries, besides Russia and Poland, would be represented for discussions of a peace between Russia "and her neighbors." The note further proposed the signing of a truce between Soviet Russia and Wrangel "under conditions of an immediate withdrawal of . . . Wrangel's forces into the Crimea and a provision that during the time of the armistice the [Perekop] Isthmus should constitute a neutral zone, and that . . . Wrangel be invited to London to discuss the fate of his troops and refugees, but not as a member of the conference." [49]

Trotsky, perhaps because he best appreciated the exhausted condition of the Red Army, advised Lenin to accept Curzon's offer and strive for peace with the Entente and Poland.[50] Instead, Lenin sent a note to Sklyansky, Trotsky's deputy in the Revolutionary War Council, in which, because of the "international situation, particularly the proposal of Curzon (the annexation of the Crimea for a peace with Poland on the Grodno-Belostok line)," he demanded, "a furious speeding up of the offensive upon Poland."

The note asked in conclusion: "Are you doing this? All of it? Energetically?" [51]

On July 17 a sarcastic note from Foreign Affairs Commissar Chicherin rejected Curzon's "ultimatum." [52] Three days later the Council of People's Commissars published a proclamation explaining this rejection to the Soviet people.

If England had not wanted war, she could easily have forestalled it [by simply refusing to give] Poland war supplies and money. But England wanted war. Though conducting talks with us in order to lull her working classes, England at the same time constantly sent war materials to Pilsudski and Wrangel [for use] against the Russian workers and peasants.

Lord Curzon refers to the League of Nations in whose name he makes his proposal. But Poland [our attacker] is a member of the League of Nations [as is] imperial Japan, which, under cover of its allies, now carries on monstrous violence in the Far Eastern Republic. If it had been the purpose of the League of Nations to further the cause of peace, it would have restrained Poland from starting war and would have demanded that Japan evacuate eastern Siberia. But this has not been the case. All the members of the League, . . . and France, England, and America in particular, are bound in mutual responsibility to the cause of the provocation of the war of Poland with the Ukraine and Russia. The most powerful members of the League . . . have helped and are helping Poland as much as they can. They did not even answer us when on March 9 we turned to them with an appeal to hold back the hand of Pilsudski's government already raised to strike its criminal blow. Now, however, that the white guard Polish troops have suffered severe blows by the Red Army, the League, . . . responsible for the war, comes with the twig of peace in its hands, or rather under the guise of peaceful intentions, and offers us its mediation in our reconciliation with Poland and the other border states. . . .

But the government of Great Britain . . . does not limit itself to the question of Poland. In his note of [July] 12 Lord Curzon proposes nothing less than that we cease the war with Baron Wrangel and promise him that he may withdraw his bands to the south of the [Perekop] Isthmus, so that he may encamp within the confines of the Crimean Peninsula, which England places at his disposal. . . .

This is not the first time that the government of Great Britain evinces its interest in . . . Wrangel and the Crimea. On April 12, when the Red forces, having smashed Denikin, were preparing to pass through the threshold of the Crimea in order to finish off the Wrangelian remains of Denikin's army, Lord Curzon came forth with precisely the same twig of peace in his hands and proposed to us the complete capitulation of Wrangel and his men under condition of an amnesty. We agreed and upon the insistence of the British government immediately drew rein to our attack. Thereupon Lord Curzon immediately changed the conditions and instead of the capitulation of Wrangel, began to speak of our not trespassing into the Crimea. At the same time the British military and naval ministry was working energetically to rearm and re-equip Wrangel's troops. The result of this harmonious collaboration of Curzon, Churchill, and Wrangel is the new offensive of the white guard troops northward from the Crimea which began early in June. It is quite evident that the offensive of Wrangel, for the purpose of which Lord Curzon had previously asked an amnesty, was in accordance with the plan of supplementing the onslaught of white guard Poland and was consequently ordered by the same London center. But now, as though nothing had happened in the past, the British minister of foreign affairs again asks us to refrain from an attack upon Wrangel and prepare to accommodate his hireling upon a part of Russian territory. . . .

The entire course of the past efforts of the British government, its allies and assistants, testifies to the fact that its intermediacy at the present time pursues but a single purpose: to save Pilsudski and Wrangel, whom they set upon us, from their deserved destruction, to give them the possibility to remedy their condition, to regroup and reman their ranks, to arm themselves and begin anew the war against Worker-Peasant Russia.

Clearly we could not inflict upon the masses of Russia and the Ukraine the dangers of a new war in which all efforts and all the sacrifices would have to be undergone again from the beginning. This is why we turned down the offer of British mediation. . . .

We know them too well to trust them. . . . The League of Nations

comes with words of peace on its lips in order to drive a new knife into
our backs. . . .

Be on guard, Red Army men, workers . . . and peasants . . . !

With the deepest desire for peace and the brotherhood of all peoples, but with deep distrust toward world imperialism, we take our
revolutionary sword in hand with redoubled strength. The battle for
the fencing off, the consolidation and thriving of our socialist republic
we shall carry on to the end against all enemies, and along with this we
will help the Polish workers and peasants to liberate themselves from
their Polish and foreign oppressors.

Forward to the complete destruction of . . . Wrangel's bands!

Forward against the bourgeois-aristocratic despoilers of Poland!

Long live the Workers' and Peasants' Red Army! [53]

Lenin, it is obvious, considered Curzon's proposals to be part of
an Entente plot to gain a respite, in order at some later date to press
a fresh onslaught against the Soviet Republic. Facing the prospect
of an interminable struggle, which to the Russian populace would
mean ever-new and exhausting sacrifices, Lenin had decided to
gamble upon a swift destruction of the Entente forward base in
Poland.[54] Until the threat from Poland was eliminated, Wrangel
could not be properly dealt with. As long as there was war on any
front, there could be no release of men from military duty for the
work of rehabilitating Russia, no progress along the lines which
Lenin, above all, hoped for.

Having arrived at the decision to carry the war into Poland proper,
Lenin also had to think about the political problems that successful
military action, would bring to life. An enduring occupation of
Poland by Russians was out of the question. Such a policy would
inevitably recall the days of tsarist imperialism. With this bloody
record, particularly as it concerned Poland, Lenin, the "liberator of
the oppressed," naturally wanted no association.[55] If on the other
hand the conquest of Poland was to be followed by an early Red
Army withdrawal from Polish soil, an Entente-supported anti-Soviet
base might once again come into being. To this problem there was,
as Lenin saw it, but one solution. The Red Army would have to facilitate a social revolution in Poland. The domination of the landowners
and the bourgeoisie would have to be replaced by that of the peasants, and particularly by that of the "pro-Soviet" industrial proletariat.

When the question of crossing into Poland came up for discussion in the party councils, Trotsky opposed the move on the ground of "the weakness of [the Soviet] forces and resources." The march on Warsaw, Trotsky believed, "could end successfully only on condition of an immediate insurrection in Poland itself, and there was absolutely no assurance of that." [56] In his doubts as to the likelihood of a Polish insurrection, Trotsky was strongly supported by Dzerzhinsky, Markhlevsky, and Radek, all of them well acquainted with Polish conditions, who pointed out that the Polish masses, including the proletarians, would not greet the Russians as liberators but oppose them as conquerors.

Since early May, when Kiev had fallen, the Red Army's counteroffensive had moved some 700 kilometers northwestward against Polish resistance. Even anticipating a more difficult campaign once the Red Army left home soil, there was at least good reason to believe that it would be able to cut successfully through Poland. Had Lenin not taken this probability into consideration, he could hardly have wished to risk the venture. Yet in arguing for a drive into Poland, Lenin made no effort to base his case upon the reasonably strong likelihood of favorable military developments. He chose instead to construct his entire argument upon the most uncertain prospect of a Polish insurrection, and did this despite the fact that he himself knew nothing of conditions in Poland and that most of the expert advice he received indicated that there would be no insurrection.

Lenin's blueprint was drawn up around August 1 and was later presented to the Poles as the Soviet proposal for peace.[57] The plan depended for its realization upon the existence of a revolutionary situation in Poland. This made it necessary for Lenin to believe that the Polish lower classes would accept the Russian army as the spearhead of their revolution. So his hope became his conviction, but an uneasy conviction it was, as may be judged by the emotional display that accompanied his argumentation. He shouted down his opponents and went so far as to term Radek a defeatist. That Lenin felt guilty for having used so unnecessarily virulent an invective may be surmised from the apologetic manner in which, months after events had proved him wrong about Poland, he was still able to recall the injustice done to Radek.[58]

In sending the Red Army into Poland, Lenin's initial objective had been the defensive one of converting that country from an Entente base for intervention into a Bolshevik satellite or buffer area. But noting his army's lightning advance to the gates of Warsaw, Lenin must have been taken with the possibility that a victorious Communist army so near the borders of Entente-hating, Versailles-embittered Germany might serve to revive the Western revolutionary spirit.[59] Thus it is quite understandable that Lenin should not have wanted to limit his range of action with a doctrinarily moderate approach to the pace of Comintern building. If one way or another Europe's proletariat suddenly became reactivated, a much more radical policy of admissions would be called for. This would seem to account for the fact that Lenin, who in the early stages of the congress and of the Red advance into Poland had been reluctant to abandon the tactics of moderation toward the centrists, found it expedient as the Red Army neared Warsaw to adopt a position roughly identical with that insisted upon by the revolution-hungry Lefts at the congress.

During the entire period of the Russian advance, it should be noted, Lenin made no public mention of its possible effect upon revolution in Europe. At no time on the floor of the congress did he refer even obliquely to the march on Warsaw. Lenin's very silence with regard to so momentous a matter would seem to provide a useful key to his thoughts. He had conceived of the advance into Poland in mid-July, at a time when he was completely reconciled to a Europe unready for revolution. Though the phenomenal military success must have excited him, it could not have made him decide overnight to discard a timetable of revolution which he had arrived at as a result of previous disappointments and after a year's study of conditions in Europe. Lenin would hardly have seen fit to commit himself to a change of views until at least Warsaw had fallen and subsequent events in Europe had given him a firm basis for optimism. In the meantime, of course, he would still have wanted to prepare his ground for a new tactical line (that is, the changed conditions of admission), in case developments progressed much more favorably than originally anticipated.

At the congress Lenin never disdained to take the floor in defense of one or another point that he deemed important. But only at the fourth and fifth sessions, when the so-called national and colonial question was on the agenda, did he undertake to lead the discussion. Only these two sessions were not devoted to European matters, and they stand out in that the Russian-stated position received enthusiastic support from a large body of non-Soviet delegates, namely, the

Asiatics. Their admiration for the Soviet Union, the Soviet system, and most of Lenin's proposals contrasted markedly with the suspiciousness and hostility expressed by so many Europeans. The difference in attitude, it might be said, revealed clearly which group considered itself as giving to, and which as taking from, the Third International then in the process of taking shape.

Lenin's Theses on the National and Colonial Question [60] disclosed above all the world-centralistic notion of Soviet Russia's role at which he had arrived. Thesis 5 reads:

> The political situation of the world has placed upon the order of the day the dictatorship of the proletariat, and all events of world politics concentrate themselves inevitably about a single central point, namely, the struggle of the bourgeoisie of the entire world against the Soviet Republic, which groups about itself inevitably, on the one hand, the Soviet movements of the advanced workers of all countries, and on the other hand, all the national-liberationist movements of the colonies and the oppressed nationalities, who are convinced from bitter experience that they have no hope except in the victory of Soviet power over world imperialism.

The countries of the West, as Lenin saw it, were grouping themselves about the Soviet Republic in the sense that the various Communist parties were uniting through the medium of the Third International. But theses 6 to 8 reveal that Lenin was already thinking of an actual union between Soviet Russia and the Asiatic countries. The "required" Bolshevik precedent for the manner in which union was to take place, Lenin readily found in the pseudo federationist process which had since early 1919 been operative in regrouping the former tsarist empire into what was later to become the USSR.

"Federation," wrote Lenin in thesis 7, "is a transitional form to complete unity of the workers of different countries." Federation, he pointed out, had proved expedient in creating working relationships of the Russian Soviet Republic to other Soviet Republics past and present, such as those of Hungary, Finland, Latvia, Azerbaijan, and Ukraine, and also "within the Russian Soviet Republic, with regard to nationalities having previously had neither independence nor autonomy (as, for instance, the Bashkir and Tartar Autonomous Republics . . . created in 1919 and 1920)."

It was the task of the Comintern, Lenin stated in thesis 8, to work toward the formation of an ever more closely knit federal union on the road to complete coalescence of the workers of the world. He explained that such close union was necessary first, because Soviet republics could not exist in a hostile imperialist world except for "the closest of unions," and second, "that a close economic union of Soviet republics was vital to the rebuilding and development of the productive forces destroyed by imperialism and the securing of the welfare of the workers." Since his reference to the rebuilding of productive forces destroyed by imperialism made sense only with respect to Soviet Russia, Lenin was in effect saying that a revived Russia was essential to the success of his scheme. Lenin advanced a third argument for close union, stating that such union was in line with a tendency on the part of the proletariat of all nations, already observable under capitalism and subject to further development under socialism.

From the point of view of an Asiatic country, Lenin's explanations of its need for a close federal union to Soviet Russia could scarcely have been more devoid of meaning. All the more is it evident how important was this idea from Lenin's level of perspective. The superficial explanations of course served merely to cover up his true designs. Where Asia was concerned the federal idea had two great advantages to Lenin. In the West he could expect to assert control over any country in which a revolution succeeded, for that would mean that the Comintern-directed Communist party had taken power. But in Asia it was more than likely that social revolution in one or another country would precede the domination by the Communist party. Federation, then, even if brought about by conquest, would provide the "legal" means through which Lenin could seize control. The concept of federalism also carried with it a notion of equality among the nations in the federation. In time Bolshevik centralism was bound to destroy the last vestige of member independence. But in the meantime, as bait for his trap, the term "federation," which traditionally conveyed the idea of diversity within unity, would be most useful to Lenin.

According to the Theses, then, the first objective of the Third International was to help a rehabilitated Russia become the ruling center of a federated, actually unified, Asia. In line with this thought the Theses went on to point out that the first duty of the Western (particularly a British) Communist was not to aid the struggle of his own country's workers against its bourgeoisie, but to aid the colonial revolutionary movement in throwing off his country's imperialist mastery. Developing this point at the fourth session, Radek informed the English workers that if "instead of fighting bourgeois prejudices," they supported imperialism or took a passive position toward it, "then they would themselves be collaborating in the suppression of the entire revolutionary movement in England itself. The English proletariat cannot free itself from the yoke of capitalism if it does not support the colonial revolutionary movement. . . . The International will judge English Communists not by the articles they write in *Call* [newspaper of the British Socialist party] . . . but by the number of comrades thrown into jail for agitation in the colonies."

"In England," Radek continued chidingly, "it is now very easy to speak against Russian intervention [even the left bourgeoisie were doing this]. It is far more difficult for English workers to struggle for the independence of Ireland and for antimilitarism. We have the right to demand of English comrades the fulfillment of this difficult task." Going on to kill two birds with one stone, Radek proceeded to demonstrate that the antiparliamentarism of the English Shop Stewards was incorrect not only because it represented "infantile leftism" but because how else, except through parliamentary participation, might a peasant in India learn that the Shop Stewards were fighting against his enslavement. But if one of the Shop Stewards "would in Parliament come right to the point and call things by their proper names, the presiding officer of the House of Commons would of course force him out of the chamber. And the Reuters Agency would not fail to inform the entire world of the fact that there sat in the English Parliament a 'traitor' who called murder what it was—murder." [61]

As to the function of Communists in Asia, Lenin's Theses contained directives similar to the tactical proposals he had made in 1905 in anticipation of the Russian revolution. The task, as he saw it, was to utilize every revolutionary force at hand (bourgeois nationalists, peasants) against imperialism and its native supporters, but at the same time to make sure that ultimate control of the revolutionary movement remained in Communist hands. A significant addition to the 1905 tactic, important because it indicated that Lenin saw Asiatic countries as skipping a capitalist-nationalist stage, was the prescription that the Communists of Asia set up "Working People's Soviets." To Lenin, of course, Russia was an example and hence a model for Asia, of the manner in which an agrarian society could pass more or less directly from medievalism to socialism. But the acceptance of this precept was otherwise necessary for Lenin, in that Asia's anti-imperialist revolution was not so much an end in itself as a means through which he intended to overthrow Western capitalism. Not wishing to wait a lifetime until Asia became industrialized through capitalism and thereafter socialistic, he was interested primarily in gaining early political control over the masses of Asia and then proceeding to the conquest of the West. After that there would be ample time in which to industrialize Asia and to introduce socialism.

Lenin could not admit that his main reason for desiring Soviets in Asia was to enable him to establish early control over the Asiatic masses. On the other hand, to advocate what he had so often termed the inevitable organizational structure for Western socialism as applicable to peasant Asia, might make it appear, as was the truth, that the Soviet form was actually more at home in a peasant country than it would be in the West. To do this would be the same as admitting that the success of this form in Russia was due to the fact that it had risen not from a proletarian but from a peasant background. Commenting on this matter before the congress, Lenin got around his dilemma by asking rather pompously whether the Soviet idea, developed in the capitalistic world, by which he meant Russia, could be applied to precapitalistic conditions. The answer, Lenin declared, was yes. "The idea of the Soviet organization," he stated, "is simple and can be applied not only to proletarian but also to peasant-feudal and semifeudal conditions." The point that the very simplicity of the Soviet system which made it applicable to Russia and, as he correctly foresaw, to Asia, might make it unsuitable in the West, Lenin did not bother to develop.

On the subject of just how the Asiatic countries might be led to bypass the capitalist phase of their development, Lenin modestly professed ignorance. "What means are necessary for this [skipping of capitalism]," he declared, "is not indicated in advance. Practical experience will show us the way." [62] In fact, Lenin already had the practical experience, as in Russia. But not wishing to link the Russian experience too closely to that of the precapitalistic countries, he professed inexperience. His real inexperience was in relation to the West. But where the West was concerned, he invariably claimed to know all that there was to know.

A set of theses, additional to those of Lenin, were drawn up by

Roy of India and presented to the congress on July 26. Roy used Lenin's dictum that Western revolution, because of the link between labor aristocracy and colonial superprofits, depended for success upon the ousting of imperialism from Asia. Therefrom he drew the conclusion that the Asian masses (he particularly lauded the political awareness of the Indian proletariat) constituted the vanguard of the world revolution.[63] Roy's position came as a nuisance to Lenin, who was interested only in promoting the idea of Russia's world leadership function. In the course of a committee discussion before July 26, Lenin had charged Roy "with going too far," and, acting the part of the man from "advanced" Russia, scoffed at the low political level of the Indian working classes.[64]

Bargaining between Roy and Lenin led to changes in both their theses as finally accepted by the congress.[65] Lenin held the whip and Roy gave up most of his stress upon Asia's claim to world revolutionary leadership. Lenin, in his turn, changed his description of the Asiatic revolutionary movement from "bourgeois-democratic" to "national-revolutionary," a label suggesting a higher level of revolutionary consciousness. But Lenin, it is clear, did this merely to soothe the feelings of his antagonist.[66]

In accordance with the line laid down in *Left Wing Communism*, thesis 9 of the original nineteen conditions for admission to the Comintern, had stipulated that each party wishing to belong to the Comintern was obliged to join already established unions and bore from within in order gradually to "conquer the trade unions for the cause of communism." [67] In the committee on the trade union question American and British delegates expressed strong opposition to the adoption of this tactic. The American argument in general ran along the following lines. Of the American labor force, 80 per cent was entirely outside the trade union movement. The 20 per cent within the AF of L consisted of skilled workers, all of whom were anxious to retain their privileged status. Also the strongly entrenched bureaucracy of the AF of L was beyond effective challenge and would not in any case have permitted revolutionary agitation within the organization.[68] As the Americans saw it, therefore, the most sensible approach to the problem was to organize the unorganized with the aim of setting up a union organization in competition with the AF of L.[69]

In Britain most of the industrial labor force had been organized for decades and was linked to the British Labour party. The well-established union bureaucracies and the Labour party stood for the acceptance of the bourgeois order. The British Shop Stewards had organized themselves precisely in order to draw the workers out of the conformist organizations and into revolutionary channels [70] and were therefore opposed to joining the existing unions. They too made reference to the all-powerful reactionary bureaucracies,[71] and, as previously mentioned, loathed the idea of joining the Labour party. Like the Americans, they would have preferred to establish new working class organizations on syndicalist principles.[72]

Committee discussions led to concessions on both sides. The Russians admitted that Americans might in some circumstances find it necessary to form new unions, but insisted that it was nonetheless their task to win over the AF of L, the nature of which had changed during the war as a result of an influx of new and more radical-minded elements.[73] To the Shop Stewards the Russians conceded the importance of maintaining organizations independent of the unions, but only within the general union framework and for the purpose of leading the workers against the reactionary leadership. The Americans and British in their turn agreed to join the existing unions. Their aim, however, would not be that of gradually winning over the membership but of destroying the unions. "The American and English delegates," as John Reed put it, "are trying to bring a new spirit into the old unions. . . . Communists must transform unions or remain in isolation . . . and become a staff without an army, for the soldiers of this army will be outside the leadership's sphere of influence."[74] The question of how to carry on the struggle within the unions became an impasse.[75] The Russians serving on the committee must have been aware of this state of affairs. But whether for lack of time, since the congress was drawing to a close, or simply because they realized that no fundamental accord was possible, Radek and Lozovsky did all in their power to prevent a thorough airing of the problem. On August 3, in any event, the trade union matter was presented to the congress as though essential agreement had been attained by the committee. Parts one and two of the three-part resolution on trade unions [76] thoroughly reflected Lenin's ideas as against the positions taken by the American and English delegates. The resolution having been read, the Russians flooded the congress with oratory, then called for a closing of discussion and an immediate vote on the resolution as drafted. John

Reed, however, insisted he be heard, and the British and others backed him up. Reed charged the Russians with trying deliberately "to shut out the English and American delegations." In the committee sessions, he recalled, Radek had abstained from discussing the union question on the ground that there were basic disagreements. "But today he says there are no disagreements." This, declared Reed, was proof that a discussion was necessary "even if it took all night, . . . for the matter has, in essence, not yet been discussed."

Radek thereupon inferred that Reed was a liar, tried in general to brush aside Reed's criticism, and made much of the shortage of time. "It seems strange," remarked MacAlpin of Ireland, "that we are so economical about time here, although it is not known that one especially values time in Russia." "One does not want to give us time to discuss the theses," Gallacher added bluntly. "We English-speaking comrades have the impression that one is simply trying to evade discussion. We want discussions continued, and we want Reed to have the chance to state his views." Zinoviev then raised objections to further discussions, maintaining that all the delegates had had plenty of time to air their opinions.

"I insist that we get the floor . . . ," exclaimed Tanner. "In the committee we were promised that the question would be thoroughly discussed since it is one of the most important questions. The theses, the amendments, the proposals were not translated and the members of the committee hardly had a chance to come to know them. You took two and a half days to discuss the question of accepting the French Socialist party and the USPD. This question, which is more important, should therefore be more fully dealt with." [77]

Vigorous though the American-British argumentation, it availed only to prolong the discussion which was resumed August 5. In the end, of course, Lenin's wishes prevailed by the usual preponderant majority.

Part three of the resolution required all Communist cells within the unions to link themselves to a so-called Red Trade Union International. The establishment of this organization had been provided for at the outset of the congress by the setting up under Lenin's sponsorship of an International Council of Trade Unions headed by Lozovsky. [78] Profintern, as the Red Union International came to be called, was to be subordinated to the Comintern and was intended to provide a center through which organized labor would be able to combat the "pernicious" influence of the International

Federation of Trade Unions. In April, 1920, as Lenin was writing
Left Wing Communism, the IFTU had linked itself to the International Labor Organization of the "anti-Bolshevik" League of Nations
and had thus, as Lenin feared, become a counterpart to the defunct
Second International as an agency of betrayers through which
bourgeois poisonings might be transmitted into the minds of Europe's
proletarians.

It was almost an absurdity to expect Communist unionists to
join an avowedly Comintern-controlled organization and, working
within the old unions, win them gradually to communism. Lenin
obviously considered as essential to his aims both the gradualistic
tactic and the Red center of guidance. Thus he simply refused to
recognize the probability that the bureaucracies of the established
unions would eject the Communists, as happened in France, Germany, and elsewhere, and that this in turn would cause the very
splitting of unions that sections one and two of the resolution were
designed to prevent.

The evening session of August 4 was devoted to a discussion of
Lenin's draft of the statutes of the International. According to
paragraph 8 of the draft, the "major work of the Executive Committee of the Comintern [was to fall] upon the party of that country
in which, upon the decision of the World Congress, the Executive
Committee [would have] its seat." The country so chosen was to
have "no less than five" members, that is, an unlimited number, in
the Executive Committee. Ten other countries were each to delegate
a single permanent member to the committee.[79]

"In reality," declared Wijnkoop, "we are not building an International Executive Committee but only an extended Russian Executive Committee." Wijnkoop did not object to this if it was necessary
and he conceded the possibility that there might be no alternative.
"But," as he remarked, "let us then say that this is a Russian Executive Committee and not pretend that we are getting an International
Executive Committee." Wijnkoop raised this point, as he said, only
because he feared that Russia's blockade-isolation would continue.
Therefore ten of the best people of the international revolutionary
movement, sent to serve in the Executive Committee, would lose
contact with their home countries and receive information only
from the Russians. "[In committee]," said Wijnkoop, "I suggested
that the Executive Committee be located outside Russia, . . . in

Italy or Norway. . . . Levi proposed Germany. . . . This is a very important matter because we are giving this . . . committee enormous power [permitting it] even to excommunicate entire parties, groups, and individuals. It can do this only if it knows exactly what the situation in each country is." [80]

Concurring with Wijnkoop in the opinion that Western revolutionary leaders would after a time in Moscow lose contact with their own countries, Levi, of the German Communist party, also took pains to weaken the note of distrust sounded by the Hollander. It was not, he said, that a delegate would be "obliged exclusively to use Russian-provided information but that once in Russia he would have at his disposal only such sources of information as were also available to the Russians." Levi did not agree with Radek, who had said that the same handicap would exist in any other country. Elsewhere, he pointed out, it would not take ten days for letters and newspapers to get through and such delays "would undoubtedly" cause "great difficulties." To overcome the inadequacy of contact, Levi suggested that a plenary conference of the International be held every three months. Criticizing the "not less than five" phrase in paragraph 8, Levi also attacked paragraph 12 of the statutes, which demanded that Communists create illegal organizations alongside their legal organizations. This point, he declared, had been sufficiently stressed in other Comintern resolutions and "many parties who were about to enter the International would find it helpful if these illegal organizations were left unmentioned." [81]

Zinoviev did not attempt to refute these objections head on but attacked them in a roundabout way. "Neither in paragraph 8 nor anywhere in the statutes," he declared, "is there a single word about Russia. [This was hardly necessary under prevailing conditions.] The statutes do say that the congress determines the location of the Executive Committee. If the proletarian revolution wins out in France or England, we shall of course agree to a transfer of the Executive Committee into one of those countries." Zinoviev agreed that "not less than five comrades" should be replaced in the statutes by the phrase "five comrades." [82] This concession removed from the statutes the most transparent of Lenin's devices for maintaining a firm hold on the reins of the International. In all other respects Zinoviev argued slyly in defense of the original draft. Recalling the long years that Bolsheviks had spent in exile without losing contact with Russia, Zinoviev refused to acknowledge that persons sent to a Russian-located Executive Committee would fail to retain touch with their organizations. He went on to oppose Levi's proposal for a plenary conference to meet every three months on the ground that the Executive Committee would have to be able to act independently and swiftly.[83] He failed to mention that the committee might desire to act arbitrarily and without constant interference from Europe.

Zinoviev insisted upon the necessity of illegal organizations. Even in the "so-called classical countries of bourgeois freedom, such as England and America," he said, Communists were being arrested by the thousands. "The German experience also supported [the] position" favoring illegal organizations, as, Zinoviev said, did the latest developments in Bulgaria.[84] Levi had not disputed the need for illegal organizations but merely, for safety's sake, their mention in the statutes. Apparently, then, there was fear that the failure to include the point of illegal party centers in the statutes might later become a pretext for allowing the concept to atrophy. But the illegal centers, since they would lend themselves much more easily to international centralization, were vital to Lenin, who in any event wanted no variations from his tactics, risen by this time to the level of sacred doctrine.

Most revealing as to the sort of Executive Committee Lenin wished to create was the selection of the countries (the final draft of the statutes called for ten to thirteen), the parties of which were each to send one delegate. Yugoslavia and Bulgaria were included but Holland was omitted. Radek's explanation to Wijnkoop of the reason for this omission makes sense enough in absolute terms. The Dutch Communist party, though worthy, was small and "played no outstanding role in international politics." But to one who reads the protocols of the Second Congress, the exclusion of Holland can only seem to have been deliberate. Time and again Wijnkoop had raised arguments which in their outspokenness had proved obstructive to the successful achievement of Lenin's aims. "This is not the first time in this congress," Radek told the bitterly challenging Wijnkoop, "that it has been necessary for me to exchange very unflattering expressions with the Dutch colleagues." [85] Lenin wanted an Executive Committee made up of smoothly functioning rubber stamps. Troublemakers of Wijnkoop's sort would hardly have been welcome in such company.

13

THE COURSE IS SET

LENIN'S IDEAS ON WORLD REVOLUTION, as expressed at the Second Congress of the Comintern, remained with him for his few remaining years. The Red Army's drive on Warsaw petered out in August, 1920, and it became the Polish turn to advance. Soon thereafter Lenin insisted that the Soviet government sue for peace. Almost all the Soviet experts disagreed with him. They argued that Russia, better equipped than Poland to continue the war, could, by holding out a bit longer, gain better peace terms and might even emerge as the victor.[1] Lenin's view prevailed and Russia signed the unfavorable Treaty of Riga on March 18, 1921.

Lenin subsequently explained that his motives for making the peace had been predicated upon the need to improve relations with Poland and to gain a free hand for crushing the sole remaining White threat as represented by Wrangel's forces in South Russia. He had, so he further explained, wished to advertise Soviet Russia as a peace-loving country, desirous neither of subjugating foreign territory nor of engaging in imperialistic ventures. As the main reason for the hasty peace, Lenin offered his reluctance "except in direst need" to permit "[our] heroic . . . workers and peasants . . . from [whom] all [had been] taken and nothing given," to endure further sufferings. The thought of another winter campaign, Lenin remarked, had been to him "unbearable." [2]

In October, 1918, Lenin had not been so solicitous about the welfare of the Russian people. On the eve of the German revolution he had pronounced the Russian masses "ready for all sacrifices in the defense of socialism" and able to "fight and die more unselfishly when the stakes [were] not Russian alone but also those of the international workers' revolution." [3] Lenin's new-found compassion for the Russian people was clearly a reflection of his changed conception of Russia's value in his scheme of the future. Before the

Notes begin on page 241.

autumn of 1919 he had considered the Russian people to be a mere auxiliary force in the attainment of Europe's revolution. Thereafter, and especially after Kolchak and Denikin had been defeated, Lenin saw the Russian masses as the force that would convert Russia into the model for the Asiatic revolution.

Russia by the beginning of 1920 had barely survived the hard years of war and revolution. In the months before the Polish invasion Lenin had been obsessed with the idea of swiftly restoring Russia's economy whatever the cost in popular sweat and toil. Instead of allowing the people a well-earned breathing spell, he employed, to the end of achieving speedy rehabilitation, the same measures of discipline as had been used in the time of "war communism."[4] Trotsky, having spent the winter months of 1920 in the Urals region, realized that Russia was on the brink of economic disintegration unless "war communism [was] abandoned" and "the element of personal interest [was] introduced" and "the home market [was] in some degree [restored]."[5]

In February, 1920, Trotsky submitted a proposal to the Central Committee, which contained the idea of taxing the peasants "in kind," thus providing them with a personal incentive.[6] Because Lenin "came out firmly" against Trotsky's proposal it was rejected by the Central Committee.[7] At the same time Lenin circulated a letter of instruction to the organizations of the party, which were then preparing to send delegates to the Ninth Party Congress. The letter declared that the main concern of the coming congress was to be "internal restoration, . . . for the main question of the whole Soviet construction in Russia (inasmuch as Russia has become the shepherd of the international revolution, this is to a large extent also a question of international communism) is the transition from bloody war to unbloody war."[8] The rehabilitation of Russia was, in short, to be carried out as a war, and there was, in Lenin's view, to be no diminution of popular effort or sacrifice.[9] But Lenin reckoned without the recalcitrance of the peasants. The latter had submitted to tremendous pressures in the civil war period because they had feared a victory of the Whites. But the peasants, once the Whites were defeated, saw no reason to continue enduring the Bolshevik squeeze. Throughout 1920 Lenin's program was confronted by ever-mounting peasant resistance and Lenin was forced to retreat. His New Economic Policy, or NEP, as adopted by the Tenth Party Congress in March, 1921, was in every essence the plan Trotsky had earlier devised.

Among Lenin's aims at the Second Congress of the Comintern had been that of establishing Communist parties which, while divorcing themselves from the personalities most obviously associated with reformism, would at the same time retain contact with reformist-oriented organizations, that is, socialist parties and trade unions. The course of events at the Second Congress had, however, led to a more rigid formulation of the conditions for admission to the Comintern than Lenin had wished. Also counter to his intentions had been the creation of a Comintern policy that was bound to result in a splitting of the trade unions. Even so, except for the fact that it was Zinoviev, not Lenin, who was in direct command of the Comintern, the decisions of the Second Congress need not have affected the socialist movement of Western Europe in a manner too greatly at variance with Lenin's designs. But Zinoviev, unlike Lenin, had never ceased to believe that an early eruption of revolutionism was likely in the West,[10] and it was in that expectation that he employed the directives of the Second Congress.

The USPD became Zinoviev's initial target, and he started his campaign with an "open letter" in the Comintern journal, which attacked the anti-Comintern leaders of the USPD. In October, Zinoviev, along with Lozovsky, attended that party's Halle congress. As in France and in England, where Lozovsky's propaganda and organizational activities in behalf of Profintern were to arouse strongly antagonistic trade unionist reactions, so at Halle did his speech attacking the Amsterdam International meet with unrestrained hostility. Zinoviev's four-hour address, on the other hand, achieved the brilliant success of splitting the USPD. The majority faction joined with the KPD to form the United German Communist party, or VKPD, having a total membership of 35,000. The KAPD, the tiny left Communist party of Germany, remained apart from the newly formed combination. At the Tours congress in December, 1920, the majority of the French Socialist party, opposing the centrist and rightist elements, voted in favor of adhering to the Comintern and organized itself as the Communist party of France. Although this must be regarded as a victory for Lenin, the shock waves set off by Zinoviev at Halle were on the whole damaging to Lenin's aims.

At the Second Congress of the Comintern, Levi, leader of the German Communists, had expressed his opposition to a Russian-controlled Executive Committee and had proposed Germany as a country suitable for the committee's seat. It is therefore understandable that Levi was piqued over Zinoviev's assumption at Halle of control over the German Communist party. Levi's personal resentment toward the Moscow "Turkestanians" mounted higher as the Central Committee of the suddenly enlarged German party came to include young and vigorous challengers for the leadership posts. The young ones, more generally rooted in the proletariat than was the old-guard leadership of Levi, Klara Zetkin, and others, were for that reason more inclined to activism.

Also voicing opposition to Lenin at the Second Congress had been Serrati. The latter, reflecting the relatively centrist mood of the Italian socialist movement, had evoked Lenin's anger by defending Turati. In the fall of 1920 the Italian revolutionary movement suffered its great fiasco and within the Italian Socialist party there rose an ever-increasing feeling of resentment against the attempts of the Comintern to dictate Italian revolutionary policy. In January, 1921, the Italian Socialist party held a congress at Leghorn in order to discuss the question of adherence to the Comintern on the basis of the twenty-one conditions. Zinoviev and Bukharin, having been denied visas for the journey to Italy—Zinoviev later complained that Serrati had exerted no effort to have the visas granted [11]—the Executive Committee sent Rakosi of Hungary and Kabakchiev, a Bulgarian, to represent the Comintern. At Leghorn the Comintern delegates proposed that Turati and the right-wingers be ousted from the ranks of the Socialist party. That proposal was rejected by Serrati's majority centrist faction, which generally displayed great malice toward the Comintern. Serrati charged that the Comintern Executive Committee was sending Russian-picked "gray cardinals" to various countries and that these made it their business to report back to IKKI (Executive Committee of the Comintern) without first consulting with national party leaders.[12] Kabakchiev, in particular, was subjected to waves of acrimony. The Bulgarian was termed a "wild dictator," and when he took the floor he was greeted with shouts of "Long live the Pope!" One prankster even turned loose a pigeon.[13] The outcome of the Leghorn Congress was the splitting off from the Socialist party of a minority Communist party headed by Bordiga. Serrati's stand, which had brought this result about, had been backed by Zetkin and Levi, the latter having come to Leghorn as a delegate from the VKPD. At the congress Rakosi had specifically requested Levi to support the position of the IKKI, but Levi had coldly turned down the request and had returned to Germany before the congress had concluded.[14]

The next stop of the two Comintern delegates was Berlin. There, before a congress of German party leaders, they, along with the Italian Terracini, bitterly denounced Levi's betrayal of the Comintern. "The comrades," in Terracini's words, "Brandler, particularly, were outraged because Levi had misinformed them [by reporting] that the real Communist masses in Italy stood behind Serrati, [and that those who called themselves Communists were] really syndicalists, anarchists, and so forth." [15] In their efforts to gain control over the German party and lead it onto the activist road, the upward-pressing lesser lights of the VKPD were able to use the charges hurled against Levi and Zetkin to good advantage. Levi was censured by the party and resigned from its Central Committee.

The lid of moderation having been removed, a few sparks were sufficient to set off the explosive mixture in the party's cauldron. Some such sparks were provided by severe anti-Communist provocation on the part of the German police. Further incendiary effects were produced by Béla Kun, another Zinoviev disciple, who arrived in Berlin early in March. Beset by panicky fears rising from the recent revolt of the Red sailors at the Kronstadt naval base and from his belief that there impended a renewed capitalist anti-Soviet onslaught, he urged the German Communists to go on the offensive. The result was the March Action, a poorly planned uprising in central Germany, which, culminating in a humiliating defeat, cost the party a great loss of prestige among the workers.

Levi soon thereafter published a pamphlet castigating his party for its foolhardy course of conduct.[16] The party expelled Levi on April 29, and he thereupon joined the Social Democrats. Klara Zetkin, the leader of an opposition group within the party's Central Committee, had also gone on record as a critic of the March Action and the "hastily thrown together 'theory of the offensive.'" [17] When she resigned from the Central Committee, the VKPD stigmatized her a "rightist" and an "opportunist." In Moscow, on the eve of the Third Congress of the Comintern, Zetkin sought out Lenin in order to unburden her soul and obtain justification for her behavior.[18] Speaking to the leader, she did not "conceal her alarm over the danger that would threaten the German party and the Comintern in the event that the [Third] World Congress was to take its stand upon the 'theory of the offensive.'"

Lenin laughingly reassured Zetkin, saying that the congress would provide "no special triumph to the 'theoreticians of the offensive.' We [Russians] are still here." Lenin characterized the "theory of the offensive" as a romantic product "adopted in the land of 'thinkers and poets' with the help of Béla Kun, who also belongs to a poetry-loving nation." Then, as though to contrast Russian lucidity with Western muddleheadedness, Lenin cautioned against "writing and dreaming":

> If we wish to win, we must soberly evaluate . . . world economics and world politics. . . . The first wave of world revolution has spent itself—the second has not yet risen. It would be dangerous if we were to cherish illusions about that. . . . The decisions of the congress on the question of the tactic of the Comintern and all questions connected with it must find themselves in agreement with our Theses on the world economic situation. . . . In any case, the Russian revolution can teach more than the German "March Action."

Lenin went on to describe the March Action as a setback for the revolutionary proletariat and an attack badly planned and organized. But clearly anxious to prevent further schisms in the German party, he refused to take a stand wholly against the "offensivists." He promised Zetkin that the congress would in the main support her basic political line, and that this would impede a repetition of the March Action. At the same time, while "wringing the neck of the famous 'theory of the offensive' [the congress would] have to give its proponents some crumbs of consolation and treat the error with 'fatherly' forbearance," lest "our dear Lefts" become "unduly provoked and return home [with] bitter feelings."

Zetkin herself was berated by Lenin for her "capital stupidity" in resigning from the Central Committee. "Did you lose your senses?" he asked. "I was upset by that, extremely upset. How could you act so recklessly . . . without letting us know about it, without asking our opinions?" Even though her reasons for resigning had been sound, she had, Lenin pointed out, "received a mandate in the Central Committee not from a group of comrades but from the party as a whole. [Therefore she] did not have the right to decline the confidence placed in [her]." For the defection of Paul Levi, whom Zetkin defended, Lenin had harsh words. He criticized Levi as a vain and egotistic person who wished to remain aloof from the workers and as one whose pamphlet "brutally cut the party to pieces." But Lenin was willing to forgive this prodigal son. The congress, said Lenin, would have to judge Levi sternly. But he would be judged not for his basic political view, which was "admittedly the correct one," but for his violation of party discipline. "Thus to Paul Levi the road to return to our ranks is wide open." Lacking a surplus of talented men, said Lenin, it was important for the cause as well as for his own sake that Levi not be lost. As proper penance for his sins, Levi might for a time drop out of political life, write anonymously for the party press and publish some good pamphlets. "After three or four months," said Lenin, "I will demand his vindication in an open letter." [19]

Zetkin's interview with Lenin provides valuable insights into Lenin's conception of himself as the high priest of the Comintern and the supreme arbiter over each nation's party and each party's individual member. In the sense too that it reveals Lenin's unqualified determination to keep the policies of the Comintern in the channels of moderation, the interview also anticipated the drift of events as they transpired at the Third Congress of the Comintern, which sat in Moscow from June 22 to July 12, 1921.

The "Theses on Tactics," drawn up by the Russians and adopted at the final session of the congress, devoted a special section to "Lessons of the March Action." In this the March Action was pronounced a mistake, in that the German party had characterized a defensive move as an offensive one. The enemy had thereby been given the opportunity to label the party a "putschist" organization. At the same time a sop was thrown to the VKPD. The Executive Committee of the Comintern hailed the March Action as a step forward, in that the VKPD had courageously placed itself at the head of the movement, thus proving itself the real party of Germany. In the future, the Theses advised, the party should devise slogans better fitting the occasion and should also be more careful in the matter of preparing for action. The Theses announced Levi's expulsion from the party, not for having been wrong in opposing the March Action, but entirely on the ground of his breach of discipline, for once a policy decision had been made, no comrade had the right to oppose it. Criticism was permissible, but only after the decision had gone into effect and then only within the party circles and press, and always with regard that such criticism did the party no damage.

The major portion of the Theses was devoted to tactics in general. World revolution, though still inevitably in the offing, would come, the Theses said, only after a long struggle—a struggle made more

difficult because of the counterrevolutionary influence exerted by
strong workers' organizations such as social democratic parties and
trade unions. The major task confronting Communists was therefore
that of winning influence over the masses. The Theses reiterated
the theme of the Second Congress of the Comintern—the need to
enter parliaments and unions—and went so far as to suggest a policy
that foreshadowed the subsequent Communist attempts to establish
temporary liaisons with existing socialist groups. The term "united
front," however, was not yet used. The Theses carefully explained
the essential difference between Communists and Social Democrats,
the latter being willing to compromise with capitalism, whereas
Communists steadfastly sought the overthrow of the bourgeoisie.
Although the Communists had no minimal program, they were to
make temporary demands that would draw people into the movement. "It is the task of the Communist parties," the Theses declared,
"to broaden, deepen . . . the developing struggles by the use of
slogans making concrete demands. . . . It is not enough merely to
shout out final goals [dictatorship of the proletariat] to the people—
one must also involve the masses in the struggle that leads to the
final goal." As an immediate tactic, the Theses suggested approaching the unemployed, whom the Social Democrats avoided. Communist parties must use the unemployed as "a gigantic factor of
revolutionary significance."

Under the heading "Preparation for the Struggle," the Theses
pointed out that Communists

> are always preparing, always trying to wake the masses. Where Social-
> ists in general will also enter upon a struggle over a certain issue,
> Communists will always indicate the possible treason of the other
> group. At the same time they will seek to sharpen the struggle and
> drive it as far as possible in order eventually to be able to carry the
> battle forward, even without help from erstwhile allies.[20]

In hammering out the tactical and organizational doctrines requi-
site for his conception of the Third International at the Second
Congress, Lenin had been compelled to wage bitter ideological
battles with the Left. At the Third Congress, however, the basic
structure of the Comintern and its tactical orientation had already
been determined. Most of those who attended acknowledged by
their presence alone that they were under discipline. There was
much argumentation and many a bitter word was spoken. But the

squabbling was like that within a large family. Most of it arose around tactical issues, and since there was no danger of a basic falling out, the Russian masters of the occasion could afford to be tolerant of criticism. As against the frequent gagging of discussion that took place at the Second Congress, only one attempt to do this occurred at the Third Congress. The fear of factionalism, and all that entailed, troubled Lenin so little that the KAPD, the so-called left Communists of Germany, had, much to the discomfiture of the VKPD, been invited to attend the congress as a sympathizing group. Given the opportunity to air their views, the KAPD delegates, among other things, criticized Lenin's injection into the Comintern of Russian-based opportunism.[21] They also took issue with the concept of the mass party as defiling to the Communist movement; declaring it essential that Communist parties remain pure. They admitted the impossibility of immediate revolutionary action, but stressed the need for purely propagandistic activity. This view the Russians refuted offhand as a counterrevolutionary and Menshevik deviation.[22]

At the time of the Second Congress, the militant-mindedness of the Western delegates and the Red Army's successes in Poland had made it impossible for Lenin to state too explicitly his case against armed revolutionary action. In the year following, great strike movements had been easily crushed in England and Czechoslovakia, and the March Action had left the German Communists licking their wounds. In Italy too, land of the greatest revolutionary promise, the proletarian movement had fizzled out. Soviet Russia, far from sending its armies westward, as in the case of the Polish campaign, had retreated into semicapitalism and had even concluded a trade agreement with Britain. The revolutionary struggle had clearly entered upon a period of quiescence. By the time of the Third Congress, then, the problem of leftism, as seen by Lenin, had dwindled in scope to the matter of preventing premature activism. Those therefore who voiced Lenin's views spoke out mainly against that danger and, in a manner of elders cautioning children about fireworks, stressed the theme of revolutionary moderation.[23]

The VKPD gave vent to its resentment over the fact that its heroically conceived March Action was adjudged an infantile stupidity, that Levi was expelled for breach of discipline but not for having erred, and that Zetkin and her opposition group were reaping most of the plaudits of the congress decision. Toward the VKPD delegates and some others who charged the Russians with having charted a rightist course, the Russians adopted a paternalistic tone. Lenin himself spoke little, being content to outline his general stand and to justify the NEP retreat on the grounds of the momentary equilibrium and the dire needs of a backward Russia in an "extreme state of ruin" after "seven years of . . . war." [24] In reply to Terracini, who made much of the victory of the small Bolshevik party in Russia, Lenin asked whether any other party in Europe had on its side its country's peasantry and half the army. Then, as though bored with the childishness of the leftists, he declared that Communists had been too long concerned with centrists. The Left, he said, seemed preoccupied with the initial anticentrist phase of party building. The second phase, he pointed out, was that of building the mass party, and he suggested that Communists proceed to that phase and stop worrying so much about the centrists.[25]

Thalheimer of the VKPD insisted that Lenin's Theses be corrected leftward. There was, he declared, *"no serious leftist danger in the International.* Comrade Lenin has stated that we have taken care of the Right, that there is no longer sport in the fight against the Right, and that it is time to start a new chapter. Unfortunately we are not yet done with the Right. Not even in the Russian party have we reached that stage." Thus by implication did Thalheimer attack the NEP's concessions to capitalism.[26]

Zinoviev, and particularly Trotsky and Radek, took turns in restating Lenin's line with regard to international tactics and took some trouble, as through superciliously explaining the obvious, to show that the Russian view was not more Right than Left. Zinoviev, whose own leftism had been temporarily subdued by the pressure of events, went so far as to admit that the Right was the enemy and that the leftists, being idealists capable of revolutionary self sacrifice, were essentially on the correct road. But that, he declared, was exactly why every error of the Left could be dangerous and why, for the greater cause, it had to be combated. "Don't," he asked, "weigh our feelings on a precision scale [and say] 'you spoke fifteen minutes against the Left, but only five minutes against the Right, ergo you are swaying rightward.' A half second suffices to say that the Rights are agents of the bourgeoisie—the study of errors of immaturity takes more time." [27]

Trotsky and Radek scoffed at the charge of Russian rightism and, counterattacking, made it quite clear where the center of authority rested.

"The Theses against which Thälmann [of the VKPD] complains," said Trotsky, "were not dictated by the Russians without consultation with others. These Theses represent long discussions and a compromise arrangement—from our point of view a compromise toward the left. . . . I want to emphasize that we regard these Theses as the maximal concessions to the [left] tendency which is being defended by so many comrades, including Thälmann." [28] Vigorously attacking the attempts of the VKPD, who wished to change the Theses into a document proving the March Action to have been a complete success, Trotsky conceded that the March Action had represented a step forward in the sense that it had demonstrated Communist independence from the USPD. "But," he went on, "it [had] nonetheless [been] a mistake, and we are not going to let the German Central Committee deceive itself and the German workers into believing otherwise." The congress, Trotsky declared, making a concession to the idea of democracy, might vote against the Russians on this point.

> And were we now to hurl Paul Levi out of the window and speaking of the March Action—say, rather confusedly, that it was the first attempt, a step forward—were we in short to camouflage our criticism through phraseology, then we should not have done our duty. We have the duty to tell the German workers with absolute clarity that we regard the offensive philosophy as the greatest danger, and that we regard it, when carried into practice, as the greatest political crime. [29]

The tactic of caution, Trotsky insisted, was not to be confused with being rightist. "The greatest danger lies in the fact that some comrades, being inexperienced in politics and in revolutionary matters, do not even understand the reality of danger. Our final task is not to pass judgment on the opportunists but to overthrow capitalism." [30]

Radek, defending the Theses against proposals for amendment, declared that it was wrong to take from Lenin's words the thought "*Roma locuta causa finita*—the Russian delegation has spoken its opinions and the matter is settled. It is not so intended." Like Trotsky, Radek insisted that the Theses came out of compromise, most of the concessions having gone to the Left. Said Radek:

> You have surely sensed that before the congress we have fought mostly against the Right. But it is not opportunism when I now say—I have seen signs of danger from the Left and one must also carry the battle against the Left. . . . In the commission we shall test whether the

amendment proposals are merely new formulations or whether they
are designed to change the basic lines [of the Theses]. The Russian
delegation will not accede to changes in the political line. This does
not mean that you can't change things. You can outvote us.[31]

Both Trotsky and Radek knew full well that the outcome of any
vote was determined in advance by the Russian position. When it
came to the vote, the Theses as originally proposed, were accepted
by unanimous decision.

Although far less conspicuous than his Europe-oriented policies,
Lenin's actions and attitudes with regard to the peoples of the East
also remained consistent with his long-range aims as formulated in
1919 and 1920. The Asians under Russian control became handy
mannequins for purposes of political display.

In 1920, in the predominantly Moslem Volga-Urals region of the
Russian Soviet Republic, Lenin was to engineer the formation of
the Bashkir and Tatar Autonomous Soviet Socialist Republics and
the Chuvash, Mari, and Votyak Autonomous Regions. The ethnic
distinctiveness of these new administrative units was of particular
importance to Lenin, since he expected through them to convey to
the East the liberal manner in which the Soviet Republic applied
the principle of national equality.

The decree on Bashkir autonomy, published in May, 1920, without
prior notice to the Bashkir leaders, in fact bound Bashkiria to Russia
more tightly than had been the case under the tsar. The Bashkir
Revolutionary Committee, considering itself duped by Moscow,
denounced "the imperialistic tendencies of the Russians, which
hinder in every manner the development of the national minorities."
A subsequent Bashkir uprising then had to be crushed by military
force. In July, when this war was going through its most brutal
stages, Lenin, at the Second Congress of the Third International,
unabashedly referred to Bashkiria as a happy example of the way
in which Soviet national groups could be brought into unity on
federal principles. The First Bashkir Congress of Soviets convened
in the fall of 1920 to elect a government. All the Bashkir delegates
to this congress were arrested as "nationalists" and the first government of the Bashkir Autonomous Republic was made up of Russians
and Tatars only. Lenin enforced political division along ethnic lines
even when this went against the desire of the natives. So the
Chuvash, who would have preferred to exist in a union with the

Tatars, were simply instructed to organize their territory into the Chuvash Autonomous Region, and this was done on June 24. The Mari and Votyak Autonomous Regions were decreed and constituted about six months later.[32]

A process generally similar to that which transpired in the Volga-Urals region also took place in the Kirgiz-Kazakh steppe region. In October, 1920, an Autonomous Kirgiz Republic was proclaimed, and its façade of freedom even displayed a government containing Commissariats of the Interior, Justice, Agriculture, and so forth, all of course duly expected to take orders from Moscow by way of the Communist party. In Turkestan, adjacent to Afghanistan and China, there appeared in 1920 and early in 1921, the Soviet People's Republics of Khorezm (Khiva) and Bukhara, which, probably to impress those south of their borders, were for the moment at least allowed a notable degree of actual national self-rule. The Russian Soviet Republic, however, retained the right to exploit natural resources, to move goods in and out, unencumbered by tariffs, and to use Russian money.[33]

On September 1, 1920, only a few weeks after the adjournment of the Second Congress of the Comintern, there convened at Baku the so-called "First Congress of the Peoples of the East." Nearly two thousand Asian delegates attended, most of them from Transcaucasia and Central Asia. The colorfully garbed assemblage was informed by Zinoviev, who presided, that it was invited to join with the Comintern in a "holy war," directed "in the first place against English imperialism." Clearly expressing Lenin's design, a speech by Radek assured the Baku congress that the Eastern policy of the Soviet government was not designed merely to win advantages for the Soviet Republic. "We are bound to you," said Radek, "by a common destiny: either we unite with the peoples of the East and hasten the victory of the Western European proletariat, or we shall perish and you will be slaves." A subsequent address by the Bolshevik Pavlovich expressed Lenin's thought to the effect that the Asiatic countries could with Russian help skip the capitalist stage of their development and enter upon the Soviet path to socialism.[34] The Bolshevik pronouncements were greeted with considerable enthusiasm, but the Baku congress was by and large nothing more than a propaganda circus. A far more significant Bolshevik move in the long run was the establishment in Moscow, in the fall of 1920, of an Institute of Eastern Studies, which would in time achieve an excellent record in training Asians to become Communist leaders. In December, 1921, the Soviet orientalists were given governmental sanction for the formation of an All-Russian Association of Eastern Studies, or VNAV. If men such as S. F. Oldenburg and V. V. Bartold, who were internationally known scholars of the Orient, hoped that their newly founded institution would devote itself to academic pursuits primarily, they were soon to be disenchanted. VNAV became a subsection of the Commissariat of Nationalities; its organ *Novi Vostok*, which first appeared in 1922, immediately adopted the line that a concern with revolutionism in the East took precedence over any purely scholarly interest in that part of the world.[35]

Through 1921 and 1922, the latter year for reasons of failing health marking the end of Lenin's effective leadership, the aim of rebuilding Russia made it necessary that the major stress of Soviet foreign policy be directed westward. Trade relations with Europe had to be re-established—hence the Anglo-Soviet trade pact of March, 1921—and Lenin also deemed it necessary to erect within Europe such hurdles as might serve to impede the constantly antici-pated onslaught of the armies of capitalism. In April, 1922, the Soviet government signed the Rapallo Agreement with Germany, and the same month marked the high point in the futile attempts of the Comintern to establish the basis for a united front among Communist and non-Communist socialist and labor organizations.[36]

During the same period Russia could hope for no economic or military support from Asiatic countries, nor for that matter could she provide any such support to them. Once indeed the economic *rapprochement* with Britain had been achieved, it had become necessary for the Comintern to soft-pedal its anti-imperialist motif. At the Third Congress of the Comintern the question of the Orient was deliberately slighted, being scheduled by the agenda for the next to last session. Roy of India was allotted five minutes of speak-ing time.[37] He complained and was reproved by the Bulgarian Kolarov, who made the point that the problems of the East had been thoroughly discussed at the Second Congress and at Baku.[38] At the moment, Lenin was in truth indifferent to the opinions of the Asiatics. That, however, does not mean that his long-range views with respect to a Russia-led Asia had undergone a change.

In his last published article, "Better Less, But Better," written in March, 1923, Lenin wrote:

Russia, India, China, and others, contain the vast majority of the world's people. This majority has driven itself ever faster in the last years into the war for its freedom, and in this sense there can be no shadow of a doubt as to the eventual decision in the world [revolutionary] struggle. In this sense the final victory of socialism is fully and unconditionally guaranteed. . . . In order to secure the existence [of Soviet Russia] until the final military conflict between the counter-revolutionary imperialist West and the revolutionary and nationalist East, between the civilized states of the world and the Eastern remainder, which, however, comprises the majority—it is necessary to succeed in civilizing this majority.[39]

NOTES

Notes to Chapter 1

1. V. I. Lenin, *Sochineniya* (2d ed., 30 vols.; Moscow, 1926–1932), IV, 382. *Sochineniya*, or "Works," of Lenin hereafter cited as *Soch.*

2. *Marx-Engels Gesamtausgabe*, ed. V. Adoratsky (Moscow, 1935), Part 3, III, 346.

3. K. Marx and F. Engels, *Sochineniya*, ed. V. Adoratsky (Moscow, 1935), XXVI, 480. Marx to Friedrich-Albert Sorge, September 27, 1877: "The crisis [the Russo-Turkish War] is the new turning point in the history of Europe. Russia . . . has long been on the eve of an overturn; all elements thereto are already present . . . the revolution will begin, as usual, in a scuffle over a constitution, but then will develop into a regular brawl. If mother nature is not too unmerciful with us we may yet live to see this event. . . . The entire structure of Russian society is now in a state of economic, moral and intellectual dissolution. The revolution this time will begin in the East, formerly the impregnable citadel and reserve army of the counter-revolution. . . . Mr. Bismarck looks with pleasure to the bloody strife but does not wish the matter to take place so fast. . . . If it comes to revolution, what becomes of the last prop of the Hohenzollern dynasty?"

4. In the foreword to *Der deutsche Bauernkrieg* Engels cites as one reason for the politically advanced position of the German working class in 1874 the fact that it had come late upon the proletarian stage and thus had learned from prior working class experiences in France and England. Lenin, by quoting this passage from Engels in his writing in 1902, means to prove that the Russian proletariat, historically the newest, had learned from the struggles of the English, French *and* German working classes and was therefore ahead of them all in terms of revolutionary wisdom (*Soch.*, IV, 381–82).

5. The bourgeoisie feared "an all too revolutionary attitude on the part of the working class which never stops with the democratic revolution but strives to achieve the socialist revolution. [The bourgeoisie] feared the total collapse of officialdom and bureaucracy whose interests are linked to those of the propertied classes by a thousand threads. One of the tasks of the proletariat is to drive the bourgeoisie forward and to place before the entire people slogans of a completely democratic revolution" (*Soch.*, VII, 346–47).

6. The Bolshevik minimum program in 1905 included demands for a republic, an armed people, an eight-hour day, full democratic rights and freedoms for national minorities, etc.

7. *Soch.*, VII, 191. See also pp. 297–98: "The Russian proletariat will know how to do its duty to the end. It will stand at the head of the people's armed uprising. It will not shrink from the difficult task of participating in the provisional revolutionary government if this task should fall to it. It will beat back

all counter-revolutionary attempts, crush without mercy all enemies of freedom, defend the democratic republic and achieve our entire minimum program by revolutionary means. . . . Having been victorious in the forthcoming revolution, we shall have taken a gigantic step forward toward our socialist goal, we shall have liberated Europe from the heavy yoke of a reactionary military power and will help our brothers, the class conscious workers of the entire world, exhausted physically and spiritually in the struggle with bourgeois reaction, to take new courage in the success of the revolution in Russia and stride to Socialism with renewed vigor. With the help of the socialist proletariat, however, we shall succeed not only in maintaining the democratic republic but we shall also be able to advance toward Socialism with seven league strides."

8. *Leninsky Sbornik* (35 vols.; Moscow, 1924–1945), V, 48–50.

9. *Ibid.*

10. *Ibid.* "The Russian revolution," Lenin had said earlier in his address, "was at the same time also proletarian not only in the sense that the proletariat was the guiding force, the avant-garde of the movement, but also in the sense that the specifically proletarian means of battle, that is, the strikes, served as the means of shaking up the masses and was the most characteristic feature in the tidal flow of decisive events.

"The Russian revolution was *the first*—it will surely not have been the last—great revolution in world history, in which the political mass strike played a great role. In fact, the events of the Russian revolution cannot be understood without a statistical knowledge of the strikes that took place" (*ibid.*, pp. 23–25).

11. In his address Lenin had stated, "The peculiarity of the Russian revolution lay in the fact that it was bourgeois-democratic by content but in its method of struggle was proletarian. It was bourgeois-democratic since the goal which it directly strove for and which it could achieve with its forces alone was the democratic republic, the eight-hour working day, the confiscation of the enormous large landowners' estates—measures which the bourgeois revolutions in France in 1792 and 1793 had achieved" (*ibid.*, pp. 23–25).

12. *Soch.*, XII, 211–12.

13. *Soch.*, XII, 211–12.

14. *Soch.*, XII, 213.

15. *Soch.*, IX, 28–36.

16. O. Gankin and H. Fisher, *The Bolsheviks in the World War* (Stanford, Calif., 1940), pp. 84–85.

17. *Ibid.*, p. 79.

18. *Ibid.*, p. 83.

19. *Ibid.*

20. As cited in Gankin and Fisher, *op. cit.*, pp. 85–86. The dates in this citation have been changed to conform to the modern calendar.

21. *Ibid.*, p. 153.

22. *Ibid.*

23. *Ibid.*, pp. 158–59.

Notes to Chapter 2

1. The actual title of this document was "Tasks of Revolutionary Social-Democracy in the European War," in *Soch.*, XVIII, 44–46.

2. Lenin was implying that the Russian proletariat was more advanced than that of Western countries; that its function, the overthrow of tsarism, was the key to the entire European revolution. Lenin as late as 1914 still referred to the tsar as the Gendarme of Europe (see G. E. Zinoviev, *Ucheniye Marksa i Lenina o Voine* [Moscow, 1931], p. 176). The Bolsheviks, as we have seen, lived up to Lenin's boast. The Bolsheviks in the Duma openly opposed the war and were arrested, tried, and convicted of treason.

3. *Soch.*, XVIII, 44–46.

4. *Soch.*, XVIII, 44–46.

5. M. Siromyatnikova, "Bernskaya Konferentsiya zagranichnikh organizatsii R.S.D.R.P. v 1915 g. (s primechaniyami G. L. Shklovskogo)," *Proletarskaya Revoliutsiya*, No. 5 (40) (1925), pp. 186–88.

6. *Soch.*, XVIII, 230–33.

7. *Soch.*, XVIII, 230.

8. For an explanation of what Lenin meant by a socialist union of free nations see S. W. Page, "Lenin and Self-Determination," *Slavonic and East European Review*, April, 1950, pp. 342–55. (See also pp. 20, 121–22.)

9. *Soch.*, XVIII, 231–32.

10. *Soch.*, XVIII, 232–33.

11. *Soch.*, XIX, 206: "We have incredibly little news from Russia. It is simply a pity that such a comparatively easy task as conspirative correspondence with Russia (*fully* possible even in wartime), proves to be so utterly *poorly* organized."

12. "The proletariat must carry the democratic revolution to the end, uniting to itself the peasant masses in order to crush by force the opposition of the aristocracy and to paralyze the untrustworthy bourgeoisie. The proletariat must complete the socialist revolution, uniting itself with the mass of semiproletarian elements of the population, in order to demolish by force the opposition of the bourgeoisie and paralyze the untrustworthy peasantry and petty bourgeoisie" (*Soch.*, VIII, 96).

13. "The pamphlet," Lenin wrote on May 9, 1917, "was written for the tsarist censor. I was therefore not only forced to limit myself exclusively to theoretical and economical analysis, but also to formulate the few essential comments on politics . . . in that accursed Aesopian language to which tsarism forced all revolutionaries wishing to write 'legal' works to resort. . . . That imperialism is on the eve of a socialist revolution . . . I was forced to say in 'slave' language" (*Soch.*, XX, 284). Lenin wrote these lines as part of a preface to the second Russian edition of *Imperialism*. In his preface to a later French edition he wrote: "The tens of millions of dead and maimed left by the war open the eyes of the tens of millions . . . downtrodden, oppressed, . . . and duped by the bourgeoisie, with unprecedented rapidity. Thus out of the universal ruin caused by a war, a world-wide revolutionary crisis is arising

which . . . cannot end in any other way than in a proletarian revolution and its victory" (Lenin, *Imperialism: The Highest Stage of Capitalism* [New York, 1939], p. 11).

14. "The workers of Russia extend their comradely hand to the Socialists who act like Karl Liebknecht" (N. Krupskaya, *Memories of Lenin* [2 vols.; London, 1930], II, 158). This was a passage in a message Lenin sent on February 14, 1915, to an inter-Allied socialist conference in London. While granting favorable mention to three or four splinter socialist groups in Europe, Lenin found only this one man worthy of being singled out as a model for the correct revolutionary attitude.

15. Through 1915–1916 Lenin and Zinoviev eagerly sniffed out every bit of information that made German revolution appear imminent. "The deadening influence of Kautskyism is still pressing strongly on some members of the German opposition. The most important thing is that the attitude of the masses has changed. Discontent is growing everywhere. It is difficult to name any large city in which there has not been a considerable demonstration against the high cost of living, etc. The discontent in the trenches is immense. The masses are becoming 'radicalized.' Should war continue until the autumn [1916], great events are inevitable" (G. E. Zinoviev, "Tsimmervald-kintal," *Sotsial-Demokrat*, Nos. 54–55 [June 10, 1916], pp. 2–4; cited by Gankin and Fisher, *op. cit.*, pp. 440–41).

16. As Lenin must have realized, it was opportune that Germany was the country that once in revolution could the most readily be counted on to overthrow the Russian monarchy—no other power being in a position to intervene. Also, in 1915–1916 Germany was the greatest internationalist force in Europe. On her side stood the Austrian conglomerate, and under her military control lay the Lowlands and parts of France, Poland, Lithuania, and half of Latvia. A revolution in Germany could therefore have swept like wildfire through most of Europe.

17. "Never, I think, was Vladimir Ilyich in a more irreconcilable mood than during the last months of 1916 and the early months of 1917. He was profoundly convinced that the revolution was approaching" (Krupskaya, *op. cit.*, II, 197).

18. "The dictatorship of the proletariat, which insures the leading role of the proletariat in the reconstruction of the entire social fabric—this is what particularly interested Vladimir Ilyich in the latter half of 1916. . . . He argued with Bukharin who underestimated the role of the state, the role of the dictatorship of the proletariat, etc. He was indignant with [Pyatakov] because the latter did not understand the leading role of the proletariat. . . . Vladimir Ilyich began diligently re-reading all that had been written by Marx and Engels on the state, and took extracts from their works. This equipped him with a particularly profound understanding of the nature of the coming revolution, and prepared him most thoroughly for the understanding of the concrete tasks of that revolution" (*ibid.*, pp. 192–93).

19. *Leninsky Sbornik*, XIV, 197–394. In a letter to Kollontai, February 17, 1917, Lenin wrote that he had "almost completed" the research for an article on the relation of Marxism to the state (*ibid.*, II, 282). In July, 1917, fearing

he might be "bumped off," Lenin wrote to Kamenev asking him to formulate and publish his notebook on "Marxism and the State." "I think you [can do] this in a week," Lenin wrote (*ibid.*, IV, 319).

20. The complete title of Lenin's book is *State and Revolution, the Teaching of Marxism About the State and the Tasks of the Proletariat in the Revolution.*

21. "But the dictatorship of the proletariat, i.e., the organization of the vanguard of the oppressed as a ruling class [note that Lenin limits the ruling class to a select few of the proletariat] for the purpose of suppressing the oppressors, cannot simply produce a mere broadening of democracy. *Along* with an immense broadening of democracy, which for the *first time* becomes democratism for the poor, for the people, and not for the well-to-do, the dictatorship of the proletariat places a series of restrictions of freedom upon the oppressors, the exploiters, the capitalists. We must suppress these if we are to liberate mankind from wage slavery; their resistance must be overcome by force; . . . it is clear that where there is suppression there is also violence, there is no freedom, no democracy" (*Soch.*, XXI, 430–31).

22. See Page, "Lenin and Self-Determination," *loc. cit.*

23. See Krupskaya, *op. cit.*, II, 191–92.

24. *Soch.*, XX, 277.

25. Gankin and Fisher, *op. cit.*, p. 309.

26. Zinoviev, who attended the preliminary conference, later reported: "I raised the question whether we should invite, for instance, the Dutch Marxists, the Polish Social Democratic opposition, the Social Democrats of Latvia, the 'Lichtstrahlen' group from Germany—and so forth. They answered: No, only those organizations who have official representation in the International Socialist Bureau are to be invited. I asked, Why is this so? This is not supposed to be an official conference, but a conference of lefts. The answer to this I received later, as the true nature of the meeting was eventually revealed. . . . It is clear that no one seriously even wishes to call a conference [of the left]" (*Leninsky Sbornik*, XIV, 161–63).

27. Krupskaya, *op. cit.*, II, 169.

28. *Ibid.* By mid-August the Bolsheviks had prepared for distribution "(1) a manifesto, (2) resolutions, (3) a draft of a declaration, which were sent to the most pronounced left comrades for consideration and discussion."

29. Gankin and Fisher, *op. cit.*, p. 311.

30. Krupskaya, *op. cit.*, II, 169.

31. *Soch.*, XIX, 54. *Imperialism*, in the process of composition at this very time, also placed heavy stress on the futility of peace among capitalist states. Such peace, Lenin tried to show, could never be more than an interlude between inevitable imperialist wars.

32. See Lenin, "The First Step," *Sotsial-Demokrat,* Oct. 11, 1915, and *Soch.*, XVIII, 297–301; also G. E. Zinoviev, "Tsimmervald-kintal," cited by Gankin and Fisher, *op. cit.*, pp. 439–51.

33. See S. W. Page, "The Role of the Proletariat in March, 1917; Contradictions Within the Official Bolshevik Version," *Russian Review,* IX (April, 1950), 146–49.

34. *Soch.*, XX, 68–70.
35. See n. 4, chap. 1.
36. See p. 6.

Notes to Chapter 3

1. "A week of bloodshed by the workers and Miliukov, Guchkov, and Kerensky in power!!" Lenin wrote to A. M. Kollontai on March 16. "The same old European pattern" (*Soch.*, XX, 5).

2. "Russian capital is but one branch of the world-wide 'firm' . . . bearing the name 'England and France.' . . . [The provisional government] bound hand and foot by Anglo-French imperialist capital [has] uttered not a word in renouncing the tsarist policy of seizing Armenia, Galitsia, . . . Constantinople" (*Soch.*, XX, 19). "[The provisional government] is carrying on a war of conquest to enable the Anglo-French capitalists *to retain* in their hands the plunder which they have taken from the German capitalists, and, at the same time, to *take from* the German capitalists the booty taken by them" (*Soch.*, XX, 49). The fall of the tsar and the seizure of power by "Miliukov, Guchkov and Co." Lenin ascribed in large part to a plot engineered by "English and French embassies with their agents and 'contacts.'" The purpose of this conspiracy, according to Lenin, had been to preclude the signing of a separate peace between Nicholas and Wilhelm that would have frustrated the imperialist aims of the Allied governments (*Soch.*, XX, 16).

3. *Soch.*, XX, 35.
4. *Soch.*, XX, 5, 13.
5. *Soch.*, XX, 5–6.
6. N. Sukhanov, *Zapiski o revoliutsii* (7 vols.; Moscow, 1922), III, 31–32. "Lenin's system of governmental organization came like a bolt from the blue not only to myself alone. None of those listening to the address in the Ksheshinskaya Palace [on April 17, when Lenin first presented his April Theses] had hitherto even mentioned anything like it. . . . The Soviets of Workers' Deputies could easily and naturally (and had already) become a source of governmental authority in the revolution; but nobody dreamed of them as organs of governmental power, that is, in themselves and on a permanent basis."
7. *Soch.*, XX, 35.
8. N. Krupskaya, *Memories of Lenin* (London, 1942), p. 253.
9. K. Marx, *Der Bürgerkrieg in Frankreich* (Moscow, 1937), p. 53.
10. *Ibid.*, pp. 54–55.
11. *Ibid.*, p. 49.
12. *Ibid.*, pp. 55–57.
13. *Soch.*, XX, 35.
14. *Soch.*, XX, 38.

15. *Soch.*, XX, 38.

16. On his arrival at the Finland Station Lenin was warmly greeted by a delegation of the Soviet Executive Committee, headed by Chkheidze. Lenin ignored the invitation to "pursue together with [the Soviet leadership] the aims [of] linking the forces of all [Russian] democracy." Turning away from Chkheidze to make his reply, Lenin greeted the throng as "the foremost units of the world proletarian army." He went on to say that the "[d]awn of world revolution was at hand, . . . Germany was all aboil, . . . any day the crash of European imperialism might explode. . . . Long live the world socialist revolution."

"This," comments Sukhanov, "was not only not a reply to Chkheidze. This was not an answer to the entire 'context' of the Russian revolution, as accepted without exception—by all its witnesses and participants. . . . This was very curious. . . . The voice of Lenin, heard directly outside the train, was 'the voice of the outside'" (Sukhanov, *op. cit.* III, 15–16).

17. This remark occurs in the "Draft Resolution on the War," presented by Lenin to the Petrograd party conference on April 29, 1917 (*Soch.*, XX, 190).

18. *Soch.*, XX, 87–90.

19. *Soch.*, XX, 100.

20. *Soch.*, XX, 102. Lenin characterized this "dual power" as a "remarkable peculiarity" of [the Russian revolution] (*Soch.*, XX, 94).

21. Lenin rather freely identified the SR leadership in the Soviet and the soldiers' deputies in the Soviet ("peasants in soldiers' uniforms") with the peasantry in general (*Soch.*, XX, 103, 94).

22. *Soch.*, XX, 102.

23. *Soch.*, XX, 103.

24. "If we organize ourselves and conduct our propaganda capably, not only the proletariat but also nine-tenths of the peasantry will be against a re-establishment of the police, against an irremovable and privileged bureaucracy, against an army separated from the people" (*Soch.*, XX, 121).

25. *Soch.*, XX, 104.

26. *Soch.*, XX, 108.

27. *Soch.*, XX, 101.

28. *Petrogradskaya Obshchegorodskaya Vserossiiskaya Konferentsiya R. S-D. R. P. (Bol'shevikov v Aprele 1917 g.)* (Moscow, 1925), pp. 14–15; hereafter cited as *Konferentsiya.*

29. *Pervi Legal'ni Peterburgsky Komitet Bol'shevikov v 1917 g.* (Moscow, 1927), p. 85; hereafter cited as *Komitet.*

30. Bogdat'ev too felt there should be no hurry about adopting the Communist title. "It is necessary now," he said, "to draw in comrades on a broad scale and not alienate them from ourselves" (*Komitet*, pp. 84–85).

31. The pamphlet was written to explain the April Theses.

32. *Soch.*, XX, 125–27.

33. *Soch.*, XX, 129. Lenin's highly dubious evidence for this contention was the press comment of "that extreme German chauvinist, Heilmann, editor of the archchauvinist *Chemnitzer Volkstimme,*" to the effect that Kautsky's "Center" and the Zimmerwald majority were "one and the same thing."

34. *Soch.*, XX, 130.

35. *Soch.*, XX, 191. "The slightest thought of a bloc with the petty bourgeoisie . . . is a betrayal of socialism. . . . With whom shall we form blocs, with the editors of *International?* But this paper has not yet appeared, consequently we don't know [its line]. Chkheidze is the worst shield for defensism. Trotsky, who edited a paper in Paris, never stated whether he was for Chkheidze or against him. . . . Trotsky has never made himself clear. How do we know that Larin, editor of *International,* does not adopt the same tactic?"

36. In the Petrograd Committee, for instance, the first vote on the Theses went: against, 13; in favor of, 2; abstaining, 1 (*Komitet*, p. xiii).

37. It was humiliating for the "old Bolsheviks" to see their wisdom so brazenly flouted by Lenin, who, barely setting foot upon Russian soil after years of exile, claimed to possess all the answers to all the problems (see Trotsky, *History of the Russian Revolution* [3 vols.; London, 1932–1933], I, 312).

38. At the first session of the first All-City Conference of Petrograd Bolsheviks, April 27, there was much disputation over Lenin's Theses, most of the sentiment running in favor of them. Toward the end of the session Zinoviev proposed that no resolution be adopted. "At this stage of the discussion," he argued, "it would be more sensible to limit the exchange of opinion on this question, the more so as the All-Russian [Bolshevik] Conference is about to begin." Kamenev protested vigorously against Zinoviev's suggestion. "Outside of these walls," he declared, "the political line of Lenin has stirred up much emotion amid the revolutionary democracy and the workers. It is essential that we determine specifically within a resolution our opinion on the provisional government and the war" (*Konferentsiya*, p. 17).

Though Kamenev knew that the resolution would go against his views, he was so frightened by the pro-Theses avalanche that he preferred even an unfavorable resolution to none at all. For if there existed no specific officially determined position of the party, what could halt the growing militancy of the "revolutionary democracy" short of recourse to armed violent action?

39. *Konferentsiya*, pp. 27–28; also *Pravda*, May 1, 1917.

40. *Konferentsiya*, pp. 26–28.

41. "The time has come," was *Pravda's* comment on May 1, "when even we, the workers of Russia, can openly celebrate the international holiday of proletarian solidarity." See also A. Kazovskaya, "Nota Miliukova i Aprel'skiye Dni," *Proletarskaya Revoliutsiya*, 1927, 4(63), p. 83.

42. Kazovskaya, *op. cit.*, pp. 84–85. "The cards lie open," Lenin wrote on May 4. "We have every reason to be thankful to Messrs. Guchkov and Miliukov for their note appearing today in all the papers" (*Soch.*, XX, 207).

43. The soldiers had been sparked into action by an independent revolutionary named Linde, who had exhorted the fully armed Finland Regiment to follow him to the Marinsky Palace. Other regiments followed suit and at six o'clock, when the factories let out, the workers spontaneously joined in the excitement (see M. N. Pokrovsky, ed., *Ocherki po istorii oktyabr'skoy revoliutsii* [2 vols.; Moscow, 1927], II, 180–81; also Kazovskaya, *op. cit*, pp. 84–85).

44. Examples: "Down with the Policy of Aggression," "Down with Miliukov" (Kazovskaya, *op. cit.*, pp. 84–85). Also "All Power to the Soviets" (*Soch.*, XX, 227).

45. An apologetic and probably inaccurate explanation, made subsequently

(May 11) by Schmidt of the Petrograd Committee, throws a revealing light upon the poor organization of the party at that time. "The All-City Conference," Schmidt reported, "discussed the [Miliukov note] and came to the conclusion that for the struggle with the provisional government, extended work was necessary. Drastic transitional steps—like the slogan of overthrowing the provisional government—were not indicated. The executive committee sat the entire night [May 3], the mood was one of alarm, and arrivals from the districts informed us that many factories were organizing meetings at which very great distrust in the provisional government was being expressed and the workers were organizing themselves. Influenced by this, many comrades expressed themselves in favor of overthrowing the provisional government, but no specific decisions were made" (Pokrovsky, *op. cit.*, II, 190).

46. *Soch.*, XX, 228.

47. *Konferentsiya*, pp. 55–56.

48. "Do not allow yourselves to be misled . . . into shouting 'Down with the Provisional Government' before the majority of the people has become fused [in purpose]. Crises cannot be overcome . . . by risings of small groups of armed people, by Blanquist attempts to seize power" (*Soch.*, XX, 228).

49. *Soch.*, XX, 252.

50. "It is explanation—without doing—that accounts for the vacillation [in the party]. I fully understand . . . that mass of workers who, hearing that their leaders propose only to explain, decided it was better to overthrow the government if only for lack of anything else to do. They went beyond the limits of the program because the political party showed them no political way out of the situation.

If you do not want such misunderstandings—then a political party cannot make it its task merely to explain. It is necessary to show the masses concrete political actions, for otherwise they will always . . . draw the direct line conclusions" (*Konferentsiya*, p. 57).

51. "Yes, our organization had flaws. . . . The policy which we mapped out is sound. In the future we shall take all measures to achieve such an organization that there will be no Petrograd Committee men disobeying the Central Committee" (*Soch.*, XX, 252–53). "Our line proves its correctness with every passing day. For perfect execution it needs an organization of the proletarian masses *three times* better than the present one. In every district, in every quarter, in each factory and [soldier's] company there must be a strong, harmonious organization capable of acting *as one* man. From each of these organizations direct threads must lead to the center, to the Central Committee, and these threads must be strong ones so that the enemy cannot tear them with a single blow. These threads must be strengthened and tested constantly, daily, hourly, *so that the enemy cannot drive us into confusion* (*Soch.*, XX, 234).

52. "We have a right to fight for and shall fight for influence and for a majority in the Soviet and in the Soviets. And we repeat: *Only then shall we be for transfer of power into the hands of the proletarians and semiproletarians, when the Soviet of Workers' and Soldiers' Deputies stands on the side of our policy and wishes to take power into its hands*" (*Soch.*, XX, 230).

53. *Soch.*, XX, 264–65.

54. *Soch.*, XVIII, 313.

55. *Soch.*, XX, 266.

56. See p. 34.

57. "You ask what is my program? . . . A peace which aims neither at domination over other peoples, nor a seizure of their national patrimony, nor a taking by force of foreign territories, a peace without annexations or indemnities based on [self determination]" (D. R. Francis, *Russia from the American Embassy, April 16–November, 1918* [New York, 1921], p. 120).

58. Tereshchenko's note: "Remaining unwaveringly true to the general Allied cause, Russian democracy hails the decision of the Allied Powers who have expressed the willingness . . . to submit the agreements concerned with war aims to a review. [The note suggested a conference to take up this question.] But one of the agreements . . . , that excluding the possibility of one of the Allied Powers concluding a separate peace—this need not be discussed by this conference" (V. Vladimirova, *Revoliutsiya 1917 goda [Khronika Sobitii]* [Leningrad, 1924], III, 255; also Francis, *op. cit.*, pp. 120–22).

59. "Free Russia," Tereshchenko declared, "must prove that she is accomplishing faithfully her fundamental [obligation toward the Allies]. . . . In the name of a peace, rapid and just, it is necessary to re-create the military power of new Russia . . . to prove really the existence of this force. . . . Now it can only be a question of an active defense [i.e., offensive] with a view to defending the national independence and liberty" (Francis, *op. cit.*, pp. 122–23).

60. F. Zalesskaya, "Iun'skaya demonstratsiya 1917 goda," *Proletarskaya Revoliutsiya,* 1927, 65–66, p. 143.

61. *Komitet,* p. 136.

62. Pokrovsky, *op. cit.*, II, 230.

63. *Ibid.;* also Zalesskaya, *op. cit.*, p. 144.

64. Pokrovsky, *op. cit.*, II, 230.

65. Zalesskaya, *op. cit.*, p. 144.

66. *Ibid.*, p. 146.

67. For exact text of the proclamation see Vladimirova, *op. cit.*, III, 268–69.

68. *Soch.*, XX, 482–88.

69. Vladimirova, *op. cit.*, III, 280.

70. *Soch.*, XX, 520.

71. "We had before us a direct order of that organization which in our opinion should have held all power," the Bolshevik declaration that called off the demonstration reads in part (Vladimirova, *op. cit.*, III, 280).

72. *Soch.*, XX, 519–21.

73. *Soch.*, XX, 524.

74. Soch., XX, 526.

75. "In the final analysis, the SRs counted, first, upon the union of urban nonpartisan Workers' Soviets, second, the All-Russian Peasant Union, and thirdly, and possibly, the previously active "Union of Unions," a union of all types of laboring intelligentsia—all of these into a federal tri-unity—giving to the entire revolution an organized, sustained and planned character" (V. Chernov, *Rozhdeniye revoliutsionnoy Rossii [Fevral'skaya revoliutsiya]* [Prague, 1934], pp. 221–22).

"The Mensheviks [Social Democrats] . . . also want to declare as national property the lands of the crown, the monasteries, the appanages . . . and large landowners, and rent this land, for small amounts. . . , to all who need land. But they will not touch the small landed property, not considering peasant lands as consignable or alienable, understanding well that until one can institute socialism on the land, one cannot succeed in bringing to life a general egalitarianism." (From a leaflet by Martov, under the pseudonym V. Ezhov, written probably in November 1917. See *Organizatsionni Komitet Rossiiskoy Sotsial-demokraticheskoy rabochei partii [Menshevikov], k viboram v Uchreditel'noye Sobraniye No. 3,* "Soldat', za kem poidesh tui na viborakh?")

76. *Soch.,* XX, 484–86.

77. *Soch.,* XX, 491–92.

78. Pokrovsky, *op. cit.,* II, 269.

79. *Ibid.,* pp. 282–83.

80. *Ibid.*

81. *Ibid.,* p. 284. Even when the machine gunners stood assembled outside the Ksheshinskaya Palace, Bolsheviks Nevsky, Sverdlov, and others still tried to turn back the demonstrators.

82. B. Elov, "Posle Iul'skikh Sobitii," *Krasnaya Letopis,* No. 7, 1923, p. 96. It was Stalin who delivered this report on the party's decision.

83. V. D. Bonch-Bruevich, *V. I. Lenin v Rossii* (Moscow, 1935), p. 86.

84. *Soch.,* XXI, 41.

85. See Chap. 2, n. 19.

86. Speaking to Ordzhonikidze soon after the July Days, Lenin said: "Power can now only be taken by armed uprising. One will not have long to wait. The uprising will not take place later than September, October. We must move the center of gravity to the factory committees. The factory committees must become the organs of uprising" (Pokrovsky, *op. cit.,* II, 332).

Notes to Chapter 4

1. This new theme is apparent in much of Lenin's writing following the July Days. The peaceable phase of the revolution, he insisted, had passed. The time had come for a "new revolution" (*Soch.,* XXI, 24), the July Days having represented a "sharp turn" (*Soch.,* XXI, 33) in the Russian revolution. "The political situation in Russia," Lenin wrote shortly after the July Days, "is now . . . basically different from the situation of the period March 12 to July 17" (*Soch.,* XXI, 33). The expression "sharp turn" suggests that a new sociopolitical trend had suddenly manifested itself. Actually the "sharp turn" was merely Lenin's own turning from a moderate program to one that would require much more decisive action, but Lenin always liked to identify his thoughts and moves with those of the masses as a whole.

2. "Such measures [the people taking power through the Soviets, the forming of a universal militia, etc.] would not yet constitute a 'dictatorship of the proletariat' but only a 'revolutionary democratic dictatorship of the proletariat and the poorest peasants' " (*Soch.,* XX, 38).

3. See p. 34.

4. *Soch.*, XXI, 370.

5. *Leninsky Sbornik* (35 vols.; Moscow, 1924–1945), XXI, 21.

6. That the question of the revolution's form was also on Lenin's mind can be gathered from the few lines he did write in starting the never-completed chap. vii. "The subject indicated in the title of this chapter ['Experience of the Russian Revolutions of 1905 and 1917'] is so vast that volumes can and must be written about it. In the present pamphlet it will be necessary to confine ourselves . . . to the most important lessons of the experience, those directly concerning the tasks of the proletariat in a revolution relative to state power" (*Soch.*, XXI, 454).

7. *Soch.*, XXI, 455.

8. See p. 70.

9. *Soch.*, XXI, 394–96. Lenin's notebook of Marx-Engels materials on the state contains the passage in Marx's letter to Kugelmann that includes the reference to the shattering of the old state machinery. But there is no comment by Lenin, who invariably made profuse marginal comments on anything he thought important in a passage, as to what Marx meant by the term "people." Before the Russian revolution, when Lenin was watching for revolution in the West, that word had escaped his interest. By August, 1917, however, the same word had become worthy of a lengthy analysis and interpretation.

10. L. Trotsky, *History of the Russian Revolution* (3 vols.; London, 1932–1933), II, 54–55, 116, 252–53; hereafter cited as *History*.

11. *Soch.*, XXI, 36. General Cavaignac headed the government forces that annihilated the French Socialists of 1848.

12. Lenin repeatedly mentions the name of the unfortunate Voinov, a Bolshevik workingman (*Soch.*, XXI, 36, 44, 57). Years later, Lenin was still able to recall Voinov by name.

13. See p. 54.

14. *Soch.*, XXI, 30. See also pp. 25, 31–32.

15. *Soch.*, XXI, 39–41, 56–57.

16. *Soch.*, XXI, 39–59 *passim*.

17. *Soch.*, XXI, 56.

18. "Do [the SRs and Mensheviks] intend to start a Dreyfusade on the eve of the convocation of the Constituent Assembly in Russia? The near future will provide an answer to [this question], the open presentation of which we regard as the duty of the free press." (From the letter written by Lenin, Zinoviev, and Kamenev to the editors of *Novaya Zhizn'*. *Soch.*, XXI, 30.) "The Constituent Assembly alone, if it convenes. . . , will have the full authority to pass upon the decree of the government ordering our arrest." (From the letter of Lenin and Zinoviev to the editors of *Proletarskaya Delo*. See *Soch.*, XXI, 32.)

19. "The July crisis struck an especially damaging blow at the Petrograd garrison. . . . The wave of hostility against Bolshevism swept up very high in the Petrograd garrison. 'After the defeat,' says the former soldier Mitrevich, 'I did not show up in my regiment as I might have been killed there before the squall passed.' It was exactly in those more revolutionary regiments which had marched in the front ranks in the July Days, and therefore received the most furious blows, that the influence of the Party fell lowest. It fell so low that even

three months later it was impossible to revive the organization. It was as though these units had been morally disintegrated by too strong a shock" (Trotsky, *History*, II, 254–55; see also pp. 256–57).

20. "Lenin is in hiding . . . intently watching the papers. . . . The masses are on the ebb. Martov, while defending the Bolsheviks from slander, is at the same time indulging in mournful irony at the expense of a party which has been so 'crafty' as to defeat itself. Lenin guesses—and direct rumors of this will soon reach him—that even some of the Bolsheviks, too, are not free from a note of repentance, that the impressionable Lunacharsky is not alone. Lenin writes of . . . the 'renegadism' of those Bolsheviks who show a disposition to respond to this whimpering" (*ibid.*, pp. 306–7).

21. *Soch.*, XXI, 91.

22. *Soch.*, XXI, 138.

23. *Soch.*, XXI, 196–97.

24. *Soch.*, XXI, 202–3.

25. "It is indisputable," Lenin wrote on October 14, "that the Bolsheviks would have achieved a great deal had they taken the offensive on the night of July 16–17, or even during July 17. Their defensive tactics were their weakness" (*Soch.*, XXI, 281). On October 29 he wrote of the "spontaneous excitement" on July 16, "which we, as a party, either did not understand or held back and channeled into a peaceable demonstration" (*Soch.*, XXI, 345).

26. *Soch.*, XXI, 323.

27. See pp. 65–67 and n. 30 of this chapter.

28. The famous "Order No. 1," for instance, announced on March 15 by the Soviet, aimed to take control of military action out of the hands of the officers.

29. *Soch.*, XXI, 133–34.

30. About two weeks after Kornilov's defeat the SRs and the Mensheviks attending the Democratic Conference (see n. 45 of this chapter) voted to exclude the Kadet party from the cabinet. For the moment (the SRs and Mensheviks later joined in a coalition which included Kadets), Lenin thought he saw a chance to woo the SRs and Mensheviks by renewing his compromise offer. "Only a union of the Bolsheviks with the SRs and Mensheviks, only an immediate passing of all power to the Soviets would make a civil war in Russia impossible [and make] a peaceful development of the revolution *possible* and *probable*. Within the Soviets the struggle of parties for power can go on peacefully. . . . The Bolsheviks will do *everything* to secure this *peaceful* course of revolutionary development" (*Soch.*, XXI, 206–10). Lenin repeated this theme in a *Rabochy Put'* article of October 9–10 (*Soch.*, XXI, 227).

31. W. H. Chamberlin, *The Russian Revolution, 1917–1921* (2 vols.; New York, 1935), I, 178–79. Vol. I is based largely on Trotsky's *History of the Russian Revolution*. Trotsky accepted Lenin's rationalizations of his July Days' motives as the real coin.

32. *Soch.*, XXI, 138–39.

33. *Soch.*, XXI, 136. In a postscript to his article "On Compromises" (because of complications rising from Lenin's underground existence he was unable to get the article printed until five days after it was written) Lenin expressed his disappointment in the SRs. "After reading Saturday's and Sunday's [Septem-

ber 15–16] papers, I say to myself: it seems that the offer of a compromise is already too late. It seems that the few days during which a peaceful development was *still* possible have passed. Yes, to all appearances they have already passed. Thanks to the inertness of the SRs . . . Kerensky will proceed to strengthen his position *without* them by joining forces with the bourgeoisie."

34. *Soch.*, XXI, 139–40.

35. *Soch.*, XXI, 193–94.

36. *Soch.*, XXI, 194.

37. *Soch.*, XXI, 196–97. It was a Marxian precept that the proper time for an uprising was the moment of greatest vacillation among the class enemies.

38. *Soch.*, XXI, 197.

39. *Soch.*, XXI, 208–9. From "The Russian Revolution and Civil War," *Rabochy Put'*, September 29.

40. *Soch.*, XXI, 209.

41. *Soch.*, XXI, 264.

42. *Soch.*, XXI, 276.

43. *Soch.*, XXI, 287–89.

44. "Events prescribe our task so clearly that hesitation positively becomes a crime. . . . To wait is a crime against the revolution" (*Soch.*, XXI, 293–94).

45. The Democratic (or State) Conference, which commenced September 27, was a meeting of representatives from Soviets, trade unions, co-operatives, Zemstvo and city governments, convoked by Kerensky when the Kadet ministers resigned from the government after the Kornilov coup. From the conference Kerensky hoped to receive an expression of support in the forming of a new coalition. The conference objected to the inclusion of Kadets in a new government, a sentiment which Kerensky disregarded. His new cabinet, formed October 8, included two Kadets. The conference proposed the establishment of a body to represent organized opinion and guide the government until the convening of the Constituent Assembly. The Council of the Republic, or pre-Parliament, which grew out of this proposal, consisted mostly of non-Socialist members. It met in Petrograd on October 20 and was expected to endure for six weeks and then be replaced by the Constituent Assembly.

46. *Soch.*, XXI, 287–89.

47. *Soch.*, XXI, 285.

48. *Soch.*, XXI, 231.

49. *Soch.*, XXI, 290.

50. *Soch.*, XXI, 235.

51. *Soch.*, XXI, 239.

Notes to Chapter 5

1. Trotsky's autobiography, referring to this incident, speaks of Lenin's "unpardonable . . . outrageous . . . horrible . . . behavior" toward "the older ones" (L. Trotsky, *My Life* [New York, 1930], p. 162).

2. *Ibid.*

3. In 1908, as Trotsky relates, he accidentally ran into Lenin, who, like himself, was on the way to the Copenhagen congress of the Second International. He told Lenin of his latest article written for *Vorwärts,* in which he had attacked the Mensheviks and also the idea of "expropriations," Lenin's favorite manner of providing funds for the Bolshevik center.

"Did you really write like this?" Lenin asked Trotsky reproachfully.

At Lenin's request Trotsky repeated from memory the principal ideas "as [he] had formulated them in the article."

"Could it be stopped by telegraph?" Lenin asked.

"No," Trotsky replied, "the article was to appear this morning—and what's the use of holding it up? It is perfectly right" (*ibid.,* p. 218).

Though Trotsky's autobiography hastens to explain that he was wrong at the time in opposing Lenin's views, what emerges, above all, is Trotsky's pride in having been independent of discipline from either side, and especially of having defied Lenin's wishes to his face. The relating of this incident is the more remarkable in that Trotsky's autobiography as a whole is devoted largely toward proving that Trotsky had always been a firm believer in Lenin. As Deutscher aptly states: "In *My Life* Trotsky sought to vindicate himself in terms imposed upon him by Stalin and by the whole ideological situation of Bolshevism in the 1920s, that is, in terms of the Lenin cult. Stalin had denounced him as Lenin's inveterate enemy, and Trotsky was consequently anxious to prove his complete devotion to, and his agreement with, Lenin" (I. Deutscher, *The Prophet Armed, Trotsky: 1879–1921* [New York, 1954], pp. vii–viii).

4. In 1912 Trotsky joined with the Mensheviks in the so-called (anti-Lenin) "August bloc," even though, as he freely admits, "I disagreed with the Mensheviks . . . in all important matters" (Trotsky, *op. cit.,* p. 225).

5. Martov, the Menshevik leader with whom Trotsky collaborated on the emigré sheets *Golos* and *Nashe Slovo,* published in Paris, was fully cognizant of Trotsky's uncomfortable position. When during the first six months of the war Trotsky became too obstreperous in his attacks upon Martov for his hesitancy to break with the traitorous Second International, Martov warned Trotsky that if he broke with the Mensheviks, he would "deliver himself into the hands of Grisha Zinoviev," that is, fall under the sway of Lenin. As it happened, Trotsky was not yet ready to go that far, though his ties with Menshevism were becoming increasingly burdensome, as evidenced by his writings in February, 1915, in which he clearly stated his contempt for the Menshevik position, past and present (see Deutscher, *op. cit.,* p. 219).

6. Trotsky, *op. cit.,* p. 224.

7. *Ibid.,* p. 185.

8. Lenin's fear of becoming lost through death to the revolution has already been illustrated by the letter to Kamenev written after the July Days. Another such illustration is found in Trotsky's autobiography: "And what," Lenin once asked Trotsky quite unexpectedly, soon after the November seizure of power, "what if the white guards kill you and me? Will Sverdlov and Bukharin be able to manage?"

"Perhaps they won't kill us," Trotsky rejoined, laughing.

"The devil knows what they might do," said Lenin, laughing in turn (Trotsky, *op. cit.,* p. 338). Trotsky does not relate this incident to display Lenin's fear of death, but rather to show that Lenin regarded Trotsky as indispensable and did not even think of Stalin as a possible successor.

9. It is interesting to note how Trotsky, in line with his attempt to prove himself a disciple of Lenin, tries to show that even though his and Lenin's views coincided in May, 1917, that was not because Lenin had become a Trotskyite, but because Lenin had independently arrived at the correct point of view. Modestly, Trotsky describes how he had scoffed at those who had remarked on Lenin's passing over to his side of the fence. But the tone of his writing reflects a glow of satisfaction in the thought that his earlier ideas had been the same as those adopted by Lenin so many years later (see Trotsky, *op. cit.,* p. 332).

10. This work, like his autobiography, was written largely to prove Trotsky's devotion to Lenin.

11. Trotsky, *History,* I, 444.

12. *Ibid.,* II, 69–73.

13. *Ibid.,* p. 68; Trotsky's italics.

14. *Ibid.,* p. 319; III, 133.

15. *Ibid.,* III, 133.

16. *Ibid.,* pp. 147–48.

17. *Ibid.,* p. 154.

Notes to Chapter 6

1. *Soch.,* XX, 265.

2. *Soch.,* XXI, 197.

3. *Soch.,* XXI, 223–24.

4. I. Volkovicher, *Brestsky Mir* (Moscow, 1928), p. 58.

5. In a speech on March 18, Lenin deploringly recalled this post-November mood in the party when the easy victories within Russia led to "the appearance in the leading circles of our party of . . . intellectual supermen, who allowed themselves to be carried away . . . who said: we can cope with international imperialism; over there, there will also be a triumphal march, over there, there will be no real difficulties" (*Soch.,* XXII, 318). See also G. Sokolnikov, *Brestsky Mir* (Moscow, 1928), p. 2: "From abroad came word of the profound impression left by the November revolution upon the working masses, upon the frontline troops. To advance . . . , gun in hand, upon the class enemy on the other side of the border, after having destroyed him at home, to throw oneself into 'the international arena of the revolution' seemed quite natural, the only possible way, following the 'triumphal' course of the November victories."

6. "Probably, for a time, the intoxication of chauvinism [resulting from a definitive German victory in the East] will weaken [the German revolution]." (*Soch.,* XXII, 198. For expressions of similar views by Bukharin and Zinoviev see

Protokoli Tsentral'nogo Komiteta RSDRP, Avgust, 1917–Fevral' 1918 [Moscow, 1929], pp. 202–4.)

7. This fear explains the Russian demand at Brest-Litovsk that the Germans remove no forces from their eastern front during the period of an armistice.

8. In January, Lenin had "no doubt whatsoever but that the peasant majority of our army at this moment would unconditionally favor an annexationist peace, and would not favor an immediate revolutionary war for the socialist cause. The reorganization of our army [into a Red Army] has barely begun" (*Soch.*, XXII, 197).

9. *Soch.*, XXII, 13–19.

10. J. Reed, *Ten Days That Shook the World* (New York, 1934), p. 131.

11. *Ibid.*, pp. 131–32.

12. J. L. Magnes, *Russia and Germany at Brest-Litovsk* (New York, 1919), p. 28.

13. *Mirniye Peregovori v Brest-Litovske*, I (Moscow, 1920), 11.

14. *Ibid.*, p. 13.

15. L. Trotsky, *My Life* (New York, 1930), p. 302.

16. For a good account of the pattern of German thinking see J. W. Wheeler-Bennett, *Brest-Litovsk, The Forgotten Peace* (London, 1938), pp. 99–111.

17. Max Hoffmann, *Der Krieg Der Versäumten Gelegenheiten* (Munich, 1923), p. 201. "I told [von Kühlmann] that I considered it impossible to let the Russians return to Petersburg holding such a belief. [It could result in] a mad indignation [on the part of the Russian masses, who would regard themselves as having been] lied to."

18. *Ibid.*, pp. 201–2; see also O. Czernin, *Im Weltkriege* (Vienna, 1919), p. 309.

19. Hoffmann, *op. cit.*, p. 199. "[Kühlmann and Czernin] had agreed upon an answer which accepted without limitations a peace without annexations 'if the Entente Powers considered themselves ready to negotiate under the same conditions.' I did not like the answer [because] it was essentially a lie. It based itself upon the condition 'if the Entente,' etc. I would have considered it more correct to place oneself specifically on a factual basis and to answer the Russians by declaring that the Central Powers were ready to discuss a general peace . . . but that the Russians had so far no authorization to speak for the other powers of the Entente."

20. *Ibid.*, p. 202.

21. *Ibid.;* Czernin, *op. cit.*, pp. 309–11.

22. A. Ioffe, "Brest-Litovsk, Vospominaniya," *Novi Mir*, VI, 1927, p. 140. "Germany and her Allies thirsted for a separate peace with Russia . . . most of all [because they believed] that public opinion in their countries would quiet down somewhat [if the peace was obtained]."

23. L. Trotsky, *Lenin* (New York, 1925), p. 103.

24. In the so-called "Theses on the Peace," which Lenin was preparing at this time, thesis 6 states that it would be a great gamble for the Soviet Republic to base its tactics on the attempt to determine whether the "European or especially the German . . . revolution would come in the nearest future." As

regards poor German prospects, thesis 7 declares that the peace talks "at the moment fully reveal the unconditional predominance of the war party" (*Soch.*, XXII, 194). Lenin's especially glum attitude toward Western Europe's revolution can be seen at this time from a list of themes he wrote down, sometime between January 6 and 10, under the caption, "Problems to be worked out." Problem 29 of the forty-four listed reads: "The difficulties of revolutions in Western European 'parasitic' countries" (*Soch.*, XXX, 367). By a "parasitic" country Lenin meant one with a large "labor aristocracy" of union leaders, socialist ministers, etc., whom he considered bribed to the side of capitalism by the superprofits that the imperialists derived from colonial exploitation.

25. Trotsky, *Lenin*, p. 103.
26. *Ibid.*, pp. 104–5.
27. *Ibid.*, p. 106.
28. *Ibid.*, p. 107.
29. *Ibid.*

Notes to Chapter 7

1. Among the forty-four themes Lenin noted down for further consideration (see n. 24, chap. 6), Nos. 20, 20a, 24–29, 40–42, and 44 concerned themselves with this problem. Of these, Nos. 20, 20a and 28 were fully developed and incorporated into his Peace Theses. No. 20: "Separate peace" its danger and its possible significance. Is separate peace "a deal" with imperialism? No. 20a: Separate peace and our duty before the international proletariat. *Die Deutschen brauchen eine Niederlage.* (The last refers to an argument then current among the proponents of revolutionary war to the effect that the German Social Democrats, having become defeatists, looked for a German military catastrophe as an impetus to German revolution. See thesis 11 of the Peace Theses.) No. 28: First defeat the bourgeoisie in Russia, then conquer the bourgeoisie of other lands. (*Soch.*, XXX, 364–68.)

2. *Soch.*, XXII, 599.
3. *Soch.*, XXII, 599.
4. *Soch.*, XXII, 599.
5. L. Trotsky, *Lenin* (New York, 1925), p. 107.
6. *Ibid.*, pp. 108–9.
7. *Ibid.*, pp. 109–10.
8. *Soch.*, XXII, 195.
9. *Soch.*, XXX, 370.
10. *Soch.*, XXX, 369–70.
11. "Youthfulness," wrote Lenin, commenting on the Moscow delegation, "this was one of the greatest virtues of this group of orators" (*Soch.*, XXX, 369–70).

12. *Protokoli Tsentral'nogo Komiteta RSDRP, Avgust 1917–Fevral' 1918* (Moscow, 1929), p. 201. Hereafter cited as *Protokoli*.

13. *Ibid.*, pp. 204–5.

14. Trotsky, *op. cit.*, p. 112.

15. *Protokoli*, p. 228.

16. Trotsky, *op. cit.*, p. 114.

17. *Protokoli*, p. 228.

18. Ioffe, not abstaining, voted against the proposition.

19. *Protokoli*, pp. 228–29.

20. *Ibid.*, p. 231. "Not an hour must be lost, for the masses do not understand the placing of the question in such a way. Either we carry on a revolutionary war for socialization of the land [thereby getting the peasants to support the war] and then the masses will understand us, or we conduct negotiations for peace."

21. *Ibid.*, p. 232.

22. *Ibid.*, pp. 233–37.

23. Trotsky, *op. cit.*, pp. 116–17. Lenin on more than one occasion mentioned the possibility of an eastern, or if necessary, Far Eastern, withdrawal. He spoke of this to Bruce Lockhart (see B. Lockhart, *Memoirs of a British Agent* [London, 1932], p. 239) and he also brought it up at the Seventh Party Congress, March 6–8, declaring it to be the "absolute truth that without a German revolution we are doomed—perhaps not in Petrograd, not in Moscow, but in Vladivostok, in more remote places to which we may have to retreat" (*Soch.*, XXII, 322). Trotsky gives no date for his account, but internal evidence suggests that Lenin uttered these words on or soon after February 18.

24. *Protokoli*, p. 240.

25. Lockhart, *Memoirs of a British Agent* (London, 1932), p. 229. Trotsky first approached Lockhart on February 15.

26. *Protokoli*, p. 244. Ioffe, on the other hand, always a stanch opponent of peace with Germany, was able to reconcile Trotsky's proposal with his own views on the grounds that "it was necessary to accept everything that contributes to our resistance, and this [tactic] would not destroy the character of the revolutionary war."

27. *Ibid.*, p. 236. Bukharin was so disgusted that he announced at the meeting that he was resigning from the Central Committee and was also giving up his post as editor of *Pravda*. "What are we doing," he exclaimed, throwing his arms about Trotsky after the session. "We are turning the party into a dung heap" (Trotsky, *My Life*, pp. 389–90). "Bukharin is generally ready with his tears," was Trotsky's sarcastic comment of years later. In all fairness to Bukharin, however, it must surely have disconcerted him no little to watch first Lenin and then Trotsky, each a living symbol of international proletarianism, seemingly flouting the first rules of the creed by which they and he lived.

28. *Ibid.*

29. "There will be no respite," said Dzerzhinsky, "our signing, on the contrary, will strengthen German imperialism" (*Protokoli*, p. 249).

30. *Protokoli*, p. 248.

31. *Ibid.*, p. 251.

32. After the vote was taken, these three signed a statement explaining their position which was virtually an echo of Trotsky's earlier declarations (*Protokoli*, p. 253.)

33. "Catastrophic for the Russian and international revolutions" (*Protokoli*, p. 253.)

34. *Protokoli*, p. 253.

35. Trotsky, *My Life*, p. 339.

36. *Ibid.*, p. 340.

37. An interesting if inadvertent revelation of the changing Trotsky may be seen in Trotsky's autobiographical comment on Liebknecht's attitude toward the Brest-Litovsk negotiations. "Liebknecht grew amazingly during the war. . . . It is necessary to say that Liebknecht was a revolutionary of endless courage. But he was only now developing himself into a strategist. This disclosed itself in questions of his personal life as well as of revolutionary policy. Considerations of personal safety were absolutely alien to him. After his arrest many friends shook their heads at his self-sacrificing 'recklessness.' Lenin, on the contrary, was always much concerned about the safety of the leadership. He was the head of the general staff, and always remembered that, during the war, he had to insure the functioning of the high command. Liebknecht was like a general who himself leads his troops to battle" (Trotsky, *My Life*, p. 391).

Substitute the name Trotsky for that of Liebknecht in the above citation and it is a good description of Trotsky's behavior before and after November. Admiring the courage and "recklessness" of the early Liebknecht (the young Trotsky), Trotsky's major approval goes to the later Liebknecht, who, like Trotsky at the time of the Brest-Litovsk negotiations, was coming to adopt the opportunistic attitude of Lenin.

38. On December 17, 27, and 29, Trotsky made announcements to the Entente governments, each time asking them to participate in the peace discussions. On the last two dates Trotsky hinted strongly that an Allied refusal to participate would force the Russians to conclude a separate peace (see Magnes, *Russia and Germany at Brest-Litovsk*, pp. 28, 40–41).

39. W. Hard, *Raymond Robins' Own Story* (New York, 1920), p. 65.

40. *Ibid.*, p. 67.

41. Robins' eager bearing of Trotsky's exciting tidings was met with utter disdain by Allied authorities. "In a few hours," Robins was told sympathetically, "this Lenin and this Trotsky will be gone. Forget them" (*ibid.*, p. 68). Bruce Lockhart, commenting years later upon a Petrograd meeting with Robins, writes that "as a dramatic performance, Robins' effort was immense. Doubtless too he had rehearsed all his effects before his shaving glass in the morning" (Lockhart, *op. cit.*, p. 226).

42. "At that moment Trotsky was not quite certain what the German reaction would be to his famous declaration . . . but he had a shrewd idea that it would be unpleasant" (Lockhart, *op. cit.*, pp. 226–27).

43. This despite the fact that Lockhart seems to have seen through Trotsky's overacting, describing him "as a man who would willingly die fighting for Russia provided there was a big enough audience to see him do it" (*ibid.*, p. 227).

44. *Ibid.*, p. 228.

45. *Ibid.*, p. 229.

46. "On the 21st of February," Trotsky wrote many years later, ". . . the French Ambassador Noulens telegraphed to me: 'In your resistance to Germany

you may count on the military and financial cooperation of France.' . . . But the French Government did not keep its word. Clemenceau proclaimed a holy war against the Bolsheviks. Then we were forced to conclude the peace of Brest-Litovsk" (Trotsky, *Stalin* [London, 1947], p. 252).

47. *Protokoli*, p. 235.

48. "[Trotsky] . . . was in the worst of tempers" (Lockhart, *op. cit.*, p. 230).

49. *Ibid.*

50. "He had disappeared for some days, and no one seemed to know what had happened to him" (M. Phillips Price, *My Reminiscences of the Russian Revolution* [London, 1921], p. 250).

51. *Ibid.*

52. L. Trotsky, *Ueber Lenin* (Berlin, 1924), p. 123.

53. *Soch.*, XXIII, 3–16.

54. In explaining his views in this report, Lenin many times referred to the "economic" basis for his conclusions.

55. Hard, *op. cit.*, pp. 2–3.

Notes to Chapter 8

1. L. Fischer, *The Soviets in World Affairs* (2 vols.; New York, 1930), I, 75–76.

2. *Soch.*, XXIII, 81–82, 94–95.

3. *Soch.*, XXIII, 195.

4. *Soch.*, XXIII, 215.

5. E. H. Carr, *The Bolshevik Revolution, 1917–1923,* (3 vols.; New York, 1950–1953), III, 96.

6. *Soch.*, XXIII, 216.

7. *Soch.*, XXIII, 217.

8. "Each of us [passionately] feels himself pressed to take a stand [on the problem raised by the Russian socialist dictatorship] . . . since the very problems which today confront our Russian comrades may tomorrow have practical significance for West Europe also. Even now they decisively affect the nature of our propaganda and tactics [referring to the influence of bolshevism upon the German Socialist movement and its developing plan for what action to take in the impending revolution]." (K. Kautsky, *Die Diktatur des Proletariates* [Vienna, 1918], pp. 1–2.)

9. "And at such a moment, Mr. Kautsky, the leader of the Second International, publishes a book on the dictatorship of the proletariat, i.e., on the proletarian revolution, a book one hundred times more shameful, more shocking, more traitorous than Bernstein's famous *Prerequisites of Socialism*" (*Soch.*, XXIII, 218).

10. "Dictatorship is power, based directly upon violence and not bound

by any laws. The revolutionary dictatorship of the proletariat is a power conquered and supported by the violence of the proletariat over the bourgeoisie,
power not bound by any laws" (*Soch.*, XXIII, 341).

11. Kautsky, Lenin wrote, was "deliberately deceiving his German readers"
(*Soch.*, XXIII, 399).

12. *Soch.*, XXIII, 385–86.

13. See pp. 23–26.

14. "Unfortunately," wrote Kautsky, after citing Marx's celebrated reference
to the transitional period of the revolutionary dictatorship of the proletariat,
"Marx neglected to explain more fully how he conceived of this dictatorship"
(Kautsky, *op. cit.*, p. 20).

15. "A state-run economy is not yet socialism. Whether it is or not depends upon the character of the nation. But Russia is a *peasant country*" (*ibid.*,
p. 55).

16. *Soch.*, XXIII, 393.

17. This process, Lenin pointed out, was "first" taking place "now, in the
summer and autumn of 1918," when "the rural districts are passing through
their 'November' [i.e., proletarian] revolution. [Note again Lenin's shading
of peasant into proletarian.] A turn is coming. The wave of kulak revolts is
giving way to a rise of the poor, to the growth of the 'Committees of Poor
Peasants'" (*Soch.*, XXIII, 117).

18. *Soch.*, XXIII, 391.

19. "The Soviets . . . represent an immeasurably higher form . . . of
democracy . . . because, by uniting and drawing *the masses of workers and
peasants* into political life, they serve as a most sensitive barometer, the one
closest to the 'people' (in the sense in which Marx, in 1871, spoke of a real
people's revolution"). (*Soch.*, XXIII, 391.)

20. *Soch.*, XXIII, 393.

21. *Soch.*, XXIII, 396.

22. "Of course several hundred state-supported agricultural communes and
Soviet farms (that is, large farms cultivated by associations of workers on behalf
of the state) are very little. But is it possible to speak of 'criticism' when Kautsky
omits to mention this fact?" (*Soch.*, XXIII, 403.)

23. *Soch.*, XXIII, 404.

24. *Soch.*, XXIII, 405–6.

Notes to Chapter 9

1. *Soch.*, XXIII, 440.

2. "The democratic republic, the constituent assembly, universal elections,
etc., constitute the dictatorship of the bourgeoisie, and for the liberation of labor
from the capitalist yoke there is no other way than to *replace* this dictatorship
by the dictatorship of the proletariat." (From an article in *Pravda*, January 3,
1919; *Soch.*, XXIII, 441–42.)

3. "In Germany, as in Austria apparently, the major question of the

revolution is now: National Assembly or the power of the Soviets" (*Soch.*, XXIII, 440; see also p. 496).

4. *Soch.*, XXIII, 496. As early as October 18 Lenin had hailed his "respected comrades" of the Spartacus League, then still attached to the USPD (Independent Socialist Party of Germany), as the group which was the most energetically "undertaking to effect the creation of . . . Soviets throughout all of Germany." He expressed the hope "that the book of renegade Kautsky against the dictatorship of the proletariat would prove useful," since it would "affirm the correctness of what the Spartacists had always said about the Kautskyites" and enable "the masses to free themselves more quickly from the influence of Messrs. Kautsky & Co., who were dragging them into the swamp" (*Soch.*, XXIX, 514).

5. "Spartacus could no longer work together with [the USPD]," Eberlein, the German delegate reported to the founding congress of the Third International on March 2, 1919. "The majority [Socialist] party is united, but it looks rotten to the Independents. Every leading [Independent] proposed a different direction and each one pressed for the formation of a new party. Lebedour and Däumig, especially, went about with the idea of forming an *allgemeine* German party and had [this] materialized, there would have come into existence another independent social democratic party. This would have leaned neither to the left nor to the right and would have stood neither for the point of view of the extreme left, that of the Spartacus League, nor for the dictatorship of the proletariat. This determined us to break unconditionally with these people and thereby to make impossible the founding of such a mish-mash party.

"The task of the Communist party was not only the founding of a new party, but, in the main, to educate the masses; to prepare them for carrying through to the socialist order . . . for among the workers the thought always comes to the fore, that the task is finished once a few ministers have been replaced by Social Democrats" (Bibliothek der Kommunistischen Internationale, VII, *Der I Kongress*, etc. [Hamburg, 1921], p. 14). The expression "crazy fringe" is taken from F. Borkenau, *The Communist International* (London, 1938), pp. 143–44. Among the Spartacus leadership, Luxemburg, at least, realized that most of the workers were, as Borkenau writes, "with the majority Socialists and not even with the USP[D], not to mention her own group," and hence was more than likely opposed to the split. Luxemburg was pushed onto the adventurist path by a small group of fanatics who had entered the Spartacus League immediately after the war had ended and who believed, like the Bolsheviks, that it was the task of a small group to establish a dictatorship and then proceed to the business of creating sentiment for the revolution (Borkenau, *op. cit.*, p. 142).

6. *Soch.*, XXIII, 495.

7. Lenin could "find no words for expressing the . . . loathesomeness . . . of this butchery perpetrated by those who passed themselves off as Socialists" (*Soch.*, XXIII, 498).

8. *Soch.*, XXIII, 498–500.

9. *Soch.*, XXIII, 494–95.

10. S. W. Page, "Lenin, The National Question and the Baltic States, 1917–1919," *The American Slavic and East European Review*, VII, No. 1 (February, 1948), pp. 19–30.

11. *Izvestiya*, February 1, 1919.

12. P. Stučka, *Pyat' Mesyatsev Sotsialisticheskoy Sovyetskoy Latvii* (Moscow, 1919), Part I, pp. 21–22.

13. At the All-Russian Conference of Bolsheviks, May 7–12, 1917, the party went along with Lenin to the extent of condemning the "Center" as the "enfeebling" element of the Zimmerwald bloc and the "Zimmerwald bloc as a whole," for "having turned down the proposal of the Left to call upon the workers of all lands to direct revolutionary struggle against their governments" and for "refusing to admit the need for a direct break with the social chauvinists." The party on this occasion also announced it as "its task in a country where revolution had begun earlier than in other countries . . . to take upon itself the initiative for the creation of a Third International," but in the same resolution refuted Lenin by voting "to remain within the Zimmerwald bloc, giving itself the task of defending therein the tactic of the Zimmerwald Left, and to charge the Central Committee with advancing quickly toward the founding of the Third International." The resolution further insisted that "a new socialist International could only be created by the workers themselves, through revolutionary struggles in their own countries." Through respectfully parroting Lenin's statements on the need for a Third International, the Russian Bolsheviks were quite unable to see its creation as their particular task. (*Vsesoiuznaya Kommunisticheskaya Partiya (b) v Rezoliutsiyakh i Resheniyakh ee S'ezdov, Konferentsii i Plenumov Ts. K. (1898–1932), Part I, 1898–1924* [Moscow, 1932], pp. 263–64.)

14. By this time Lenin's desire to bring about a new International was shared by the Bolsheviks in general as well as by the Left SRs, who, nominally at least, shared governmental authority with the Bolsheviks (*Soch.*, XXIV, 723–24).

15. Among those who attended the meeting were Stalin, representing the Bolsheviks, Haglund and Grimlund for the Swedish Marxist Left party, Nissen for the Norwegian Social Democrats, Natanson and Ustinov for the Russian SRs, Petrov for the English Socialist party, Bazhor for the Rumanian Social Democrats, Radoshevich for the Yugoslav Social Democrats, and Reinstein for the American Socialist Labor party (*Soch.*, XXIV, 723–24).

16. *Soch.*, XXIV, 724.

17. *Bor'ba Bol'shevikov za Sozdaniye Kommunisticheskogo Internatsionala* (Moscow, 1934), pp. 105–6.

18. *Ibid.*, pp. 113–16. This proclamation is included in Trotsky's *Collected Works*, but the 1935 edition of Lenin's *Collected Works (Sochineniya)* XXIV, ascribes its authorship to Lenin and Bukharin. It may well be true, as E. H. Carr notes, that Trotsky had been falsely deprived of his author's credits. Regardless of who actually set the words to paper, the tract contains all of Lenin's then-important ideas on the subject. Lenin had made his decision to send out the appeal after discussing his intentions with Fineberg of England, Sirola, a Finn, and Chicherin, at an informal conference held in the Kremlin bedchamber of the former tsar. Fineberg later wrote "that the consultation before the birth of the Communist International took place in the royal bedchamber of Nicholas the Last" (S. Fineberg, "The Formation of the Communist International," *The Communist International*, Nos. 9–10 [1929], pp. 443–45).

19. "When I asked Lenin whether or not to go to the Ukraine, he en-

couraged me to do so. But when I expressed my fear that [while I was gone] the international congress would take place, he quieted my fears: 'In all probability nothing will come of the whole business. If, however, as I do not believe, something were nonetheless to materialize, then you and Rakovsky will come at once on a special train'" (A. Balabanova, *Erinnerungen und Erlebnisse* [Berlin, 1927], p. 225).

20. Jacques Sadoul had originally come to Russia as an officer attached to the French military mission. He appeared as the French delegate at the founding congress of the International, but was given only a consultative voice. He opened his address on March 3 with apologies for speaking "neither German, the language of international socialism, nor Russian, the language which tomorrow will be that of international communism. I have a somewhat fluent command only of the French language, which at this moment, I regret to say, must be designated as the language of the revolution of the past" (Bibliothek der Kommunistischen Internationale, VII, *I Kongress*, p. 62).

21. Boris Reinstein, "delegate" of the American Socialist Labor party, had lived in Russia the two years past, and in his report on March 2 had to apologize for "being unable . . . to provide [the comrades] with any fresh information about America" (Bibliothek, VII, *I Kongress*, p. 35). Sadoul had not seen France for eighteen and a half months. However, this was in the tradition of Marx, who in 1864, having lived in England for thirteen years, was nonetheless the delegate from Germany to the founding congress of the First International.

How flimsy a contact was required to establish a comrade as delegate of a particular country may be seen from the following statement of a report made on March 3 by Chicherin, speaking on behalf of the committee for the validation of delegates' mandates:

"We consider the revolutionary parties the representatives of the revolutionary party of the country even though its number is momentarily not formally very large. . . . Comrade Rutgers represents Holland with a consultative vote. He has no mandate but may speak for the party. At the same time he has a consultative vote for the American League for Socialist Propaganda. But since he was in Japan only in the process of passing through, he can, where Japan is concerned, not be regarded as an outstanding member of a movement or as a mandate bearer with consultative voice. Hence it was necessary to cross the Japanese group from our list" (Bibliothek, VII, *I Kongress*, p. 56). Had Rutgers stopped overnight in Tokyo, he would, it seems, have been able to represent three continents.

22. "Upon [the] arrival of [Balabanova] in Moscow, the conference was in full course. Participating in it besides a few comrades who had come from Germany for just that purpose, were mostly ex-prisoners of war and a few revolutionaries who had been in Russia" (Balabanova, *op. cit.*, p. 225). Since only one delegate came from Germany proper, Balabanova, by Germany, may have meant the West in general.

"In fact, the only delegates that I can recall who came directly from abroad were comrade Eberlein, . . . comrade Rutgers and several Finnish comrades. The other foreign parties represented at the Congress were represented by those parties then in Moscow" (Fineberg, *op, cit.*, p. 444).

23. H. Eberlein, "The Foundation of the Comintern and the Spartakus-bund," *The Communist International*, Nos. 9–10 (1929), p. 437.

24. "Lenin," she wrote, "says the bourgeois state is an instrument of oppression of the working class; the socialist state of the bourgeoisie. To a certain extent, he says, it is only the capitalist state stood on its head. This simplified view misses the most essential thing: bourgeois class rule has no need of the political training and education of the entire mass of people, at least not beyond certain narrow limits. But for the proletarian dictatorship that is the life element, the very air without which it is not able to exist. . . . Socialism in life demands a complete spiritual transformation in the masses degraded by centuries of bourgeois class rule; social instincts in place of egotistical ones, mass initiative in place of inertia . . . etc., etc. No one knows this better . . . than Lenin. But he is completely mistaken in the means he employs. Decree, dictatorial force of the factory overseer, draconic penalties, rule by terror—all these things are but palliatives. The only way to a rebirth is the school of public life itself, the most unlimited, the broadest democracy and public opinion. It is rule by terror which demoralizes.

"When all this is eliminated, what really remains? In place of the representative bodies created by general, popular elections, Lenin and Trotsky have laid down the soviets as the only true representation of the laboring masses. But with the repression of political life in the land as a whole, life in the soviets must also become more and more crippled. Without general elections . . . freedom of press and assembly, . . . a free struggle of opinion, life dies out in every public institution, becomes a mere semblance of life, in which only the bureaucracy remains as the active element. Public life gradually falls asleep, a few dozen party leaders of inexhaustible energy and boundless experience direct and rule. Among them, in reality, only a dozen outstanding heads do the leading and an elite of the working class is invited from time to time to meetings where they are to applaud the speeches of the leaders, and to approve proposed resolutions unanimously—at bottom, then, a clique affair—a dictatorship, to be sure, not the dictatorship of the proletariat, however, but only the dictatorship of a handful of proletarians . . . in the sense of the rule of the Jacobins. . . . Yes, we can go even further: such conditions must inevitably cause a brutalization of public life: attempted assassinations, shooting of hostages, etc." (R. Luxemburg, *The Russian Revolution* [New York, 1940], pp. 44–48.)

25. R. Luxemburg, "Organisationsfragen der russischen Sozialdemokratie," *Die Neue Zeit*, No. 42, 22 Jahrgang, II, (1903–1904), 486–87.

26. "In Russia . . . there is being attempted the experiment of creating a social democracy [before the establishment of] the political regime of the bourgeoisie. This has lent a quite peculiar form not only to the matter of the transplantation of socialist teachings to Russian soil, but also to the problem of agitation and [party] organization. . . . To the social democracy of Russia has fallen the task to interfere deliberately with a portion of the historical process and to lead the proletariat directly out of political atomization, which is the basis of the absolute regime, to the highest form of organization—as an aim-conscious fighting class. The question of organization is, therefore, particularly difficult for Russian social democracy, above all, because it must, lacking the political raw material, . . . create out of empty air, like God Himself, out of

nothing, that, which ordinarily is previously prepared by the bourgeois society" (*ibid.*, pp. 485–86).

27. Luxemburg, *The Russian Revolution*, p. 54.

28. "The danger begins only when [the Bolsheviks] make a virtue of necessity and want to freeze into a complete theoretical system all the tactics forced upon them by these fatal circumstances, and want to recommend them to the international proletariat as a model of socialist tactics . . . [thus] they render a poor service to international socialism for the sake of which they have fought and suffered; for they want to place in its storehouse as new discoveries all the distortions prescribed in Russia by necessity and compulsion—in the last analysis only by-products of the bankruptcy of international socialism in the present war.

"Let the German Government Socialists cry that the rule of the Bolsheviks in Russia is a distorted expression of the dictatorship of the proletariat. . . . All of us are subject to the laws of history, and it is only internationally that the socialist order can be realized. The Bolsheviks have shown that they are capable of everything that a genuine revolutionary party can contribute within the limits of the historical possibilities. They are not supposed to perform miracles. For a model and faultless proletarian revolution in an isolated land, exhausted by world war, strangled by imperialism, betrayed by the international proletariat, would be a miracle.

"In the present period . . . the most important problem of socialism was and is the capacity for action of the proletariat, the strength to act, the will to power of socialism as such. In this, Lenin and Trotsky and their friends were *first*. . . . They are the *only ones* up to now who can cry with Hutten, 'I have dared!'

"This is the essential and *enduring* in Bolshevik policy. . . . In Russia the problem could only be posed. It could not be solved in Russia. And in this sense, the future everywhere belongs to Bolshevism" (*ibid.*, pp. 55–56).

29. "The Communist International," Luxemburg told Eberlein, "should be definitely founded only when in the revolutionary mass movements sweeping over . . . Europe, Communist Parties have arisen" (Eberlein, *op. cit.*, p. 437). "She was thoroughly afraid of an international mainly led by the Russian Bolsheviks, whom she distrusted. . . . Oral evidence which I collected for several years from many of her collaborators—including the late Ernst Meyer—entirely confirms [this view]." (Borkenau, *op. cit.*, p. 87.)

30. "Next to the Russian Communist Party, the greatest prestige and respect were enjoyed by the members of the German Communist Party. . . . That feeling was passed on to its representative at the Congress . . . Eberlein. Apart from . . . Lenin, there was hardly another comrade whose opinion and wishes were so much respected, owing to the party which he represented, as was comrade [Eberlein]. Everybody was in the mood to do anything to meet the demands of his party half way" (B. Reinstein, "On the Road to the First Congress," *The Communist International*, Nos. 9–10, [1929], p. 432).

31. *Soch.*, XXIV, 725.

32. Bibliothek der Kommunistischen Internationale, VII, *Der 1 Kongress der Kommunistischen Internationale, Protokoll der Verhandlungen in Moskau vom 2 bis zum 19* [a misprint, should be 6] *März, 1919*. (Hamburg, 1921), p. 8. (Hereafter cited as *I Kongress.*)

33. *Ibid.*, pp. 76–77.

34. *Ibid.*, p. 94.

35. E. Korotky, B. Kun, O. Pyatnitsky, eds., *Protokoli Kongressov Kommunisticheskogo Internatsionala, Pervi Kongress Kominterna, Mart, 1919 g.* (Moscow, 1933), p. 87. (Hereafter cited as *Pervi Kongress.*)

36. "We traveled like apprentice craftsmen all the way. On tenders, locomotives, . . . in cattle cars, on foot through the Ukrainian and Polish robber bands, always in danger of losing our lives—always with the most fervent thoughts. To Moscow. We want to get to Moscow. We must get to Moscow, and nothing can stop us from getting there. We have reached our goal. We are among you, our comrades" (*I Kongress,* p. 105).

37. *Ibid.*, pp. 104–5.

38. Balabanova, *op. cit.*, pp. 225–26; Reinstein, *op. cit.*, p. 434.

39. "Everybody was astounded by [Eberlein's] proposal [that the founding of the International be delayed]. Everybody had come [to Moscow] with the first intention of laying the foundation of the Comintern and could in no wise agree with comrade [Eberlein's] arguments" (Reinstein, *op. cit.*, p. 433).

40. "But how Steinhardt spoke! It is difficult to convey the impression. He seemed to electrify his audience, infecting them with his boundless enthusiasm, audacity and faith in the strength of our movement" (*ibid., p.* 434).

41. "[Eberlein] had won a temporary victory, but it was merely temporary, lasting only a few hours. None of those who had voted for the decision were satisfied with it. They all felt that an error had been committed under pressure and were eager for a suitable moment to put it right" (*ibid.*).

42. "There were comrades who saw in [Eberlein's arguments] the expression of the timidity and scepticism of the Spartacus comrades themselves on the question of the expediency of establishing a new international. Certain of them said that Rosa Luxemburg had also been against the immediate foundation of a special Communist International. Others went further and considered that the position of [Eberlein] indicated that the Spartacists and Luxemburg had not yet ceased to regard the social-democrats as their deluded party comrades, had not yet given up hope that they would some time or other be united again; and so were endeavoring to postpone the foundation of the Comintern, since the latter would interfere with their hopes" (*ibid.*, p. 433).

43. Balabanova, *op. cit.*, pp. 225–26.

44. *Pervi Kongress,* p. 98.

45. *I Kongress,* p. 129. Lenin's optimistic evaluation of the Soviet movement in England was derived from Fineberg's exaggerated report on the English situation delivered earlier. "In the Shop Stewards' Committees, in the workers' committees and in the national conference of the Shop Steward Committees," Fineberg had declared, "we already have an organization similar to those upon which the Soviet Republic rests" (*I Kongress,* p. 72).

46. *Pervi Kongress,* p. 107.

47. *I Kongress,* pp. 129–30.

48. *Pervi Kongress,* pp. 118–19.

49. *I Kongress,* p. 132.

50. *Ibid.*, p. 133.

51. *Ibid.*

52. *Ibid.*, p. 134.

53. *Ibid.*, pp. 135–36.

54. Bibliothek der Kommunistischen Internationale, I., *Manifest, Richtlinien, Beschlüsse des ersten Kongresses, Aufrufe und offene Schreiben des Exekutiv-Komitees bis zum zweiten Kongress* (Hamburg, 1920), p. 20.

55. *Ibid.*, p. 49.

56. *Ibid.*, p. 52.

Notes to Chapter 10

1. These territories included most of the land east of the Urals, much of South Russia and the Ukraine, as well as North Russia, Transcaucasia, and the Crimea.

2. *Pervi Kongress*, p. 217.

3. "One must not overlook the fact that the young Russian industry has never done without foreign aid. The Entente paralyzes the organization of the new economic life in that it forbids foreign specialists, the actual [managers] of Russian industry, to return to Russia, . . . it destroys industry and imposes upon the people the consequences of unemployment [possibly a hint at unemployment in the West] in that it forbids the importation into Russia of machines, railway cars, and locomotives. Even the harvest is threatened since peasants no longer receive from abroad the necessary farm equipment and instruments. . . . The Soviet Republic has numerous times officially expressed its desire to utilize, even in the future, the help of foreign industries and specialists; [the Soviet Republic] has declared its readiness to pay dearly for their services, necessary at the present time for the prosperity of Russian economic life." The message further appealed to liberal elements in the Entente countries, as to proletarians, to demand, among other things, "the renewal of trade relations [between Russia and the West and] the delegating to Russia of several hundreds or even thousands of organizers, engineers, instructors and skilled workers, particularly metal workers . . . particularly for [the restoration of the means of communication and] the organization of transportation" (*ibid.*, pp. 216–18).

4. "When our Central Committee," said Lenin in his March 18 address, "was obliged to take up the question of partaking in the Prinkipo Island conference together with the Whites—which would in essence have led to their annexation of all territories they occupied—this question of a truce produced not one unfavorable voice among the proletariat, and this was the case in the party too. At least we were not obliged to hear of dissatisfaction or demurrers. This happened because our lesson in international politics [at the time of Brest-Litovsk] had yielded results" (*Soch.*, XXIV, 119).

5. *Soch.*, XXIV, 55–59.

6. "There are conditions when violence is necessary and useful, and there are conditions when it can give no results. . . . However, . . . these differences

have not been clear to all. . . . In November [1917] violence . . . had a brilliant success.

"Why? Because first, the masses were organized in Soviets, and second, because the enemy—the bourgeoisie . . . was undermined, worn down by the long political period from March to November . . . like a piece of ice in thawing water, and already quite powerless internally—and that is why the movement in November, comparing it with the present revolutionary movement in Germany, so easily gave us a complete, brilliant triumph of revolutionary violence.

"Can one assume that this path, this form of struggle, the easy triumph of revolutionary violence is feasible without these conditions?

"To assume this would be the greatest error. And the greater the revolutionary victory, sustained under certain conditions, the oftener there exists the danger that we permit ourselves to be beguiled by these triumphs, not considering cold-bloodedly, calmly, and attentively the conditions that made the victory possible."

[The Kerensky government blew away like a piece of fluff.]

"But is this situation similar to that which now faces us as a practical problem with regard to world imperialism? Of course not.

"This is why in the sphere of foreign policy the question of Brest-Litovsk caused such difficulties. The mass character of the movement helped to overcome these.

"But in what lay the source of the errors which made a section of our comrades think that we had committed an unheard of crime? And even now there are odd birds among those people, who are able to hold a pen and imagine that they are somebodies . . . who still believe that this was collaborationism with German imperialism.

"Yes, this was collaborationism—but of the same sort as when we 'collaborated' with the tsar, entering the disgustingly reactionary Duma to destroy it from within.

"Can one count, by the application of violence alone and without a corresponding development of the proletariat in these imperialist countries, upon overthrowing world imperialism?

"To pose the problem in this manner (which we must do as Marxists), then to employ violence there would be absolute absurdity . . . and a complete misunderstanding of the conditions under which the policy of violence succeeds.

"Now we see this. We are rich in experience.

"At the time, in the period of the Brest peace, when we had to gather our resources and lay the foundation of a new army in a country ruined and worn out by war, as no other country on earth, . . . at this time the imperialism of other countries was being undermined by internal decay, by the growing protests, and was weakened. Just as revolutionary violence won a victory in Germany only after a struggle of many months had undermined imperialism in that country, so now the pattern repeats itself to a certain degree, if not fully, in the countries of the Allies. . . .

"This is why that policy which we were obliged to conduct in the course of the most bestial, violent, degrading Brest peace, was the only correct policy.

"And I believe that it would not be without purpose once more to recall this policy when we view our position in relation to the . . . Allies, who are just as full of the mad desire . . . to crush Russia, in order to divert from themselves the growing wrath of the toiling masses.

"Looking squarely at the facts [we have to admit] that the Entente is militarily stronger than we are, . . . but this strength of the Allies—is not for long; they stand on the eve [of revolution]; . . . if they succeed [in concluding a peace] without flying at each other's hair and throats, then this peace will be the beginning of a quick crash, because to pay the unheard of debts and get out of the desperate ruin, when in France the production of fowl has dropped to less than half, and hunger knocks at every door, and the productive forces have been destroyed—they are not capable of solving this dilemma.

"If one faces the facts, one must admit that the ability to evaluate events, which served so well in the Russian revolution, is helping every day to confirm the world revolution. We know that the streams which are making inroads upon the icy blocks of the Entente, . . . capitalism and imperialism, are growing with every day.

"On the one hand the Allies are stronger than we, on the other, they can, in view of their internal conditions, not last much longer.

"Our most essential experience was the Brest peace. . . . We had to wait, retreat, maneuver, sign the most degrading peace, which gave us the chance to build the new foundation of the new socialist army. But we laid the foundation and our once all-powerful enemy is already powerless" (*Soch.*, XXIV, 55–59).

7. *Soch.*, XXIV, 157. At 5:00 P.M., March 22, the Central Committee of the Hungarian Communist party radioed to Moscow a report on the seizure of power and greetings to Lenin, "the leader of the international proletariat" (*Soch.*, XXIV, 768).

8. *Soch.*, XXIV, 178.

9. From the archives of the Soviet War Commissariat, as cited by Louis Fischer, *The Soviets in World Affairs* (2 vols.; New York, 1930), I, 194.

10. "Previously," he declared on April 5, "lies were told, scaring the European workers about Russia's anarchy . . . violaters . . . usurpers. But Hungary provided an example of revolution which developed differently. . . . Our difficult situation lay in the fact that we had to produce Soviet power against patriotism. We had to smash patriotism and conclude the Brest peace. This was a most desperate, mad, and bloody smashing. Bolshevism—this means the use of bloody means to smash even patriotism. [Violence when necessary is all right.] In the neighboring countries they have seen who must rule. Who else but the Soviets? This is like old times, when princes saw that their power was weakened, they said: 'A constitution is necessary—let the bourgeoisie take over.' . . . When the . . . imperialists made fantastic demands upon the Hungarian capitalists, the latter said, 'We cannot fight. Behind us the people will not march; but we as Hungarian patriots want to offer resistance. What kind of power shall there be?—Soviet power'" (*Soch.*, XXIV, 178).

"The Hungarian bourgeoisie displayed before the entire world that it voluntarily retired and that there is only one power in the world capable of leading the people in a difficult moment, the power of the Soviets. This is why the Hungarian revolution, by the fact that it was born quite differently from ours, shows the whole world that which was hidden in relation to Russia, namely, that bolshevism is connected with the new proletarian workers' democracy which stands in the place of the old parliament" (*Soch.*, XXIV, 219).

11. *Soch.*, XXIV, 219.

12. *Soch.*, XXIV, 181.

13. *Soch.*, XXIV, 195.

14. *Soch.*, XXIV, 262. The world significance of the spreading Sovietism was also acknowledged by the Communist party of Soviet Latvia. "But it does move—the revolution," proclaimed a manifesto of April 9. "First Hungary—now Bavaria. . . . Read this, German workers in soldiers' uniforms who are here fighting against your Latvian brothers. . . . Your lying prophets who have always declared that only in dark Russia could a Soviet Republic arise, have now been answered by Hungary. Your social traitors who tell you that a Soviet regime is not suited to Germany are today refuted by—Bavaria. And tomorrow —Württemberg and Austria. It is the final hour. Who is not with us is against us" (*Rote Fahne* [Riga], April 9, 1919).

15. *Soch.*, XXIV, 313–16.

16. *Soch.*, XXIV, 181.

17. In a letter dated April 22, 1919, Kun assured Lenin that he was doing everything possible to guide the Hungarian revolution in a manner that Lenin would approve of. "I do not believe there is even a single action or enactment [of the government] based on a principle that you could raise objection to. Our present situation in foreign politics is worse by far than that of Russia. Yet I believe no objections can be made to our actions even from the point of view of pure principle. The conciliation [with the Social Democrats], brought about on the basis of this programme, is doubtless one of principle and tactics, that is to say, a real unity. The members of the extreme right have been pushed out of the party, and the old trade union bureaucracy is gradually being sifted out. I know very well that not I, but the proletariat itself, will decide its own fate, but I beg you to keep your confidence in me" (*The Communist International*, No. 2, June, 1919, p. 225).

18. *Soch.*, XXIV, 195.

19. *Soch.*, XXIV, 264.

Notes to Chapter 11

1. That Lenin conceived of Asia in terms of his Russian perspective can be adequately surmised from the Russian yardstick which he employed in commenting upon the Chinese revolution of 1911. "Chinese freedom," he wrote in November, 1912, "was won by a union of peasant democracy and liberal bourgeoisie. It remains to be seen whether the peasants, not led by a proletarian party, can support their democratic position *against* the liberals—who await only the appropriate moment to turn to the right" (*Soçh.*, XVI, 189).

2. "In Asia, everywhere the mighty democratic movement grows. . . . The bourgeoisie *still* moves with the people against the feudal reaction. *Hundreds* of millions of people are there awakening to life, to light, to freedom. What joy this world movement evokes in the hearts of all conscious workers, knowing that the path to collectivism lies through democracy—with what feelings of sympathy to young Asia are all honest democrats filled!

"But 'progressive' Europe? It robs China and helps the enemies of democracy, the enemies of freedom in China! . . .

"All those who command Europe, the entire European bourgeoisie, is *in* league with all the forces of reaction and medievalism in China.

"However, all of young Asia, i.e., the hundreds of millions of toilers of Asia, have a trustworthy ally in the person of the proletariat of all the civilized countries. No power on earth can stop his victory, which will liberate both the peoples of Europe and the peoples of Asia" (*Soch.*, XVI, 395–96).

3. A proclamation of December, 1917, signed by Lenin and Stalin, was directed to the "Laboring Moslems of Russia and the East." It promised to those whose "beliefs and customs [had] been tramped upon by the tsars" the right "under the mighty protection of the Revolution" to "organize [their] national life in complete freedom" (R. Pipes, *The Formation of the Soviet Union, Communism and Nationalism, 1917–1923* [Cambridge, Mass., 1954], citing L. I. Musulman, *Revue du Monde* [1922], Part I, pp. 7–9).

4. *Zhizn' Natsional' nostei*, No. 24, Nov., 1918; cited in Pipes, *op. cit.*, p. 160.

5. *Soch.*, XXIV, 360. "And now, a half year after November 9 and the German defeat," Lenin declared in a July 5 address, "the French and English imperialists have made a peace . . . This showed all the workers who had formerly supported the cause of the French and English imperialists [how matters really stood]. These workers who had favored war to the end are now coming over to our side, not by days but by the hour, and are saying: 'They deceived us for four years. In the name of freedom they promised us the defeat of Germany, the victory of freedom, equality and democracy. Instead they gave us the Peace of Versailles, an unworthy violent peace in the interests of plunderers.' " On July 15 Lenin remarked, "As Brest for Germany, so Versailles for France and England will end in the downfall of the capitalists and the victory of the proletariat" (*Soch.*, XXIV, 401).

6. At this congress held on March 2–6 Haase said: "The [National] Assembly is a fact, and one must not demand its removal. But it requires supplementation by a system of Soviets. The question is not whether [we should have] a National Assembly or Soviets but rather how to join the two. The tendency is in this direction" (*Soch.*, XXIV, 782).

7. *Soch.*, XXIV, 135. Lenin made this comment in March, 1919, at the Eighth Party Congress.

8. This commission was appointed by the Soviet government when the Soviet armies captured Orenburg in January, 1919. Among its members were M. V. Frunze and V. V. Kuibyshev, commander and commissar respectively of the Fourth [Soviet] Army. The course of military affairs delayed the commission's originally intended direct departure for Tashkent (Pipes, *op. cit.*, p. 181).

9. So dismal a report was sent back to Moscow that the party's Central

Committee dispatched a bitterly critical letter to "All Organizations of the Communist Party of Turkestan."

"The toiling masses of Kirgiz, Sarts, Uzbeks, and Turkmens," the letter declared in part, "do not as yet know what Soviet power and the Communist party really are—the defender of all oppressed and exploited peoples" (G. Safarov, *Kolonial'naya Revoliutsiya [Opit Turkestana]*, [Moscow, 1921], p. 133).

10. *Soch.*, XXIV, 811.

11. *Soch.*, XXIV, 531.

12. Cited in Pipes, *op. cit.*, p. 169.

13. *Soch.*, XXIV, 542–51.

14. The British Socialist party, the Socialist Labour party, the Workers' Socialist Federation, the South Wales Socialist Society. For a detailed account of the formation of the British Communist party see S. R. Graubard, *British Labour and the Russian Revolution, 1917–1924* (Cambridge, Mass., 1956), pp. 115–39.

15. *Soch.*, XXIV, 437–42.

16. *Soch.*, XXIV, 478.

17. *Soch.*, XXIV, 480.

18. *Soch.*, XXIV, 481.

19. "Even now, two years after the conquest of state power, we have not yet ended our struggle with the remains of the Menshevik trade unions. How long a process this is! How strong in certain localities and in certain professions is the influence of petty-bourgeois ideas!" The following out of the same tract is noteworthy above all because of the farfetched illustration in Lenin's attempt to link the Russian experience with that of Germany. "The history of our revolution, for instance, showed that the sympathy of the majority of the workers . . . in the Urals regions and in Siberia was not revealed by elections, but by the experiences of the year-long domination of General Kolchak over the Urals and Siberia. Incidentally, the power of Kolchak also came into existence out of a 'coalition' of Scheidemannists and Kautskyans (in Russian, 'Mensheviks' and 'Socialist-Revolutionaries,' partisans of the Constituent Assembly), as in Germany now the Messrs. Haase and Scheidemann, by their 'coalition' pave the way to power of von [der] Goltz or Ludendorff" (*Soch.*, XXIV, 480–81).

20. *Soch.*, XXIV, 482.

21. *Soch.*, XXIV, 480.

22. *Soch.*, XXIV, 502.

23. *Soch.*, XXIV, 504.

24. *Soch.*, XXIV, 810.

25. During 1917 Lenin had numerous times declared that only in "free" Russia was it possible for a party seeking the overthrow of its government to preach and practice toward this end with almost complete impunity to counteraction.

26. *Soch.*, XXV, 241–42.

27. Lenin attacked the German "left-communist" contention that parliamentarism had become "historically obsolete." He admitted as "beyond dispute" that "in the world historical sense . . . the *epoch* of bourgeois parliamentarism [had] come to an end and the *epoch* of the proletarian dictatorship

[had] *begun."* (The italicizing of the words *epoch* and *begun* should be especially noted.) But the world historical yardstick, Lenin continued, "is one of decades. Ten or twenty years sooner or later makes no difference from the standpoint of the world historical yardstick; in terms of world history it is a trifle which cannot be calculated even approximately. But precisely for that reason it is a gross theoretical error to use the world historical measure in matters of practical politics" (*Soch.*, XXV, 200). In his "Theses on the Basic Tasks of the Second Congress of Comintern," written July 4, Lenin admitted that in most capitalistic countries even the preparatory beginnings of proletarian revolution had not yet been made. At the same time he declared that this did not mean that proletarian revolution was impossible in the near future, "for the entire economic and political situation was extraordinarily rich in explosive materials and in possibilities for sudden eruptions." In the general condition of "crisis in all the dominant and in all the bourgeois parties" Lenin saw a further "circumstance tending to revolution." But from these observations Lenin drew the conclusion that the "immediate task of the Communist party was not that of hastening revolution, but that of further enhancing the preparedness of the proletariat" (*Soch.*, XXV, 315–16).

28. *Soch.*, XXV, 207.

29. *Soch.*, XXV, 207.

30. *Soch.*, XXV, 175.

31. *Soch.*, XXV, 174.

32. *Soch.*, XXV, 177–79. The pamphlet's object, Lenin explained, was "to apply to Western Europe whatever [was] of general application, general validity and general binding force in the history and the present tactic of bolshevism" (*Soch.*, XXV, 192).

33. M. Rafail, "God bez Lenina na Vostoke," *Lenin i Vostok, Sbornik Statei* (2d ed.; Moscow, 1925), p. 7.

Notes to Chapter 12

1. *Vtoroy Kongress Kominterna, Iul'—Avgust 1920g* (Moscow, 1934), p. 29.

2. The Dutch Tribunists and the Spanish National Confederation of Labor (CNT).

3. The British and Scottish Shop Stewards and a French group, which in May, 1919, designated itself as the "Committee for Adhesion to the Third International."

4. "This method ensured that every delegation 'went to school' on the first principles of the new movement under the direction and tuition of one of the Russian communist leaders" (J. T. Murphy, *New Horizons* [London, 1941], p. 147). The membership of the committees is listed in *Vtoroy Kongress*, pp. 627–28.

5. For expressions of reverence with respect to Russia and bolshevism see Murphy, *op. cit.* "The crossing of the Russian frontier . . . was the moment of a lifetime, to be remembered forever" (p. 105). "Then Lenin, the master of us all, took the floor" (p. 149). See also Balabanova, *Erinnerungen und Erlebnisse,* "At the Congress, Serrati acted heroically. He defended his point of view even when it opposed that of Lenin" (p. 259).

6. "When any particular country was considered, the discussion usually resolved itself into a debate between the delegation from that country and the Russians. When a general or principal question was under consideration, every delegation approached the question from the angle of his or her own particular country. Only the Russians showed any real knowledge and sense of internationalism. We from England were very insular and knew little of the life of other countries and their parties. . . . Lenin, Trotsky and Radek were far ahead of any in the Congress in their knowledge both general and particular of other countries and their parties" (Murphy, *op. cit.,* p. 150).

7. The three other members were Levi (Germany), Rosmer (France), and Serrati (Italy).

8. By the term "Soviet bloc" is meant not only delegates supposedly representing one or another part of Bolshevik-held Russia but also delegates, such as those of Poland, Eastern Galitzia, Lithuania, Latvia, etc., whose designation had emanated from Russia and not from the countries officially ascribed to them.

9. *Vtoroy Kongress,* pp. 619–25. This official source admits that the cited numbers of delegates and votes is not exact.

10. Germany, Austria, Bulgaria, Finland, Yugoslavia, Czechoslovakia, and Switzerland.

11. Dutch East Indies (2 votes), Korea (1 vote), Persia (1 vote), Turkey (3 votes). China and India were represented but without decisive votes.

12. *Vtoroy Kongress,* p. 59.

13. *Ibid.,* p. 61.

14. " . . . upon whom we count especially as the representatives of the mass movement" (*ibid.,* p. 68).

15. *Ibid.,* pp. 68–69.

16. S. R. Graubard, *British Labour and the Russian Revolution, 1917–1924* (Cambridge, Mass., 1956), p. 116.

17. The British delegation was made up of Tom Quelch and William Mac-Laine of the British Socialist party; Sylvia Pankhurst; Jack Tanner, Dave Ramsey, and J. T. Murphy of the Shop Stewards; Willie Gallacher, as a dissident from the Glasgow-based Socialist Labour party, and the independents, Helen Crawford and Dick Beech (*ibid.,* p. 130).

18. *Vtoroy Kongress,* p. 69.

19. *Ibid.,* p. 70.

20. *Soch.,* XXV, 281.

21. *Vtoroy Kongress,* pp. 90–96.

22. That the added names were not on Lenin's original list does not mean that Lenin had ever desired any form of compromise with such "archbetrayers." Lenin had probably intended that the mention of the two Italian prototypes would stand for his views on reformists in general. That he had selected pre-

cisely these two as bad examples is readily explained by the fact that at the time when he was drawing up his theses the problems facing the Communist movement in Italy had been his particular preoccupation. The appearance of German, French, British, and American names in the revised thesis 7 shows that Lenin wanted to brush off the stigma of opportunism that the Lefts had flung at him. The additional names did not seriously alter the meaning of the message contained in the original wording of thesis 7, but they did create a tougher impression. "The committee," Zinoviev announced, "has decided more correctly to name not only Italian opportunists: we are, after all, the Communist International and must therefore decry reformists of other countries also. The committee has decided to name at least one [reformist] for each country" (*ibid.*, p. 162). As far as one can judge it was not at this time but at a subsequent date that the committee also decided to add the name of Hilferding to the list (*ibid.*, p. 449).

23. *Ibid.*, p. 163.

24. *Ibid.*

25. The French socialist leadership, he said, had shown a willingness to accept Woodrow Wilson as a man of good will. The party's press was still running articles by Rights and centrists and had referred to Renaudel as "our friend." The USPD was still under the influence of Kautsky. The Italian party was better than the others but erred greatly in refusing to eject Turati, a man who could make a speech in parliament proposing that workers and bourgeoisie should help each other. "Now mind you, Turati, as a member of the Italian party is also a member of the Third International. Tell me, . . . isn't this shameful!" Bombacci, one of the Italian delegates at the Congress, on occasion of sharing a speaker's platform with Turati, had refused to label him "our class enemy." The Swedish, Norwegian and Yugoslav parties had also shown tolerance toward reformism (*ibid.*, pp. 170–76).

26. *Ibid.*, p. 177.

27. Concluding on a flag-waving, tub-thumping note, Zinoviev declared that whatever attitude the leaders of the USPD or the French Socialist party took, "the hearts of the workers of all countries belong to us; . . . the last hour of the bourgeoisie and the semibourgeois Second International has struck. The hour for the real struggle for socialism has arrived" (*ibid.*, pp. 177–78).

28. *Ibid.*, pp. 196–97.

29. *Ibid.*, p. 653.

30. *Ibid.*, pp. 199–200.

31. *Ibid.*, p. 212.

32. *Ibid.*, pp. 215–16.

33. *Ibid.*, p. 223.

34. *Ibid.*, p. 225.

35. *Ibid.*, pp. 240–44.

36. *Ibid.*, pp. 249–50.

37. *Ibid.*, pp. 274–76.

38. *Ibid.*, p. 281.

39. *Ibid.*, p. 450.

40. *Ibid.*, p. 451.

41. *Ibid.*, pp. 13–29.

42. On every other controversial issue to arise at the congress, the opposi-

tion to Lenin came only from the delegates of one or two countries, other delegations not considering themselves especially affected. In their opposition to the idea of the essentiality of a party, the English Shop Stewards found support in no other delegation. In their stand on the trade union question the Shop Stewards were joined only by the American contingent. Lenin's tactical proposals with regard to the middle peasantry aroused none but the Germans of the USPD. Equally isolated were the Italians in explaining their reluctance to break with reformist leaders on the grounds of working class attitudes peculiar to Italy. But the question of what groups to admit to the Comintern, since it brought to the fore the fury of the revolutionary-minded toward those whom they considered traitors to the cause, brought a strong reaction from all the important delegations.

43. "It is doubtful whether we who were visitors in 1920 fully appreciated the circumstances that were developing before our eyes. Perhaps we were too occupied with the romantic aspects of the revolution to measure correctly the drama in which we were participating. Maybe our heads were too full of the burning question of world revolution to appreciate the nature of the problem of successfully consolidating what had been won in the vast country in which we were guests" (Murphy, *op. cit.*, p. 114; see also p. 144).

44. J. T. Murphy, a delegate of the Shop Stewards, was later to write that in 1920 the revolutionary tide "beyond the frontiers of Soviet Russia . . . was already on the ebb." As evidence, Murphy cited the defeat of the Hungarian revolution, the failure of the German revolution to make headway, the passing of the peak of the strike wave in Britain, etc. "These things, however, did not stand out clearly before us. We thought of ourselves as at the centre of the revolution which would spread and spread, wave on wave. Yes, there would be setbacks here and there, . . . but these would be incidental to the onward movement of the great army of workers and oppressed. These were the mistaken ideas at the back of our minds as we entered the Kremlin gates. . . . We were playing leap-frog with history and did not know it" (J. T. Murphy, *op. cit.*, p. 135).

45. *Ibid.*, p. 113.

46. See Trotsky, *My Life*, p. 456.

47. Alleging that the Allied Supreme Council had been under the influence of Russian Whites when it had determined the Polish-Russian border, the Bolsheviks offered to revise the line in Poland's favor.

48. S. Rabinovich, *Istoriya grazhdanskoy voini* (Moscow, 1933), p. 96.

49. Iu. V. Kliuchnikov and A. V. Sabanin, *Mezhdunarodnaya Politika noveishego vremeni v dogorogakh, notakh i deklaratsiyakh,* Part III (Moscow, 1928), pp. 34–35.

50. "After the terrific effort that enabled the Fourth Army to cover 650 kilometres in five weeks, it could drive forward only through inertia. Everything hung on nerves and these were but thin threads. I demanded an immediate conclusion of peace before the army should grow too exhausted" (Trotsky, *My Life*, p. 457).

51. Trotsky Archives (Harvard University).

52. Chicherin's note expressed "the great satisfaction" of the Soviet government with "the British wish to facilitate the establishment of peace in Eastern

Europe," but expressed sorrow over the fact that just before the Polish invasion of Russia the British government had not expressed the wish to facilitate peace in Eastern Europe. Similarly, Britain had not co-operated with Soviet attempts to make peace with other border states, and in December, 1919, when Estonia was preparing to sign a peace with Soviet Russia, the Allied Supreme Council had warned Estonia not to do so (Kliuchnikov and Sabanin, *op. cit.*, pp. 35–36).

53. *Ibid.*, pp. 41–45.

54. The trend of Lenin's thinking may be safely inferred from an address he delivered on May 5, shortly before the Poles entered Kiev. "The rule which we have held to in all previous years, we must unchangingly adhere to at the present time also. The rule consists of this: once matters have come to war, then everything must be subordinated to the interests of war, all internal life of the country must be subordinated to war and on this score not the slightest vacillation is permissible" (*Soch.*, XXV, 261).

55. To a congress of Cossacks on March 1, 1920, Lenin had said: "True, [the Entente] can still send Poland against us. The Polish landlords and capitalists . . . hurl threats that they want the territory [held by Poland in] 1772, that they wish to subjugate the Ukraine. . . . And we say to the Polish comrades that we respect Polish freedom as we do the freedom of any other peoples, that the Russian worker and peasant, having experienced the tsarist yoke knows well what this means. We know that the greatest crime was the partitioning of Poland among German, Austrian, and Russian capital, that this partitioning condemned the Polish people to long years of oppression, when the use of the native language was considered a crime, when the entire Polish people was brought up on one idea—to free itself from this triple yoke. That is why we understand the hatred that permeates the spirit of the Poles, and we say to them that we shall never cross the boundary upon which our troops now stand— and they stand a great distance away from where the Polish people live. We propose peace on this basis, because we know that this will constitute an immense acquisition for Poland. We do not want war to rise over a territorial boundary because we wish to wipe out the accursed past when every Great Russian considered himself an oppressor" (*Soch.*, XXV, 58).

56. L. Trotsky, *Stalin* (London, 1947), p. 328.

57. The draft treaty was presented to a Polish delegation at Minsk on August 17. The Soviet government offered territorial conditions identical to those proposed to Poland before the start of hostilities. This seemingly generous stipulation, however, was not made to the same (Pilsudski) government but to the "Polish people," to whom the Soviet government also conceded the "unconditional right to arrange its life" as it saw fit and to establish whatever form of governmental authority it desired.

The draft treaty in fact dictated an alteration of Poland's social structure. Article 12 demanded that the "Polish Republic [undertake] to pass legislation for the free division of the land, granting it in the first instance to the families of Polish citizens killed, wounded, or incapacitated in the war or as a result of the war." Most of the war casualties were naturally members of the lowest classes. The treaty stipulated that the Polish army should be the size of an internal police force, but demanded at the same time the establishment of a "people's militia," clearly intended to be under Bolshevik control. The projected treaty further forbade Poland to allow groups hostile to the Soviet Republic within her territory, to produce arms, or to receive supplies of military materials from foreign countries (Kliuchnikov and Sabanin, *op. cit.*, pp. 47–49).

58. "All the talents of Budënny and of other . . . army leaders," Lenin was subsequently to tell Klara Zetkin, "could not counterbalance our military and technical shortcomings and, even less, our false political reckoning, our hope in the Polish revolution. Incidentally, Radek foretold how everything would happen. He warned us. I was terribly angry with him and called him a defeatist —but in the main he proved to be right. He knows the situation in the West better than we do and he is talented. He is very helpful to us" (L. Fischer, *The Soviets in World Affairs*, I, 271).

59. For an account of the great excitement, revolutionary and otherwise, generated in Germany by the Red advance, see E. H. Carr, *The Bolshevik Revolution, 1917–1923* (3 vols., New York, 1950–1953), III, pp. 323–28.

60. *Vtoroy Kongress,* pp. 646–50.

61. *Ibid.,* pp. 113–14.

62. *Ibid.,* pp. 101–02.

63. *Ibid.,* 105–7. Note the striking parallel to Lenin's opportunistically contrived thesis of 1902 with regard to the world revolutionary role of Russia's proletariat. See p. 4.

64. A. S. Whiting, *Soviet Policies in China, 1917–1924* (New York, 1954), pp. 54, 295.

65. For Roy's revised theses see *Vtoroy Kongress,* pp. 496–99.

66. Whiting, *op. cit.,* pp. 51–52, 294–95.

67. *Soch.,* XXV, 282.

68. *Vtoroy Kongress,* pp. 338, 346.

69. *Ibid.,* p. 338.

70. During the war when the British union leadership had refused to sanction strikes, strike committees were formed from among the rank and file—thus originating the Shop Stewards Committees.

71. According to Gallacher, it was "ridiculous to think of conquering the old trade unions and their ossified bureaucracies. . . . To speak of conquering the trade unions from within is as nonsensical as to dream of conquering the capitalist state from within" (*Vtoroy Kongress,* pp. 426–27).

72. "The English and the American comrades," said Gallacher, "need to gain the opportunity to conduct the battle for communism outside the trade unions" (*ibid.,* p. 427). Before leaving Moscow, Gallacher had come around to an acceptance of Lenin's position (W. Gallacher, *Revolt on the Clyde* [London, 1936], pp. 251, 253).

73. *Vtoroy Kongress,* p. 339.

74. *Ibid.,* p. 426.

75. A further opponent of Lenin's line was Bombacci, for many years a leader in the Italian union movement, who regarded the trade unions as having "no revolutionary function whatsoever."

76. Schism in the union movement, the Americans were told, was permissible, but only in cases of vital necessity. The final test of its necessity had always to be the consideration of whether the schism would lead to an isolation of the Communists from the working class. However, even if the creation of revolu-

tionary unions did prove necessary, this was still not supposed to signify the exit of Communists from opportunistic unions, "which [were] in a process of fermentation and transition toward a class struggle orientation." It was "on the contrary" the task of Communists "to expedite the evolution of the mass unions" and lead the organized workers into a "conscious struggle for the overthrow of capitalism."

The second part of the resolution was aimed at the British and conceded that the factory-shop, or shop-steward, committee was a vital transmission belt through which the workers could be drawn from their wage-hour conception of the union struggle to the conception of acquiring control of production itself. But it added that the factory-shop committees must not limit their membership to workers already willing to accept the dictatorship of the proletariat but must make recruits among the politically backward, thus deepening the mass awareness of the fact that an improvement of the economic basis of capitalism had already ceased to be possible. The resolution informed the Shop Stewards that it was not their function to replace the unions, but to remain within them until the seizure of power had taken place. Only then, under Communist party guidance, were the factory-shop committees to "build factory cells of the unions, which together with the workers' power in the localities and the center [would] construct special economic organs" (see *Vtoroy Kongress*, pp. 659–64).

77. *Ibid.*, pp. 362–63.

78. For the "Declaration of the Organization of the International Council of Trade Unions" see *Pravda*, July 18, 1920. Other members of the council were L. D'Aragona, of the Italian Labor Confederation, A. Pestagna, of the Spanish National Confederation of Labor, and A. Rosmer, of the revolutionary syndicalist minority of the French General Confederation of Labor.

79. *Vtoroy Kongress*, p. 406.

80. *Ibid.*, pp. 397–99.

81. *Ibid.*, pp. 399–400.

82. *Ibid.*, p. 406.

83. *Ibid.*, p. 407.

84. *Ibid.*, pp. 408–9.

85. *Ibid.*, p. 453.

Notes to Chapter 13

1. K. Zetkin, *Vospominaniya o Lenine, Sbornik statei i vospominaniya* (Moscow, 1933), p. 41.

2. *Ibid.*, p. 42.

3. See p. 113.

4. "We have begun the great war, which we will not win quickly; that is the bloodless war of the toilers' armies against hunger, cold, and ruination—for a civilized, bright, abundant, and healthy Russia." (From a speech given

January 26, 1920; see *Soch.*, XXV, 16.) "The country is in the final stages of ruin. . . . We must concentrate in the main upon gathering bread and bringing it to the center. Any deviation from this task, even the slightest dispersion of effort, would be [fatal] to our cause. . . . We must throw all our forces upon the front of labor . . . and do it with warlike and merciless determination." (From a speech of January 27; see *Soch.*, XXV, 19; see also *Soch.*, XXV, 24–25.)

5. Trotsky, *My Life*, p. 463.

6. Trotsky's proposal contains the following passage: "The food resources are threatened with exhaustion, a contingency that no amount of improvement in the methods of requisition can prevent. These tendencies toward economic decline can be counteracted as follows: (1) The requisition of surpluses should give way to payment on a percentage basis (a sort of progressive income tax in kind), the scale of payment being fixed in such a way as to make an increase of the ploughed area, or a more thorough cultivation still yield some profit; (2) a closer correspondence should be established between the industrial products supplied to the peasants and the quantities of grain they deliver" (Trotsky, *My Life*, p. 464).

7. *Ibid.*

8. *Soch.*, XXV, 43.

9. "From this victory," Lenin declared at the Ninth Congress, "we are now proceeding . . . to those tasks of peaceful economic development, the solution of which is the main function of our congress. . . . Yes, the task now is to apply to the peaceful work of economic development, to the restoration of our shattered industry, everything that can weld the proletariat into an absolute unity. Here we need the iron discipline, the iron system without which we could not have held out for two months, let alone for over two years. We must be able to utilize our success. On the other hand, it must be realized that this transition will demand many sacrifices of which the country has already borne many" (*Soch.*, XXV, 103).

10. In the course of the Second Congress of the Comintern, Zinoviev, clearly departing from Lenin's position, had more than once appended to his comments a declaration indicating his belief in an imminent eruption of revolution in the West (see *Vtoroy Kongress*, pp. 178, 385).

11. *Protokoll Des III Kongress Der Kommunistischen Internationale (Moskau, 22 Juni bis 12 Juli 1921)*, (Hamburg, 1921), p. 168. Hereafter cited as *III Kongress*.

12. *Ibid.*, p. 171.

13. *Ibid.*, p. 167.

14. *Ibid.*, p. 329.

15. *Ibid.*, p .330.

16. The pamphlet was entitled *Our Path, Against Starting Explosions*.

17. Zetkin, *op. cit.*, p. 43.

18. "My conscience was greatly troubled over the fact that I, in breaking discipline, found myself in sharp opposition to those who stood closest to me politically and personally—my Russian friends" (*ibid.*, p. 44).

19. *Ibid.*, pp. 45–53.

20. Bibliothek der Kommunistischen Internationale, XX, *Thesen und Reso-*

lutionen des III Weltkongresses der Kommunistischen Internationale (Moskau, 22 Juni bis 12 Juli 1921), (Hamburg, 1921), pp. 31–63.

21. *III Kongress*, p. 341.

22. *Ibid.*, p. 444. At the July 2 session Zinoviev had pointed out that it was the "leftist tendency" rather than organized leftist groups that were to be feared (*ibid.*, p. 626).

23. Lenin's discussion with Zetkin reveals the scorn toward "infantile leftism" of a man whom events had proved indisputably correct. To Trotsky, at the time of the Third Congress of the Comintern, Lenin said, "In July [1917] we committed not a few blunders." Lenin, as Trotsky writes, had in mind "our hasty armed uprising, the much too aggressive form of the demonstration which was in no proportion to our forces in the scale of the country" (Trotsky, *Lenin*, p. 77). Although Trotsky's interpretation of Lenin's thoughts is incorrect (see p. 77), it is nonetheless clear that Lenin had become so antioffensivistic that the July demonstrations, which the Bolsheviks had not initiated but merely sanctioned and which, in September and October, 1917, Lenin had deplored as a lost opportunity for seizing power, he could in retrospect remark upon as an act of undue Bolshevik recklessness.

24. *Soch.*, XXVI, 429.

25. *III Kongress*, p. 518.

26. *Ibid.*, p. 596.

27. *Ibid.*, p. 627.

28. *Ibid.*, p. 638.

29. *Ibid.*, p. 646.

30. *Ibid.*, p. 650.

31. *Ibid.*, pp. 665–66.

32. Pipes, *The Formation of the Soviet Union*, pp. 167–72.

33. *Ibid.*, p. 255; see also A. Park, *Bolshevism in Turkestan* (New York, 1957), pp. 63–87.

34. Carr, The Bolshevik Revolution, III, 262–63.

35. Z. Laqueur, "The Shifting Line in Soviet Orientology," *Problems of Communism*, V, No. 2, March–April, 1956, p. 21.

36. Carr, *op. cit.*, 407–12.

37. *III Kongress*, p. 1018.

38. *Ibid.*, p. 1035.

39. *Soch.*, XXVII, 416–17.

BIBLIOGRAPHY

Balabanova, A. *Erinnerungen und Erlebnisse.* Berlin, 1927.

Bonch-Bruevich, V. D. *V. I. Lenin v Rossii.* Moscow, 1935.

Bor'ba Bol'shevikov za Sozdaniye Kommunisticheskogo Internatsionala. Moscow, 1934.

Borkenau, F. *The Communist International.* London, 1938.

Carr, E. H. *The Bolshevik Revolution, 1917–1923.* 3 vols. New York, 1950–1953.

Chamberlin, W. H. *The Russian Revolution, 1917–1921.* 2 vols. New York, 1935.

Chernov, V. *Rozhdeniye revoliutsionnoy Rossii (Fevral'skaya revoliutsiya).* Prague, 1934.

Czernin, O. *Im Weltkriege.* Vienna, 1919.

Der I Kongress der Kommunistischen Internationale, Protokoll der Verhandlungen in Moskau vom 2 bis zum 19 März, 1919. Hamburg, 1921.

Deutscher, I. *The Prophet Armed, Trotsky: 1879–1921.* New York, 1954.

Die Rote Fahne. Riga.

Eberlein, H. "The Foundation of the Comintern and the Spartakusbund." *The Communist International,* Nos. 9–10, 1929.

Elov, B. "Posle Iul'skikh Sobitii." *Krasnaya Letopis,* No. 7, 1923.

Fineberg, S. "The Formation of the Communist International." *The Communist International,* Nos. 9–10, 1929.

Fischer, L. *The Soviets in World Affairs.* 2 vols. New York, 1930.

Francis, D. R. *Russia from the American Embassy, April 16–November, 1918.* New York, 1921.

Gallacher, W. *Revolt on the Clyde.* London, 1936.

Gankin, O. and H. Fisher. *The Bolsheviks in the World War.* Stanford, Calif., 1940.

Graubard, S. R. *British Labour and the Russian Revolution, 1917–1924.* Cambridge, Mass., 1956.

Hard, W. *Raymond Robins' Own Story.* New York, 1920.

Hoffmann, M. *Der Krieg Der Versäumten Gelegenheiten.* Munich, 1923.

Ioffe, A. "Brest-Litovsk, Vospominaniya." *Novi Mir,* VI, 1927.

Izvestiya.

Kautsky, K. *Die Diktatur des Proletariates.* Vienna, 1918.

Kazovskaya, A. "Nota Miliukova i Aprel'skiye Dni." *Proletarskaya Revoliutsiya,* 1927, 4 (63).

Kliuchnikov, Iu. V. and A. V. Sabanin. *Mezhdunarodnaya Politika noveishego vremeni v dogorogakh, notakh i deklaratsiyakh,* Part III. Moscow, 1928.

Krupskaya, N. *Memories of Lenin.* 2 vols. London, 1930.

———. *Memories of Lenin.* London, 1942.

Laqueur, Z. "The Shifting Line in Soviet Orientology." *Problems of Communism.,* V, No. 2, March–April, 1956.

Lenin, V. I. *Sochineniya,* 2d ed. 30 vols. Moscow, 1926–32.

———. *Leninsky Sbornik.* 35 vols. Moscow, 1924–45.

Lockhart, B. *Memoirs of a British Agent.* London, 1932.

Luxemburg, R. "Organisationsfragen der russischen Sozialdemokratie." *Die Neue Zeit,* No. 42, 22 Jahrgang, II, 1903–4.

———. *The Russian Revolution.* New York, 1940.

Magnes, J. L. *Russia and Germany at Brest-Litovsk.* New York, 1919.

Manifest, Richtlinien, Beschlüsse des ersten Kongresses, Aufrufe und offene Schreiben des Exekutiv-Komitees bis zum zweiten Kongress. Hamburg, 1920.

Marx, K. *Der Bürgerkrieg in Frankreich.* Moscow, 1937.

Marx, K. and F. Engels. *Sochineniya,* XXVI. Moscow, 1935.

Marx-Engels Gesamtausgabe, Part 3, III. Moscow, 1935.

Mirniye Peregovori v Brest-Litovske. Vol. I. Moscow, 1920.

Murphy, J. T. *New Horizons.* London, 1941.

Organizatsionni Komitet Rossiiskoy Sotsial-demokraticheskoy rabochei partii (Menshevikov), k viboram v Uchreditel'noye Sobraniye No. 3, "Soldat', za kem poidesh tui na viborakh?" November[?], 1917.

Page, S. W. "Lenin and Self-Determination." *Slavonic and East European Review,* April, 1950.

———. "Lenin, The National Question and the Baltic States, 1917–1919." *The American Slavic and East European Review,* VII, No. 1, February, 1948.

———. "The Role of the Proletariat in March, 1917; Contradictions Within the Official Bolshevik Version." *Russian Review*, IX, April, 1950.

Park, A. *Bolshevism in Turkestan*. New York, 1957.

Pervi Legal'ni Peterburgsky Komitet Bol'shevikov v 1917 g. Moscow, 1927.

Petrogradskaya Obshchegorodskaya Vserossiiskaya Konferentsiya R. S-D. R. P. (Bol'shevikov v Aprele 1917 g.) Moscow, 1925.

Pipes, R. *The Formation of the Soviet Union, Communism and Nationalism, 1917–1923*. Cambridge, Mass., 1954.

Pokrovsky, M. N. *Ocherki po istorii oktyabr'skoy revoliutsii.* 2 vols. Moscow, 1927.

Pravda

Price, M. Phillips. *My Reminiscences of the Russian Revolution*. London, 1921.

Protokoli Kongressov Kommunisticheskogo Internatsionala, Pervi Kongress Kominterna, Mart, 1919 g. Moscow, 1933.

Protokoli Tsentral'nogo Komiteta RSDRP, Avgust 1917–Fevral' 1918. Moscow, 1929.

Protokoll Des III Kongress Der Kommunistischen Internationale (Moskau, 22 Juni bis 12 Juli 1921). Hamburg, 1921.

Rabinovich, S. *Istoriya grazhdanskoy voini*. Moscow, 1933.

Rafail, M. "God bez Lenina na Vostoke." *Lenin i Vostok, Sbornik Statei,* 2d ed. Moscow, 1925.

Reed, J. *Ten Days That Shook the World*. New York, 1934.

Reinstein, B. "On the Road to the First Congress." *The Communist International*, Nos. 9–10, 1929.

Safarov, G. *Kolonial'naya Revoliutsiya (Opit Turkestana)*. Moscow, 1921.

Siromyatnikova, M. "Bernskaya Konferentsiya zagranichnikh organizatsii R.S.D.R.P. v 1915 g. (s primechaniyami G. L. Shklovskogo)." *Proletarskaya Revoliutsiya*, No. 5(40), 1925.

Sokolnikov, G. *Brestsky Mir*. Moscow, 1928.

Stučka, P. *Pyat' Mesyatsev Sotsialisticheskoy Sovetskoy Latvii*. Moscow, 1919.

Sukhanov, N. *Zapiski o revoliutsii*. 7 vols. Moscow, 1922.

Thesen und Resolutionen des III Weltkongresses der Kommunistischen Internationale (Moskau, 22 Juni bis 12 Juli 1921). Hamburg, 1921.

Trotsky, L. Archives. (Harvard University.)

———. *History of the Russian Revolution.* 3 vols. London, 1932–33.

———. *Lenin.* New York, 1925.

———. *My Life.* New York, 1930.

———. *Stalin.* London, 1947.

———. *Ueber Lenin.* Berlin, 1924.

Vladimirova, V. *Revoliutsiya 1917 goda (Khronika Sobitii),* III. Leningrad, 1924.

Volkovicher, I. *Brestsky Mir.* Moscow, 1928.

Vsesoiuznaya Kommunisticheskaya Partiya (b) v Rezoliutsiyakh i Resheniyakh ee S'ezdov, Konferentsii i Plenumov Ts. K. (1898–1932), Chast' I, 1898–1924. Moscow, 1932.

Vtoroy Kongress Kominterna, Iul'-Avgust 1920 g. Moscow, 1934.

Wheeler-Bennett, J. W. *Brest-Litovsk, the Forgotten Peace.* London, 1938.

Whiting, A. S. *Soviet Policies in China, 1917–1924,* New York, 1954.

Zalesskaya, F. "Iun'skaya demonstratsiya 1917 goda." *Proletarskaya Revoliutsiya,* 1927, 65–66.

Zetkin, K. *Vospominaniya o Lenine, Sbornik statei i vospominaniya.* Moscow, 1933.

Zinoviev, G. E. *Ucheniye Marksa i Lenina o Voine.* Moscow, 1931.

INDEX

Allied Supreme Council, 135, 169, 238–39
American Federation of Labor, 179–80
American League for Socialist Propaganda, 225
American Socialist Labor party, 224–25
Amsterdam International, *see* International Federation of Trade Unions
Axelrod, P., xiv, xvi, 74

Balabanova, A., 225
Bartold, V., 198
Bashkir Autonomous Soviet Socialist Republic, 175, 196
Bavarian Soviet regime, 139, 142
Bazhor, 224
Beech, D., 236
Bernstein, E., xv, 221
Berzin, P., 21
Bogdat'ev, S., 36
Bombacci, N., 237, 240
Bordiga, A., 162, 166, 188
Brandler, H., 189
British Communist party, 146, 234
British Labour party, 158, 180
British Socialist party, 158, 177, 234, 236
Bubnov, A., 101, 107
Budënny, S., 240
Bukhara, Soviet People's Republic of, 197
Bukharin, N., 97, 99, 100, 106–8, 128, 132, 154, 188, 204, 215–16, 219, 224
Bullitt, W., 136

Call, British Socialist party organ, 177
Chernov, V., 45, 62
Chicherin, G., 170, 224–25, 238
Chkheidze, N., 207, 208
Churchill, W., 135, 171
Chuvash Autonomous Region, 196–97
Clemenceau, G., 135, 221
Comintern, Executive Committee of, 162–63, 166, 182–84, 188, 191

Communist party of Soviet Latvia, 232
Congresses and Conferences
Bolshevik and Communist:
Sixth Congress of the Russian Social Democratic Workers' Party (January, 1912), xviii; Bern Conferences (1915), 13, 15, 21, 22; Petrograd (All-City) Conferences of Bolsheviks (1917), 39, 52, 72, 209; All Russian Party Conference (May, 1917), 20, 42, 81; Seventh Party Congress (March, 1918), 107; Congress of Moslem Communists (November, 1918), 142; First Congress of Latvian Soviets (January, 1919), 122; Heidelberg Conference of German Communists (October, 1919), 149; Second All-Russian Congress of Communist Organizations of the Peoples of the East (November, 1919), 144–45; Ninth Party Congress (March, 1920), 186, 242; Tenth Party Congress (March, 1921), 186
Socialist Congresses and Conferences:
First Congress of the Russian Social Democratic Workers' party (Minsk, 1898), xv, Second Congress of the Russian Social Democratic Workers' party (Brussels-London, 1903), xvi, 18, 74, 75; Congress of the Second International (Copenhagen, 1908), 215; Congress of the Second International (Basel, 1912), 7–9; Bern Conference (July, 1915), 21; Zimmerwald Conference (September, 1915), 21–23, 28, 32, 33, 37, 75, 122, 207, 224; Kienthal Conference (1916), 22, 23; Stockholm Conference (1917), 122; Bern Conference (February, 1919), 123, 130, 132; Congress of the USPD (March, 1919), 143, 233; Italian Socialist Congress (Bologna, October, 1919),

Congresses and Conferences (*Cont.*)
149; USPD Congress at Halle
(October, 1920), 187–88; Leghorn
Congress of Italian Socialist party
(January, 1921), 188
All-Russian Congresses of Soviets:
First, 32, 46, 47, 49; Second, 73,
79, 84; Third, 93; Fourth, 108
Constituent Assembly (Russian), 36,
69, 71, 121, 148, 212, 214, 234
Council of the Republic, 72, 214
Crawford, H., 236
Crispien, A., 163–65
Curzon, G., 169–72
Czernin, O., 88, 217

D'Aragona, L., 166, 241
Däumig, E., 160–61, 165–66, 223
David, E., 25
Debs, E., 120
Democratic Conference, *see* State Conference
Denikin, A., 135, 169, 171, 186
Dittman, W., 164
Dutch Communist party, 160–61, 165,
184, 235
Dzerzhinsky, F., 96, 101, 173, 219

Eberlein, H., 126–32, 223, 225, 227–28
Economists, xv
Engels, F., 19, 20, 34, 201, 204, 212
English Communists, 149, 152, 159,
177
English Fabians, 25
English Labour party, 123
English Socialist party, 224

Federation of Foreign Groups of the
Russian Communist party, 111
Fineberg, S., 125, 224, 228
First Congress of the Peoples of the
East, 197
French Communist party, 187
French General Confederation of Labor, 241
French Socialist party, 159–60, 162,
164–66, 181, 187, 237
French Youth League, 162
Frunze, M., 223

Gallacher, W., 181, 236, 240
German Communist party (KPD),
119–20, 126, 146–50, 152, 161, 163,
187, 227

German Communist Workers' party
(KAPD), 149, 163, 187, 193
German Independent Socialist party
(USPD), 119, 143, 154, 158–63,
165–66, 181, 187, 195, 223, 237–38
German National Assembly (1919),
119, 143, 223, 233
German United Communist party
(VKPD), 187–89, 191, 193–95
Goldenberg, I., 162, 164
Gorter, H., 161
Grimm, R., 143
Grimlund, O., 129, 131–32, 224
Guchkov, A., 44, 206, 208
Guesdes, J., 49

Haase, H., 25, 49, 233–34
Haglund, 224
Hilferding, R., 141, 237
Hillquit, M., 161
Hoffmann, M., 88, 91, 100
Hungarian Soviet regime, 137–39, 143,
175, 231

IKKI, *see* Comintern, Executive Committee of
International Federation of Trade
Unions, 143, 182, 187
International Labor Organization
(ILO), 182
International Socialist Bureau, 23, 205
Ioffe, A., 87, 88, 97, 99–101, 111, 219
Iskra, xvi, xvii, 74
Italian Communists, 149, 151, 188
Italian Labor Confederation, 241
Italian Socialist party, 21, 149, 154,
188, 237

Kabakchiev, K., 188
Kadets (Constitutional Democratic
Party), 28, 64, 213–14
Kalinin, M., 35, 36, 94
Kamenev, L., 8, 32, 39–41, 54, 59, 65,
73, 88, 205, 208, 215
KAPD, *see* German Communist Workers' party)
Kapp Putsch, 160
Kascher, 129
Kautsky, K., xii, xv, 6, 25, 28, 37, 57,
114–18, 124, 147–48, 161–62, 165,
168, 204, 207, 221–23, 234, 237
Kerensky, A., 45, 51, 64, 65, 68, 69,
72, 137, 206, 214, 230
Khorezm, Soviet People's Republic of,
197

Kirgiz Autonomous Soviet Socialist Republic, 197
Kolarov, V., 198
Kolchak, A., 135, 143, 186, 234
Kollontai, A., 21, 204, 206
Kornilov, L., 64, 65, 67, 68, 71, 72, 78, 213–14
Kossior, S., 96
KPD, see German Communist party
Krestinsky, N., 97, 101
Kuibyshev, V., 233
Krylenko, N., 96, 97
Kugelmann, L., 57, 212
Kun, B., 125, 137–39, 189–90, 232
Kuusinen, O., 128

Latvian Soviet Republic, 121, 175, 232
Lazzari, C., 120
League for the Liberation of Labor, xi
League of Nations, 124, 170–71, 182
Lebedour, G., 223
Lenin's more important writings: April Theses, 32, 33, 35, 36, 39–41, 44, 62, 77, 134, 137, 156, 206; Declaration on Peace, 84; Farewell Letter to the Swiss Workers, 23–26, 116; Imperialism, 19, 132, 141–42, 205; Left Wing Communism, 152, 159, 167–68, 179, 182; Letters from Afar, 27–30; On the United States of Europe Slogan, 15, 16; State and Revolution, 20, 29, 56–58, 70, 113, 115, 118; The Proletarian Revolution and the Renegade Kautsky,114; Theses on the National and Colonial Question, 175–78; Theses on the Peace, 93, 96, 217–18; Theses on the War, 12; What Is to Be Done, xv, 1
Levi, P., 161, 183–84, 187–91, 193, 195, 236
Liebknecht, K., 19, 25, 37, 38, 50, 119–20, 126, 147, 204, 220
Lloyd George, D., 106, 135
Lockhart, B., 100, 104–6, 219–20
Lomov, A., 97, 100
Longuet, J., 161
Loriot, F., 120
Lozovsky, A., 180–81, 187
Lunacharsky, A., 59, 213
Luxemburg, R., 14, 15, 119–20, 126, 128, 223, 227–28

MacAlpin, 181
MacDonald, R., 161

MacLaine, W., 236
MacLean, J., 37, 50, 120
March Action, 189–91, 193, 195
Mari Autonomous Region, 196–97
Markhlevsky, Y., 173
Martov, J., xv, xvi, xvii, 213, 215
Marx, K., xi, 1, 2, 19, 20, 29–31, 34, 36, 55, 57, 58, 116–17, 201, 204, 212, 222, 225
Mehring, F., 119
Meyer, E., 227
Miliukov, P., 40, 44, 206, 208, 209
Modigliani, G., 159
Münzenberg, W., 163, 165
Murphy, J., 236

Narodnik, xii, xiii, 33, 55
Natanson, M., 224
NEP, see New Economic Policy
Nevsky, 45, 211
New Economic Policy (NEP), 186, 194
Nicholas I, 1
Nicholas II, 42, 206, 224
Nissen, 224
Norwegian Labor party, 154
Norwegian Social Democrats, 224
Noulens, J., 220

Oldenburg, S., 198

Pankhurst, S., 146, 236
Pannekoek, A., 37, 161, 165
Paris Commune, 6, 27, 29–36, 55, 58
Pavlovich, M., 197
Pestagna, A., 241
Petrov, P., 224
Pilsudski, J., 169–70, 239
Platten, F., 129, 132
Plekhanov, G., xiv–xvi, 58
Pokrovsky, M., 88
Potressov, A., xv, xvi
Prinkipo Island, 136, 229
Profintern, 181, 187
Pyatakov, G., 204

Quelch, T., 236

Radek, K., 14, 21, 114, 149, 156, 160–61, 164, 166, 173, 177, 180–81, 183, 194–97, 236, 240
Radoshevich, 224
Rahja, I., 132
Rakosi, M., 188
Rakovsky, K., 129, 131, 225
Ramsey, D., 236

Red Trade Union International, *see* Profintern

Reed, J., 84, 125, 180–81

Reinstein, B., 125, 224–25

Renaudel, P., 25

Riga, Treaty of, 185

Robins, R., 103–5, 109, 220

Rosmer, A., 236, 241

Roy, M., 179, 198, 240

Rudnyanszky, A., 125, 129

Rumanian Social Democrats, 224

Rutgers, S., 225

Sadoul, J., 125, 225

Scheidemann, P., 25, 49, 119–20, 147–48, 234

Second International, 7, 8, 9, 12, 21, 22, 28, 33, 37, 49, 75, 113, 120, 122, 124–25, 127, 130, 132, 143, 154, 156, 158, 168, 182, 215, 221, 237

Serrati, G., 120, 149, 164–65, 188–89, 236

Shklovksy, G., 13–15

Shlyapnikov, A., 11

Shop Stewards, 156–58, 177, 180, 228, 235–36, 238, 240–41

Sirola, Y., 224

Sklyansky, E., 170

Smilga, I., 46, 49, 77, 97, 100

Socialist Labour party, 234, 236

Sokolnikov, G., 97

Sorge, F., 201

Sotsial-Demokrat, bolshevik paper, 8, 15, 42

South Wales Socialist Society, 234

Spanish National Confederation of Labor, 235, 241

Spartacus League or Spartacist, 22, 114, 119–20, 124, 223, 228

Stalin, J., 32, 95–97, 142, 144, 151, 211, 215–16, 224, 233

State Conference, 72, 213–14

Steinhardt 128–29, 131, 228

Stoecker, W., 165–66

Stolypin, P., 9

Stučka, P., 121–22

Südekum, 119

Sultan-Galiyev, M., 144

Sverdlov, Y., 97, 100, 101, 122, 211, 215

Swedish Marxist Left party, 224

Tanner, J., 156–58, 181, 236

Tatar Autonomous Soviet Socialist Republic, 175, 196

Thalheimer, A., 194

Thälmann, E., 195

Tereshchenko, M., 45, 210

Terracini, U., 189, 194

Theory of the offensive, 189–90

Third International, as an idea, 23, 33, 36–38, 115, 119–20, 122–32, 224, 228

Tomsky, M., 52

Tribunists, *see* Dutch Communist party

Trotsky, L., and NEP, 186, 242; "no war-no peace," 90, 91, 93, 96, 104, 105; "permanent revolution," 43, 76, 77, 102; Polish war, 170, 173, 238

Tseretelli, I., 45–47

Turati, F., 159, 164–65, 188, 237

Turkmen Communists, 143–44, 234

Ulyanov, A., xiii

Uritsky, M., 97, 101

USPD, *see* German Independent Socialist party

Ustinov, 224

Van Leeven, 160–61

Versailles, Treaty of, 142, 174, 233

VKPD, *see* German United Communist party

Von Kühlmann, R., 88, 89, 96, 217

Votyak Autonomous Region, 196–97

Walcher, 164

Wijnkoop, D., 160–61, 163, 165, 182–84

Wilhelm II, 42, 206

Wilson, W., 135–36, 237

Workers' Socialist Federation, 146, 234

Wrangel, P., 169–72

Yedinstvo, Menshevik paper, 39

Yudenich, N., 135

Yugoslav Social Democrats, 224

Zasulich, V., xvi, 74

Zetkin, K., xv, 119, 188–91, 193, 240, 243

Zhizn' Natsional'nostei, 144

Zinoviev, G., 21, 45, 58, 73, 95, 96, 127, 131–32, 155–57, 161–62, 165–66, 181, 183–84, 187–89, 194, 197, 204, 205, 208, 215–16, 237, 242–43